HULK
BROKEN WORLDS

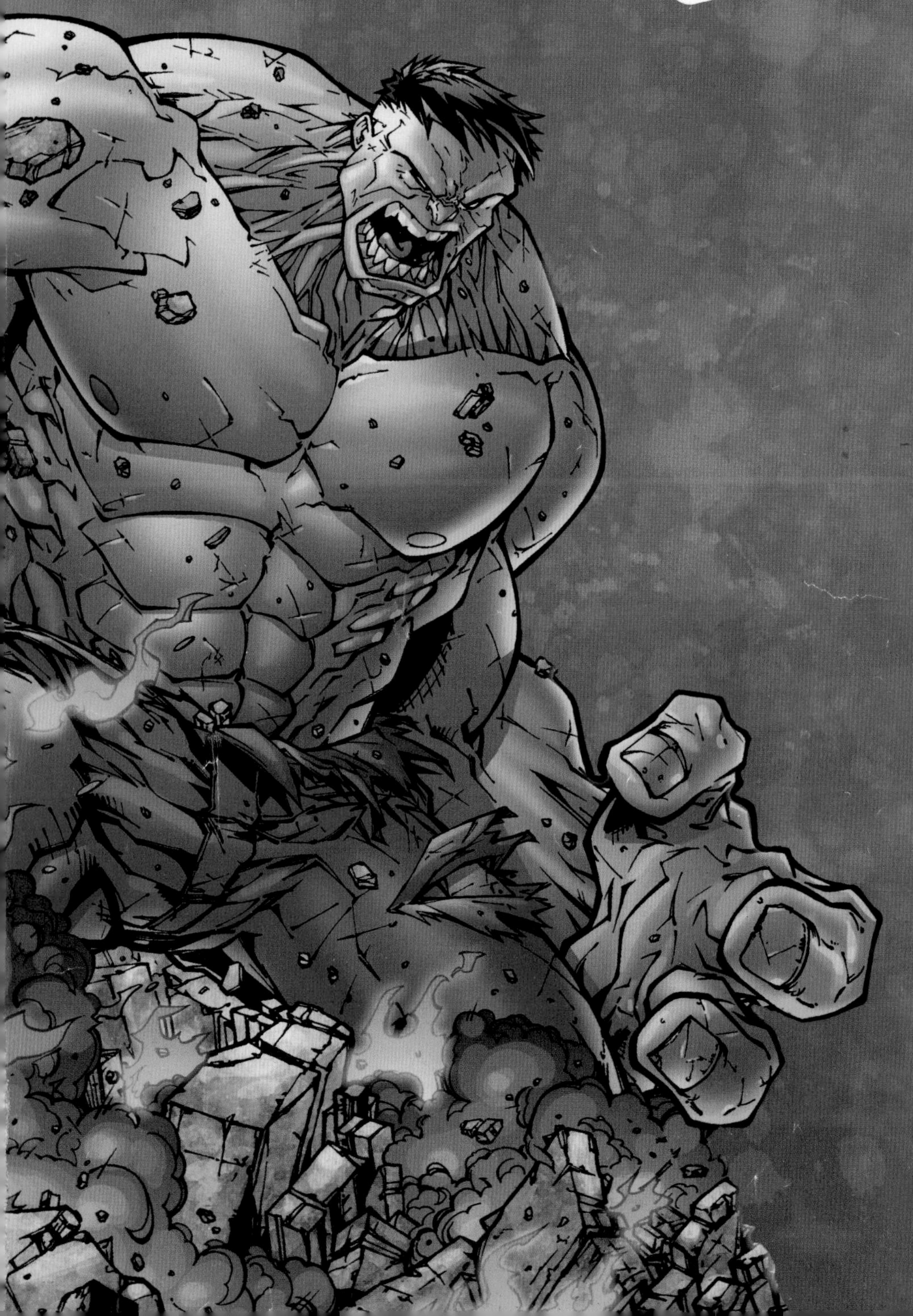

HULK: BROKEN WORLDS

BROKEN WORLDS

WRITERS: **FRED VAN LENTE, ROY THOMAS, PAUL BENJAMIN, PETER DAVID, MARC SUMERAK, ADAM WARREN AND JASON HENDERSON**

ARTISTS: **CLAYTON HENRY, HERB TRIMPE & KARL KESEL, DIEGO LATORRE, RODNEY BUCHEMI & GREG ADAMS, JONBOY MEYERS & MARK IRWIN. KELSEY SHANNON, STEVE SCOTT AND JUAN SANTACRUZ**

COLORS: **EMILY WARREN, MOOSE BAUMANN, JUNE CHUNG, LEE LOUGHRIDGE AND ANGEL MARIN**

LETTERS: **VC'S JOE CARAMAGNA AND DAVE SHARPE**

COVER ARTISTS: **MARK BROOKS & PAUL PELLETIER, RICK MAGYAR AND KRISTEN SOREN**

ASSISTANT EDITOR: **JORDAN D. WHITE**

EDITOR: **MARK PANICCIA**

HULK FAMILY: GREEN GENES

WRITERS: **FRED VAN LENTE, GREG PAK AND PAUL TOBIN**

ARTISTS: **SCOTT CLARK & GREG ADAMS, JHEREMY RAAPACK & GREG ADAMS, BENTON JEW AND DIEDRICH O'CLARK & AL VEY**

COLORS: **ULISES AREOLA, CHRIS SOTOMAYOR, MOOSE BAUMANN AND LEE LOUGHRIDGE**

LETTERS: **VC'S CORY PETIT AND JOE CARAMAGNA**

COVER ARTIST: **MARKO DJURDJEVIC**

ASSISTANT EDITOR: **JORDAN D. WHITE**

EDITOR: **MARK PANICCIA**

X-MEN VS. HULK

WRITER: **CHRIS CLAREMONT**

ARTISTS: **JHEREMY RAAPACK & LARRY WELCH**

COLORS: **CHRIS SOTOMAYOR**

LETTERS: **ED DUKESHIRE**

COVER ARTISTS: **DAVID YARDIN & WIL QUINTANA**

ASSISTANT EDITOR: **CHARLIE BECKERMAN**

EDITOR: **MARK PANICCIA**

COLLECTION EDITOR: **CORY LEVINE** • EDITORIAL ASSISTANT: **ALEX STARBUCK**

ASSISTANT EDITOR: **JOHN DENNING** • EDITORS, SPECIAL PROJECTS: **JENNIFER GRÜNWALD & MARK D. BEAZLEY**

SENIOR EDITOR, SPECIAL PROJECTS: **JEFF YOUNGQUIST** • SENIOR VICE PRESIDENT OF SALES: **DAVID GABRIEL**

PRODUCTION: **JERRY KALINOWSKI** • BOOK DESIGN: **SPRING HOTELING**

EDITOR IN CHIEF: **JOE QUESADA** • PUBLISHER: **DAN BUCKLEY**

EXECUTIVE PRODUCER: **ALAN FINE**

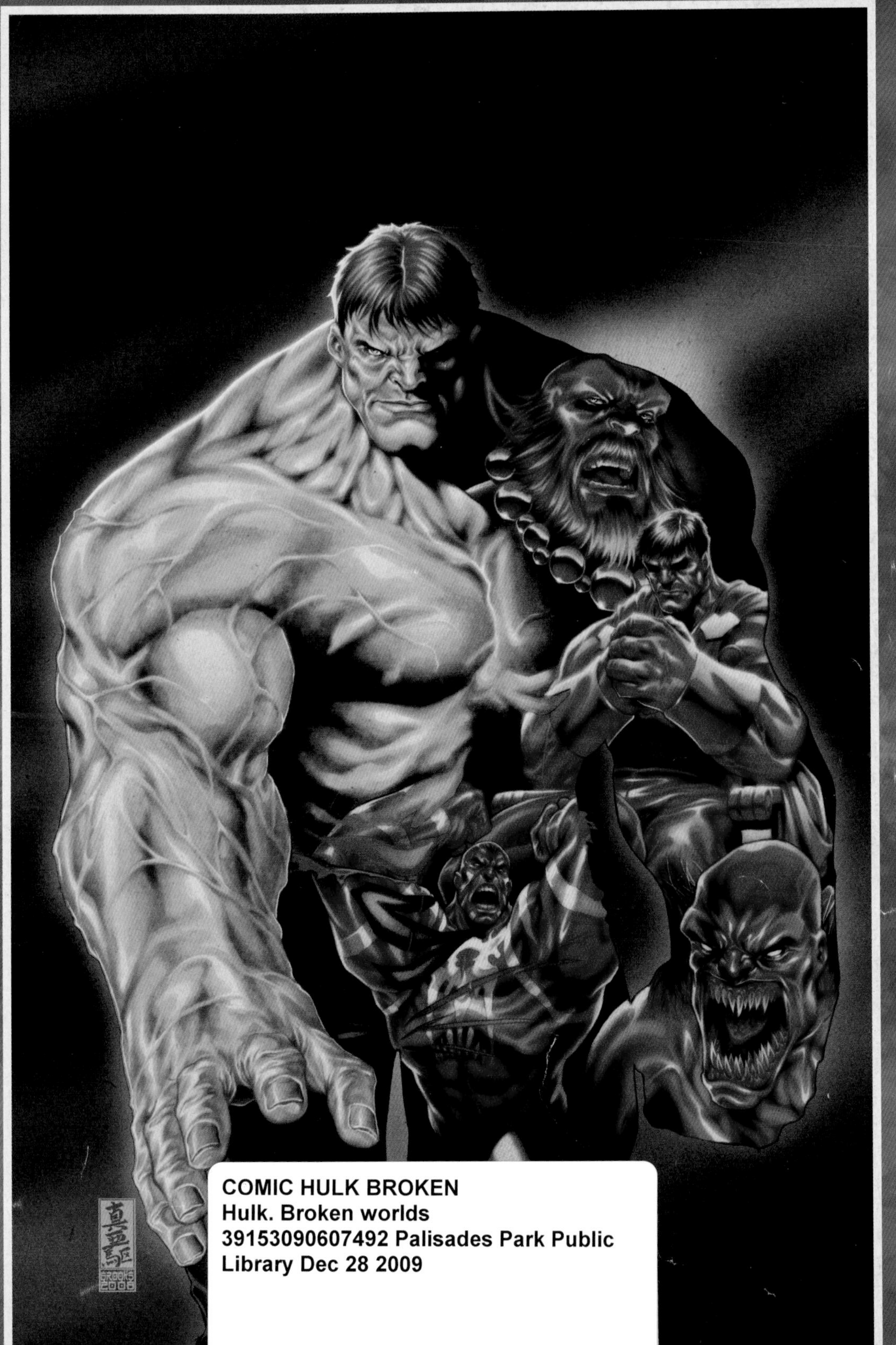

BROKEN WORLDS: BOOK ONE

HULK
BROKEN WORLDS

HULK:

CAUGHT IN A BLAST OF GAMMA-RADIATION, BRILLIANT SCIENTIST BRUCE BANNER NOW FINDS HIMSELF CURSED TO TRANSFORM IN TIMES OF STRESS INTO THE LIVING ENGINE OF DESTRUCTION KNOWN AS **THE INCREDIBLE HULK**…OR SO IT IS ON THE EARTH WE KNOW. BUT WHAT OF OTHER WORLDS?

HOUSE OF M:

A WORLD WHERE MAGNETO RULES OVER GENOSHA AND MUTANTS ARE THE DOMINANT CLASS ON THE PLANET. AFTER GAINING A SEMBLANCE OF PEACE AMONG THE ABORIGINAL PEOPLE OF AUSTRALIA, HULK ROSE AGAINST MAGNETO'S REACH, BECOMING RULER OF THE LAND DOWN UNDER.

MICROVERSE:

A PARALLEL UNIVERSE REACHED BY COMPRESSING ONE'S MASS DOWN TO A CERTAIN POINT, FORCING IT THROUGH AN ARTIFICIALLY CREATED NEXUS. IN THE PAST, THE HULK TRAVELLED TO THE MICROSCOPIC KINGDOM OF K'AI WHERE HE FELL IN LOVE WITH THE BEAUTIFUL PRINCESS JARELLA.

HULK 2099:

IN THE YEAR 2099, NORTH AMERICA IS A POLICE STATE RULED BY MEGA-CORPORATIONS. RUTHLESS MOVIE PRODUCER JOHN EISENHART WAS ACCIDENTALLY TRANSFORMED INTO A MONSTER BY THE KNIGHTS OF BANNER. NOW, HE TRAVELS THE COUNTRY SEEKING REDEMPTION FOR THE SINS OF HIS PAST.

FUTURE IMPERFECT:

POST-APOCALYPTIC ALTERNATE FUTURE WHERE THE MAESTRO, WHO COMBINED BANNER'S INTELLECT WITH HULK'S AGGRESSION AND POWER, TOOK CONTROL OF WHAT WAS LEFT OF SOCIETY. JUST BARELY DEFEATED BY A TIME-DISPLACED "PROFESSOR HULK," THE WORLD NOW FINDS ITSELF WITHOUT A RULER.

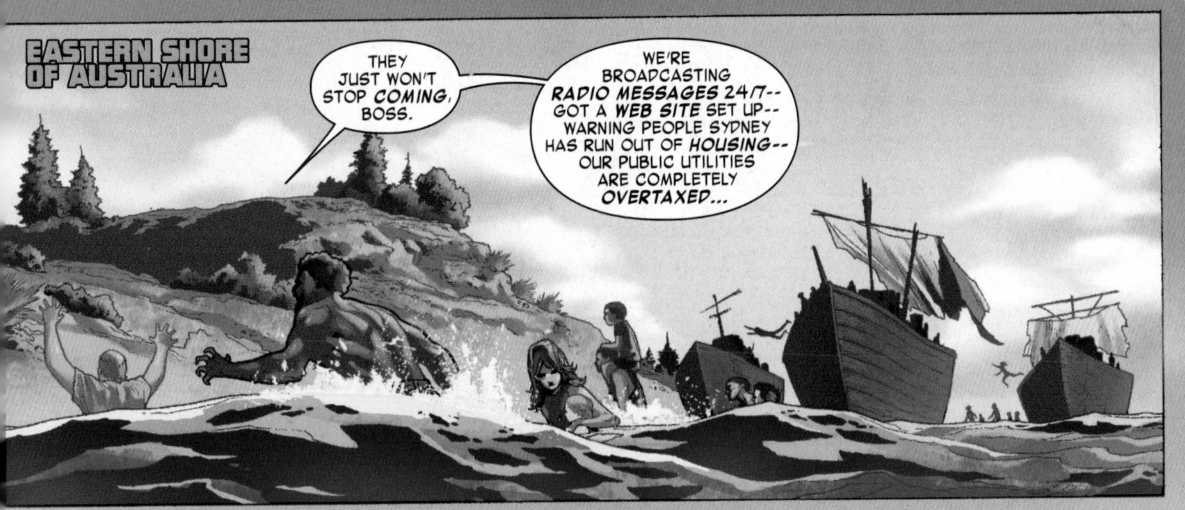
EASTERN SHORE OF AUSTRALIA
THEY JUST WON'T STOP COMING, BOSS.
WE'RE BROADCASTING RADIO MESSAGES 24/7-- GOT A WEB SITE SET UP-- WARNING PEOPLE SYDNEY HAS RUN OUT OF HOUSING-- OUR PUBLIC UTILITIES ARE COMPLETELY OVERTAXED...

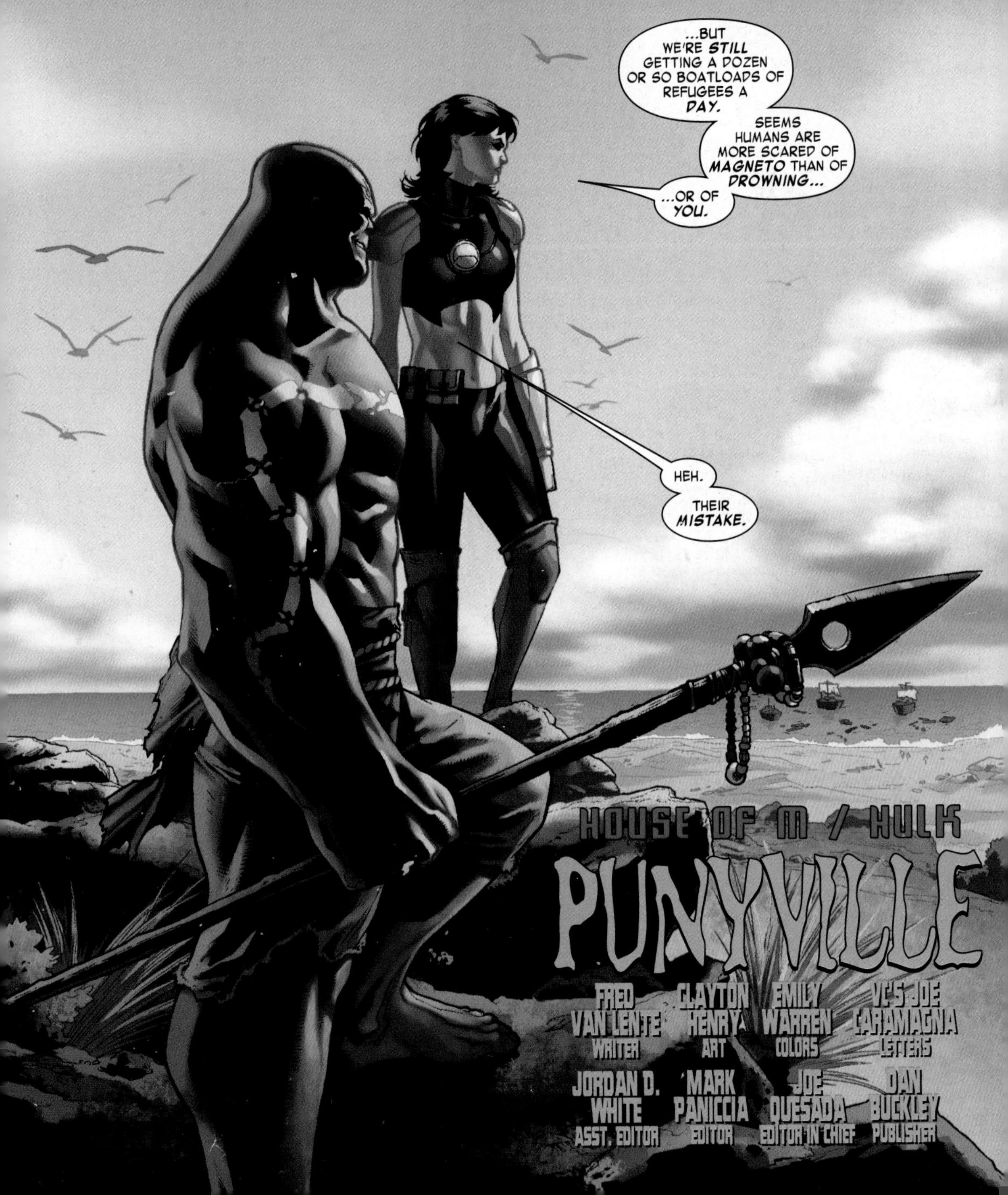
...BUT WE'RE STILL GETTING A DOZEN OR SO BOATLOADS OF REFUGEES A DAY.
SEEMS HUMANS ARE MORE SCARED OF MAGNETO THAN OF DROWNING...
...OR OF YOU.
HEH.
THEIR MISTAKE.
HOUSE OF M / HULK
PUNYVILLE
FRED VAN LENTE WRITER
CLAYTON HENRY ART
EMILY WARREN COLORS
VC'S JOE CARAMAGNA LETTERS
JORDAN D. WHITE ASST. EDITOR
MARK PANICCIA EDITOR
JOE QUESADA EDITOR IN CHIEF
DAN BUCKLEY PUBLISHER

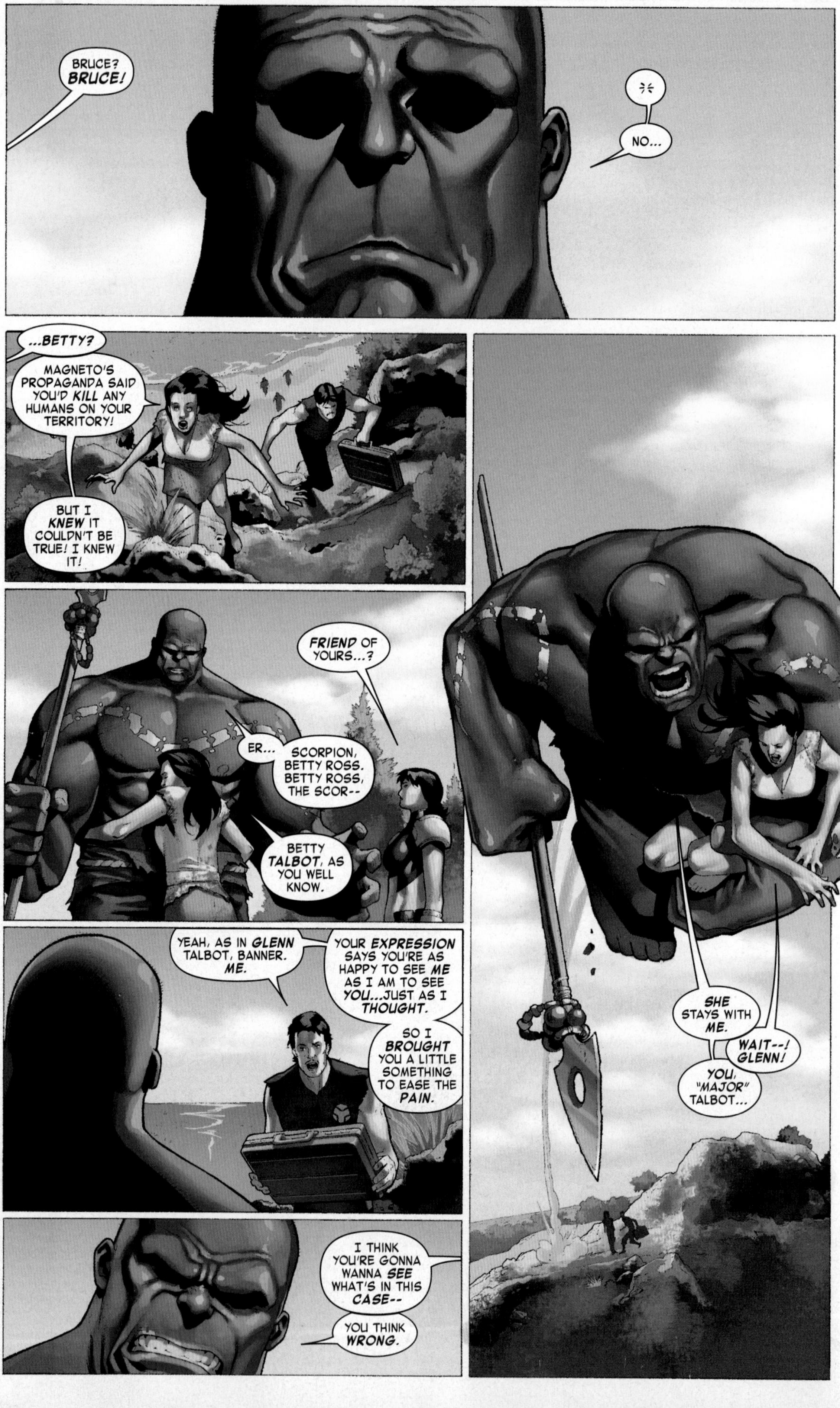

BRUCE? BRUCE!
NO...
...BETTY?
MAGNETO'S PROPAGANDA SAID YOU'D KILL ANY HUMANS ON YOUR TERRITORY!
BUT I KNEW IT COULDN'T BE TRUE! I KNEW IT!
FRIEND OF YOURS...?
ER...
SCORPION, BETTY ROSS. BETTY ROSS, THE SCOR--
BETTY TALBOT, AS YOU WELL KNOW.
YEAH, AS IN GLENN TALBOT, BANNER. ME.
YOUR EXPRESSION SAYS YOU'RE AS HAPPY TO SEE ME AS I AM TO SEE YOU...JUST AS I THOUGHT.
SO I BROUGHT YOU A LITTLE SOMETHING TO EASE THE PAIN.
I THINK YOU'RE GONNA WANNA SEE WHAT'S IN THIS CASE--
YOU THINK WRONG.
SHE STAYS WITH ME.
YOU, "MAJOR" TALBOT...
WAIT--! GLENN!

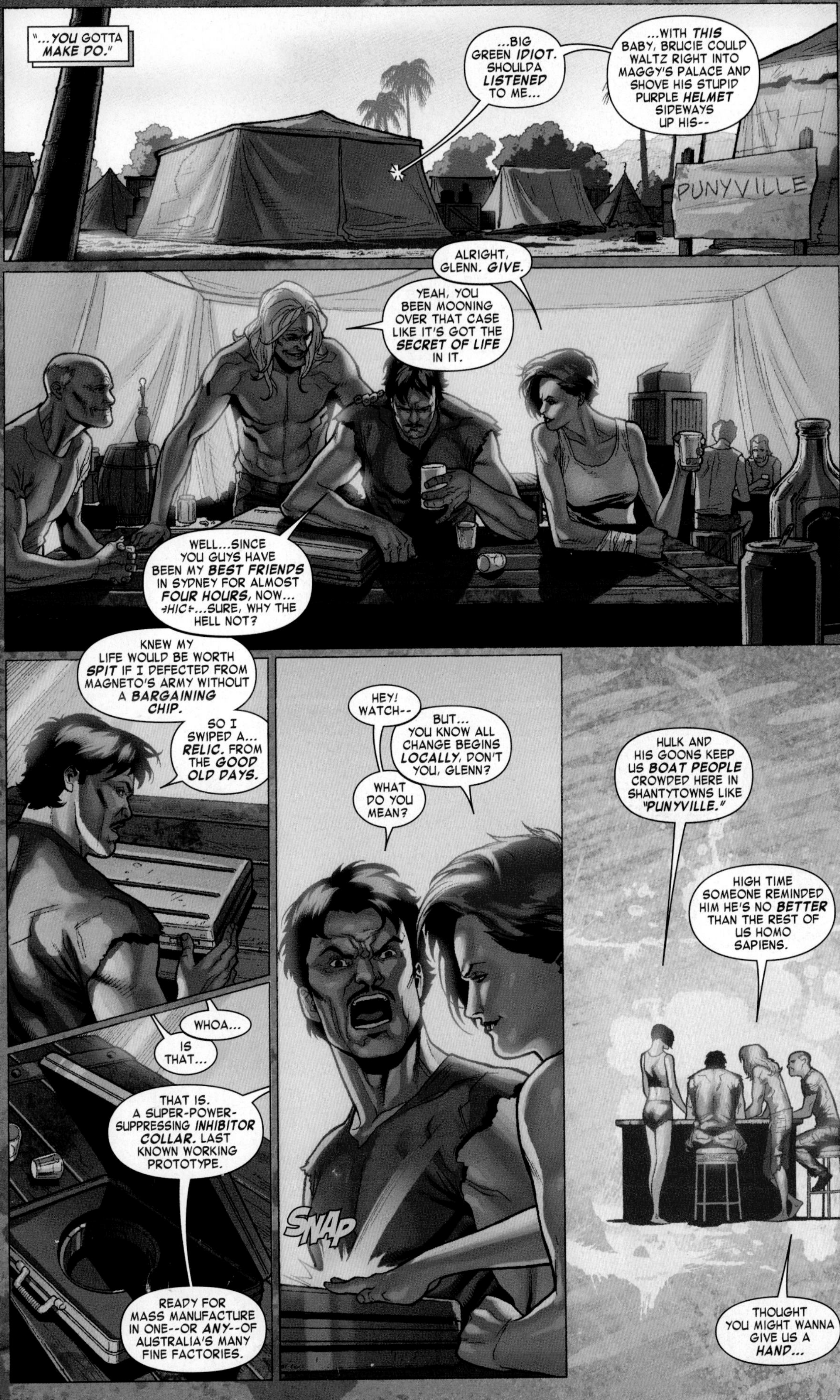

"...YOU GOTTA MAKE DO."
...BIG GREEN IDIOT. SHOULDA LISTENED TO ME...
...WITH THIS BABY, BRUCIE COULD WALTZ RIGHT INTO MAGGY'S PALACE AND SHOVE HIS STUPID PURPLE HELMET SIDEWAYS UP HIS--
PUNYVILLE
ALRIGHT, GLENN. GIVE.
YEAH, YOU BEEN MOONING OVER THAT CASE LIKE IT'S GOT THE SECRET OF LIFE IN IT.
WELL...SINCE YOU GUYS HAVE BEEN MY BEST FRIENDS IN SYDNEY FOR ALMOST FOUR HOURS, NOW... +HIC+...SURE, WHY THE HELL NOT?
KNEW MY LIFE WOULD BE WORTH SPIT IF I DEFECTED FROM MAGNETO'S ARMY WITHOUT A BARGAINING CHIP.
SO I SWIPED A... RELIC. FROM THE GOOD OLD DAYS.
WHOA... IS THAT...
THAT IS. A SUPER-POWER-SUPPRESSING INHIBITOR COLLAR. LAST KNOWN WORKING PROTOTYPE.
READY FOR MASS MANUFACTURE IN ONE--OR ANY--OF AUSTRALIA'S MANY FINE FACTORIES.
HEY! WATCH--
BUT... YOU KNOW ALL CHANGE BEGINS LOCALLY, DON'T YOU, GLENN?
WHAT DO YOU MEAN?
SNAP
HULK AND HIS GOONS KEEP US BOAT PEOPLE CROWDED HERE IN SHANTYTOWNS LIKE "PUNYVILLE."
HIGH TIME SOMEONE REMINDED HIM HE'S NO BETTER THAN THE REST OF US HOMO SAPIENS.
THOUGHT YOU MIGHT WANNA GIVE US A HAND...

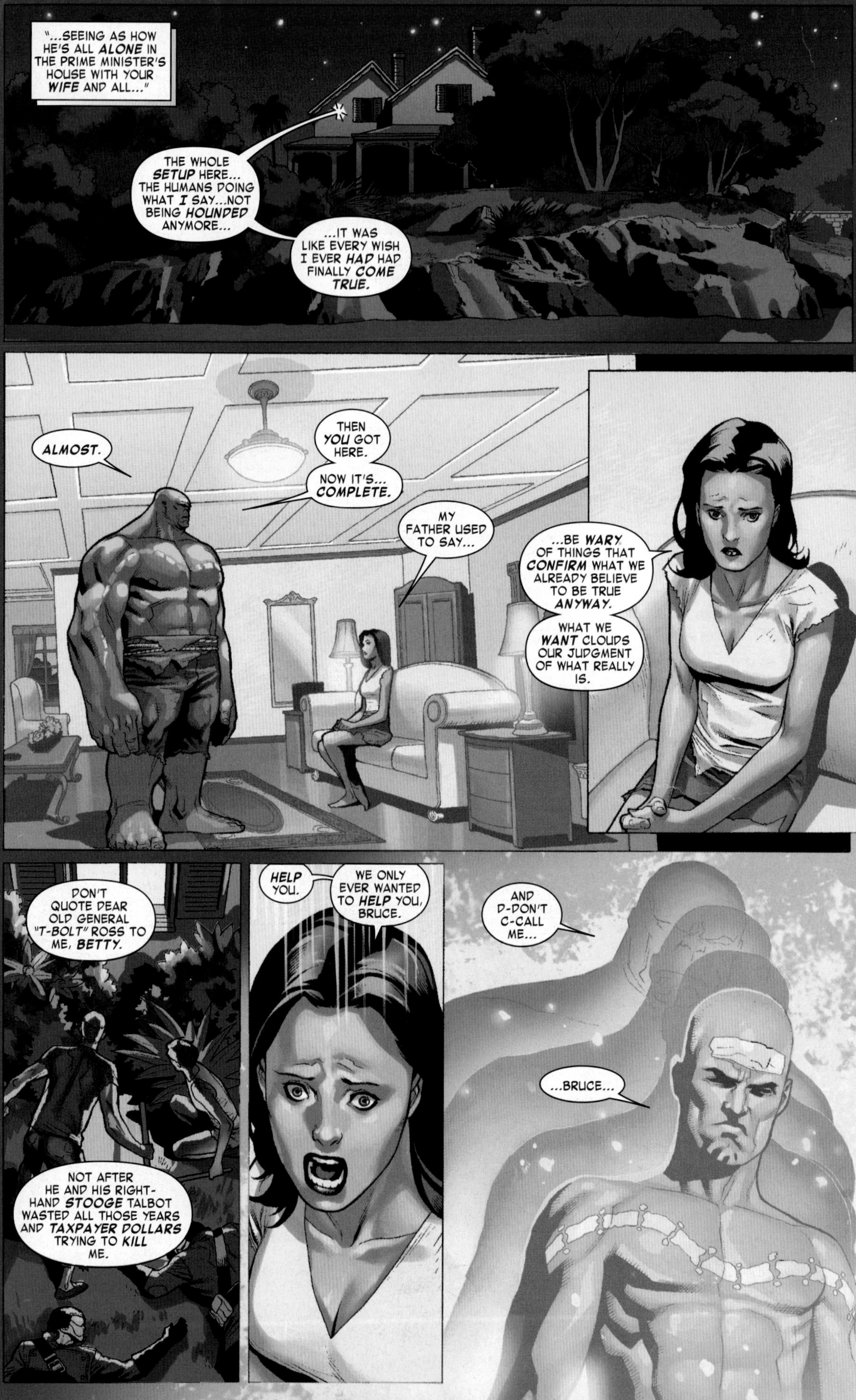
"...SEEING AS HOW HE'S ALL ALONE IN THE PRIME MINISTER'S HOUSE WITH YOUR WIFE AND ALL..."
THE WHOLE SETUP HERE... THE HUMANS DOING WHAT I SAY...NOT BEING HOUNDED ANYMORE...
...IT WAS LIKE EVERY WISH I EVER HAD HAD FINALLY COME TRUE.
ALMOST.
THEN YOU GOT HERE.
NOW IT'S... COMPLETE.
MY FATHER USED TO SAY...
...BE WARY OF THINGS THAT CONFIRM WHAT WE ALREADY BELIEVE TO BE TRUE ANYWAY.
WHAT WE WANT CLOUDS OUR JUDGMENT OF WHAT REALLY IS.
DON'T QUOTE DEAR OLD GENERAL "T-BOLT" ROSS TO ME, BETTY.
NOT AFTER HE AND HIS RIGHT-HAND STOOGE TALBOT WASTED ALL THOSE YEARS AND TAXPAYER DOLLARS TRYING TO KILL ME.
HELP YOU.
WE ONLY EVER WANTED TO HELP YOU, BRUCE.
AND D-DON'T C-CALL ME...
...BRUCE...

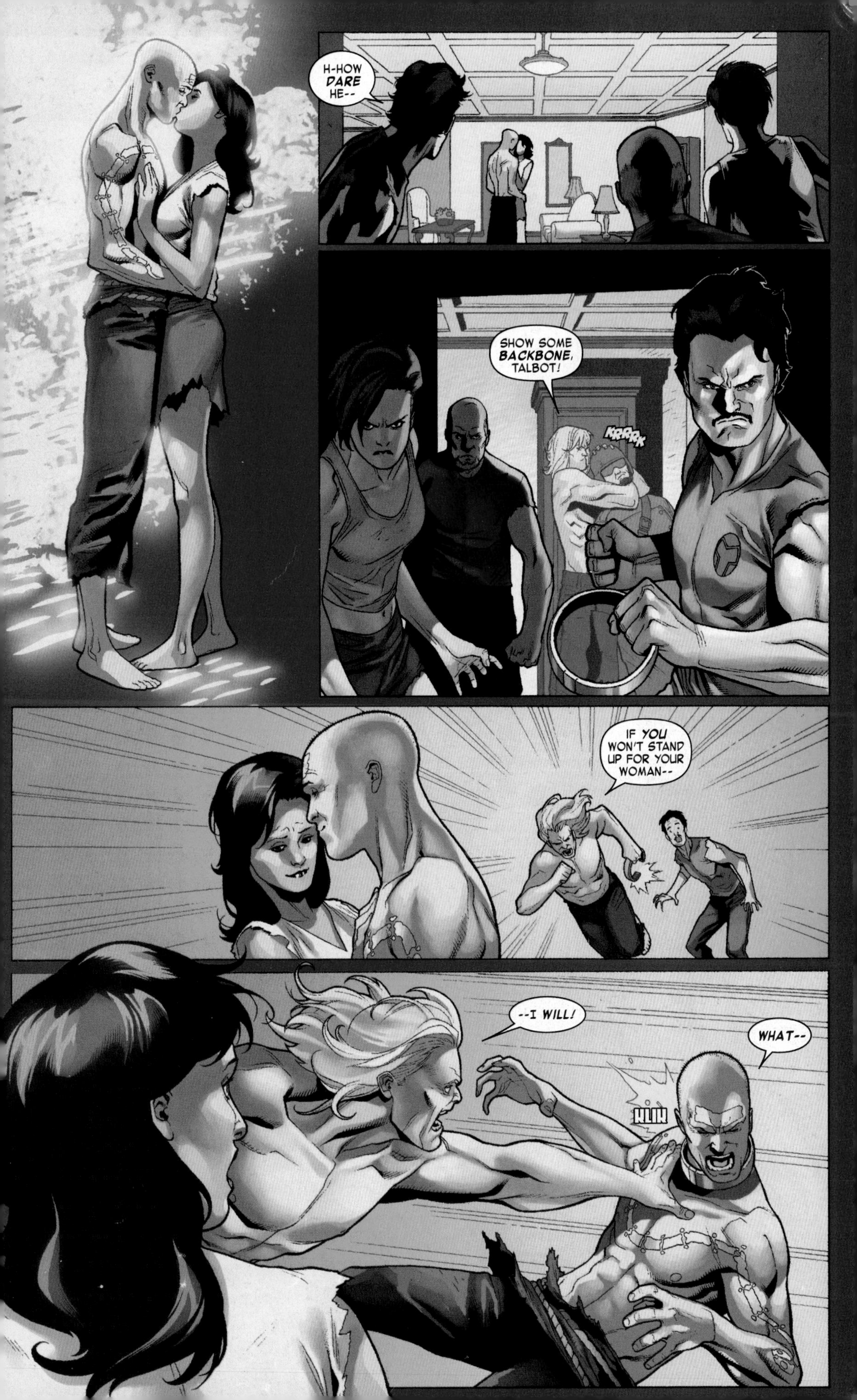
H-HOW DARE HE--
SHOW SOME BACKBONE, TALBOT!
KRRRK
IF YOU WON'T STAND UP FOR YOUR WOMAN--
--I WILL!
WHAT--
KLIK

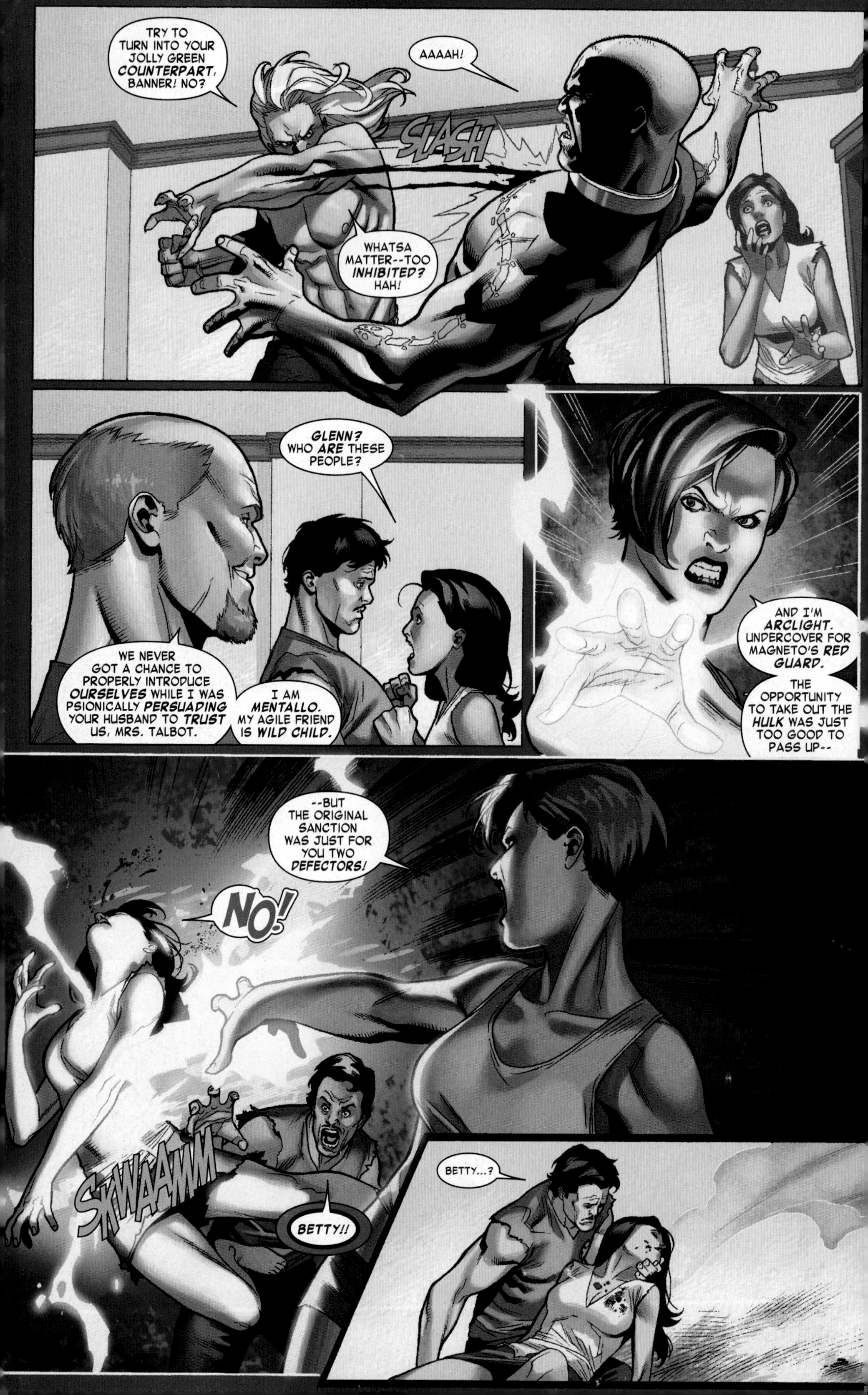
TRY TO TURN INTO YOUR JOLLY GREEN COUNTERPART, BANNER! NO?
AAAAH!
SLASH
WHATSA MATTER--TOO INHIBITED? HAH!
GLENN? WHO ARE THESE PEOPLE?
WE NEVER GOT A CHANCE TO PROPERLY INTRODUCE OURSELVES WHILE I WAS PSIONICALLY PERSUADING YOUR HUSBAND TO TRUST US, MRS. TALBOT.
I AM MENTALLO. MY AGILE FRIEND IS WILD CHILD.
AND I'M ARCLIGHT. UNDERCOVER FOR MAGNETO'S RED GUARD.
THE OPPORTUNITY TO TAKE OUT THE HULK WAS JUST TOO GOOD TO PASS UP--
--BUT THE ORIGINAL SANCTION WAS JUST FOR YOU TWO DEFECTORS!
NO!
SKWAAMM
BETTY!!
BETTY...?

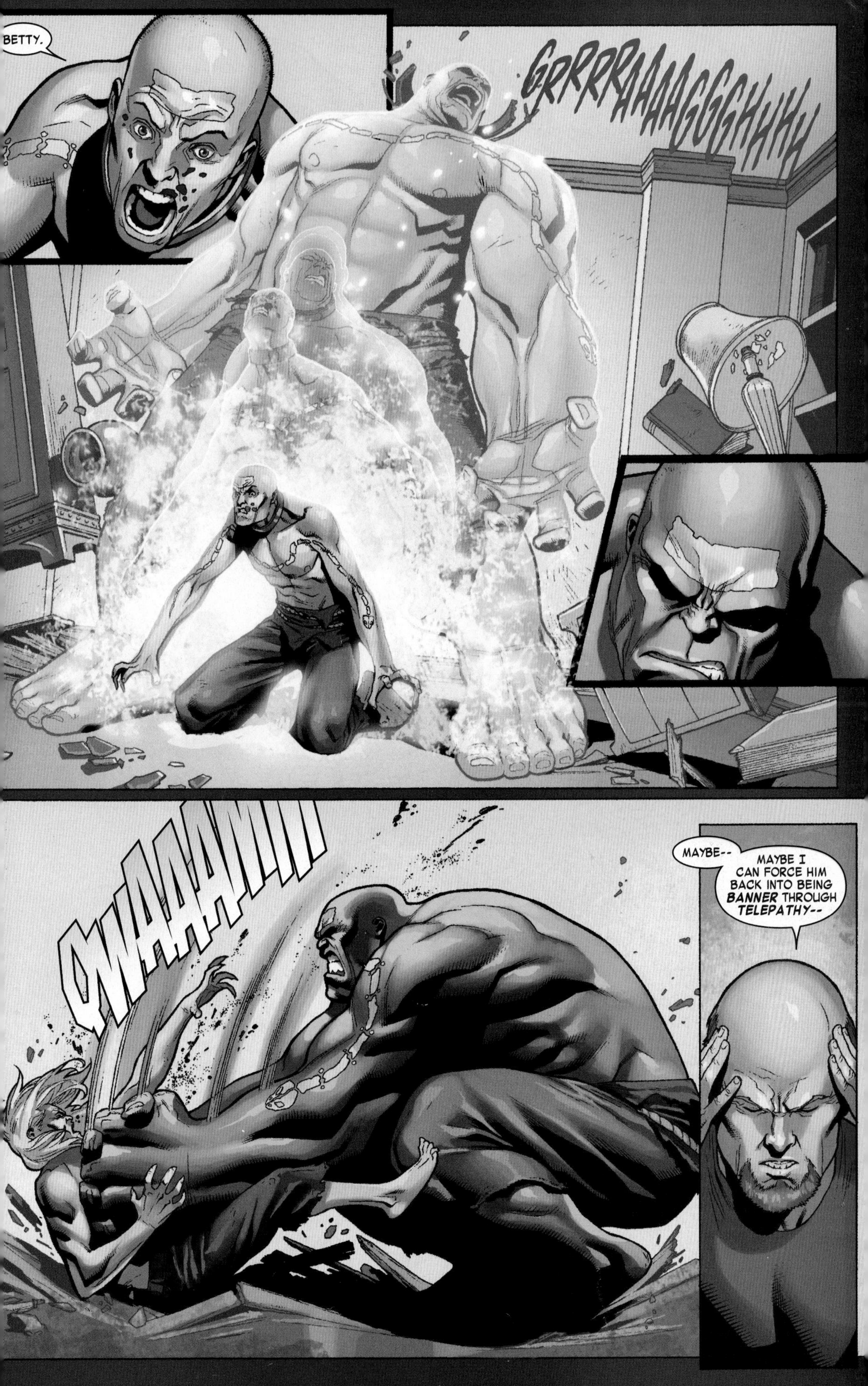
BETTY.
GRRRRAAAAGGGHHHH
QWAAAMMM
MAYBE--
MAYBE I CAN FORCE HIM BACK INTO BEING BANNER THROUGH TELEPATHY--

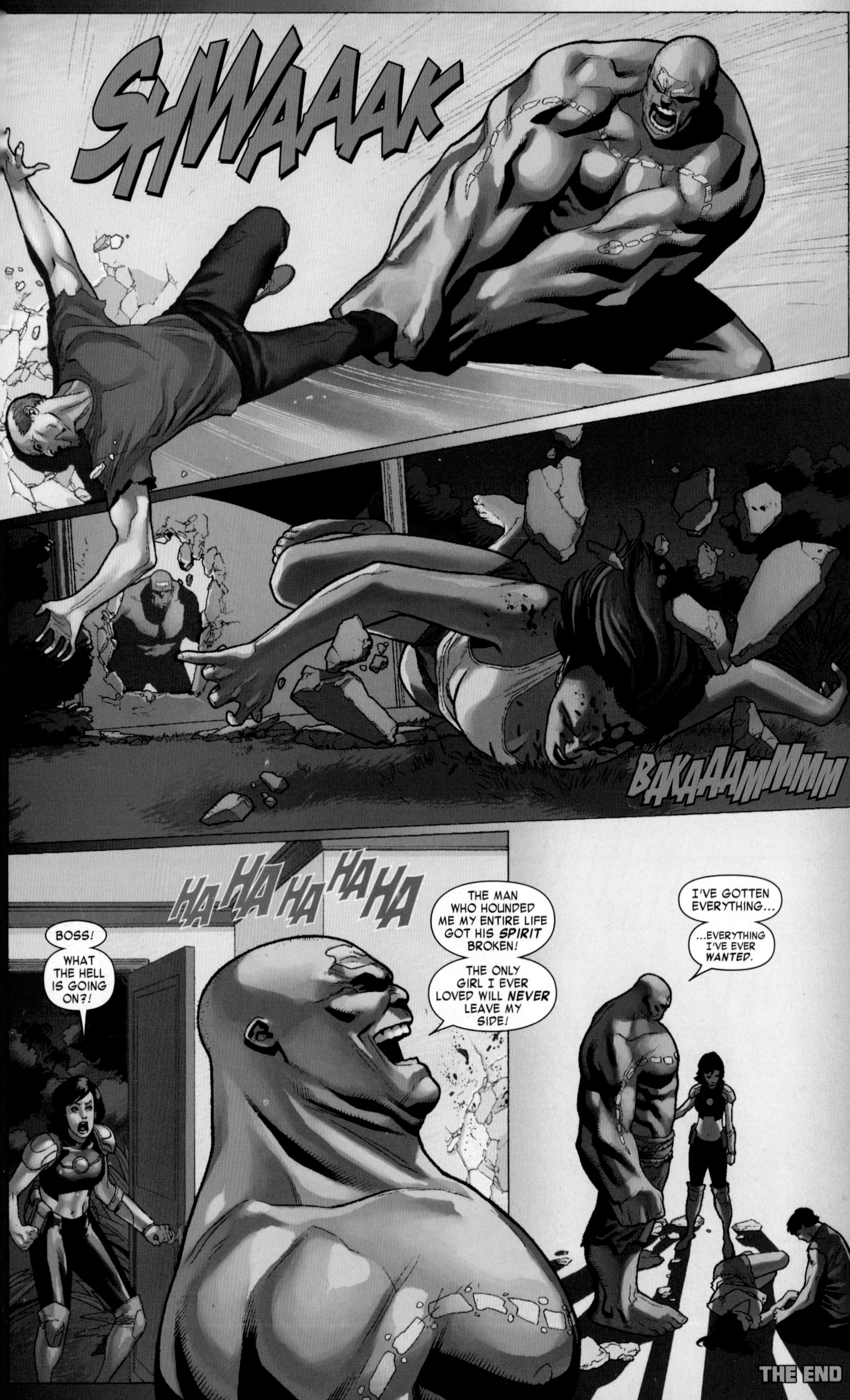

SWAAAK
BAKAAAMMMM
HA HA HA HA HA
BOSS! WHAT THE HELL IS GOING ON?!
THE MAN WHO HOUNDED ME MY ENTIRE LIFE GOT HIS SPIRIT BROKEN!
THE ONLY GIRL I EVER LOVED WILL NEVER LEAVE MY SIDE!
I'VE GOTTEN EVERYTHING...
...EVERYTHING I'VE EVER WANTED.
THE END

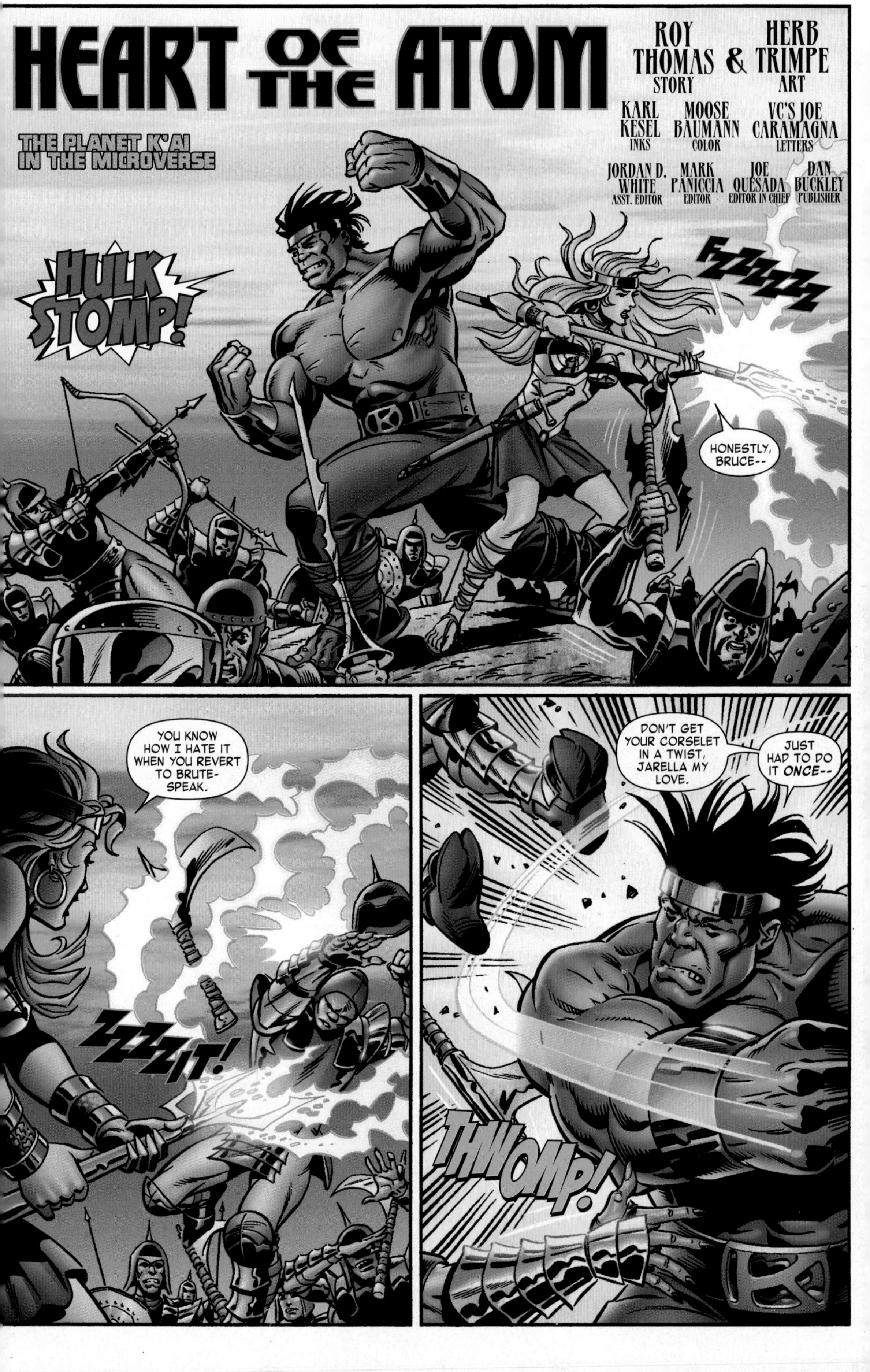
HEART OF THE ATOM
ROY THOMAS STORY & HERB TRIMPE ART
KARL KESEL INKS
MOOSE BAUMANN COLOR
VC'S JOE CARAMAGNA LETTERS
JORDAN D. WHITE ASST. EDITOR
MARK PANICCIA EDITOR
JOE QUESADA EDITOR IN CHIEF
DAN BUCKLEY PUBLISHER
THE PLANET K'AI IN THE MICROVERSE
HULK STOMP!
FZZZZZZ
HONESTLY, BRUCE--
YOU KNOW HOW I HATE IT WHEN YOU REVERT TO BRUTE-SPEAK.
ZZZZIT!
DON'T GET YOUR CORSELET IN A TWIST, JARELLA MY LOVE.
JUST HAD TO DO IT ONCE--
THWOMP!

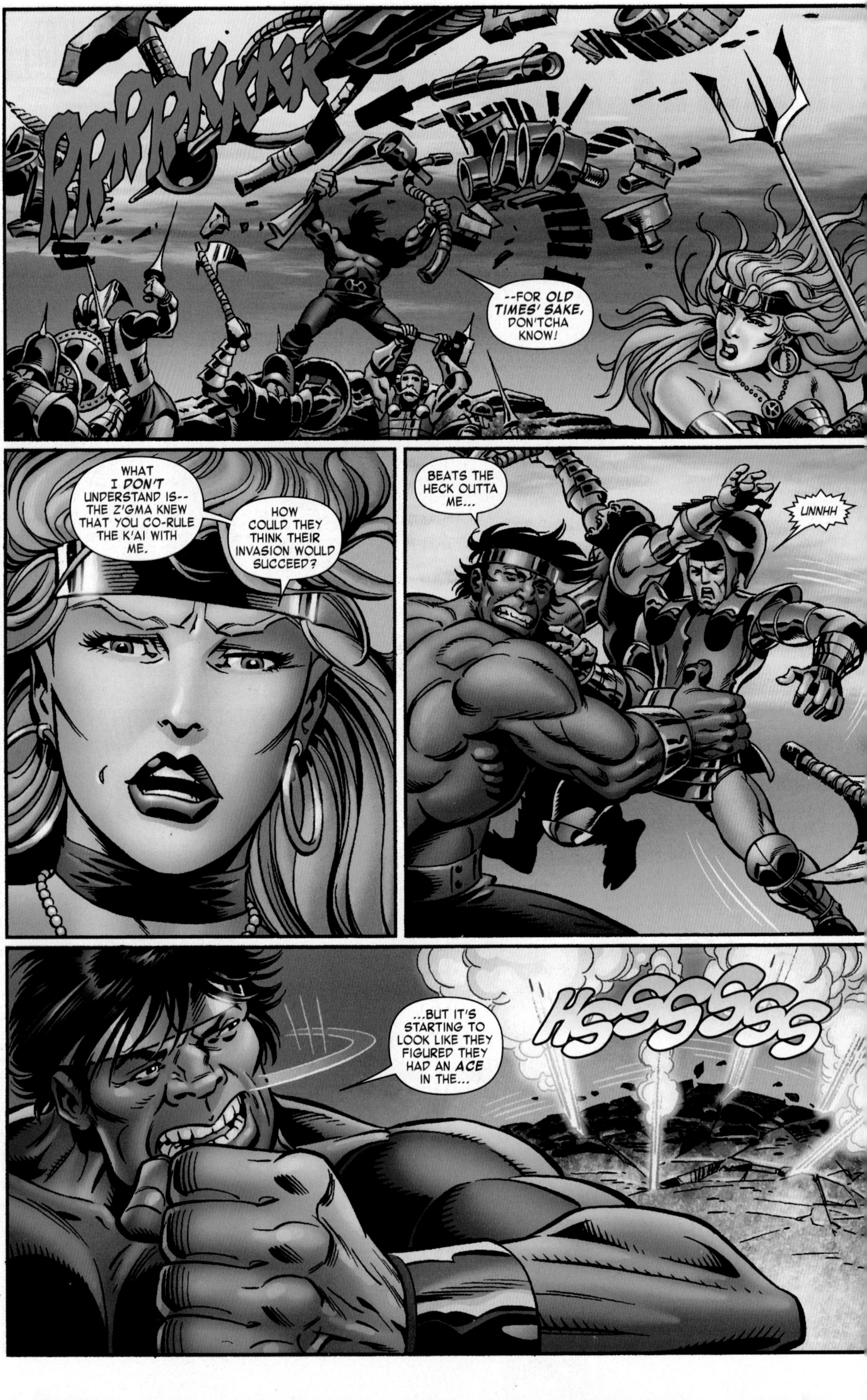

RRRRKKKK
--FOR OLD TIMES' SAKE, DON'TCHA KNOW!
WHAT I DON'T UNDERSTAND IS-- THE Z'GMA KNEW THAT YOU CO-RULE THE K'AI WITH ME.
HOW COULD THEY THINK THEIR INVASION WOULD SUCCEED?
BEATS THE HECK OUTTA ME...
UNNHH
...BUT IT'S STARTING TO LOOK LIKE THEY FIGURED THEY HAD AN ACE IN THE...
HSSSSSS

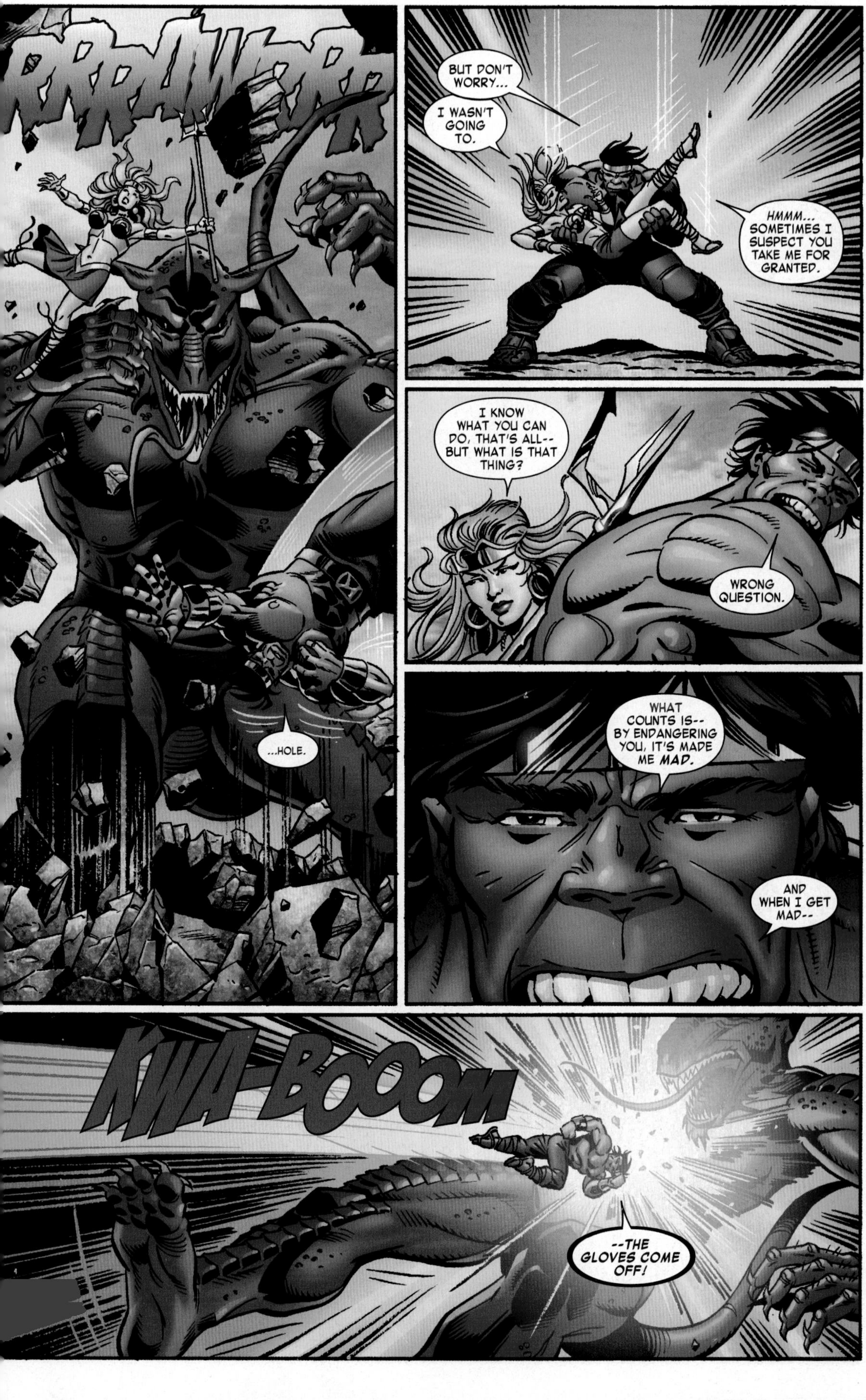
RRRAWRRR
...HOLE.
BUT DON'T WORRY...
I WASN'T GOING TO.
HMMM... SOMETIMES I SUSPECT YOU TAKE ME FOR GRANTED.
I KNOW WHAT YOU CAN DO, THAT'S ALL-- BUT WHAT IS THAT THING?
WRONG QUESTION.
WHAT COUNTS IS-- BY ENDANGERING YOU, IT'S MADE ME MAD.
AND WHEN I GET MAD--
KWA-BOOOM
--THE GLOVES COME OFF!

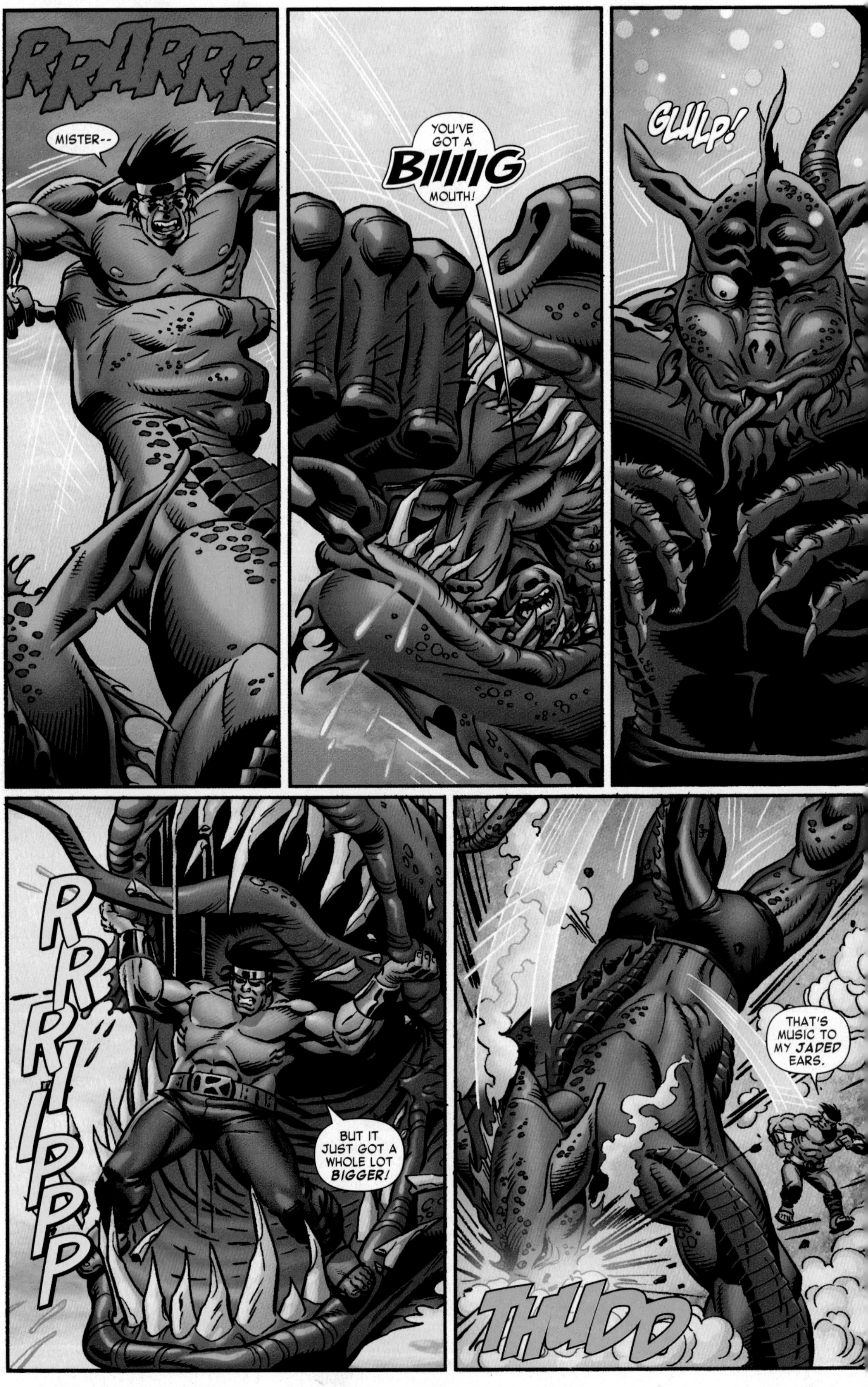
RRARRR
MISTER--
YOU'VE GOT A BIIIIG MOUTH!
GLULP!
RRRIPPP
BUT IT JUST GOT A WHOLE LOT BIGGER!
THUDD
THAT'S MUSIC TO MY JADED EARS.

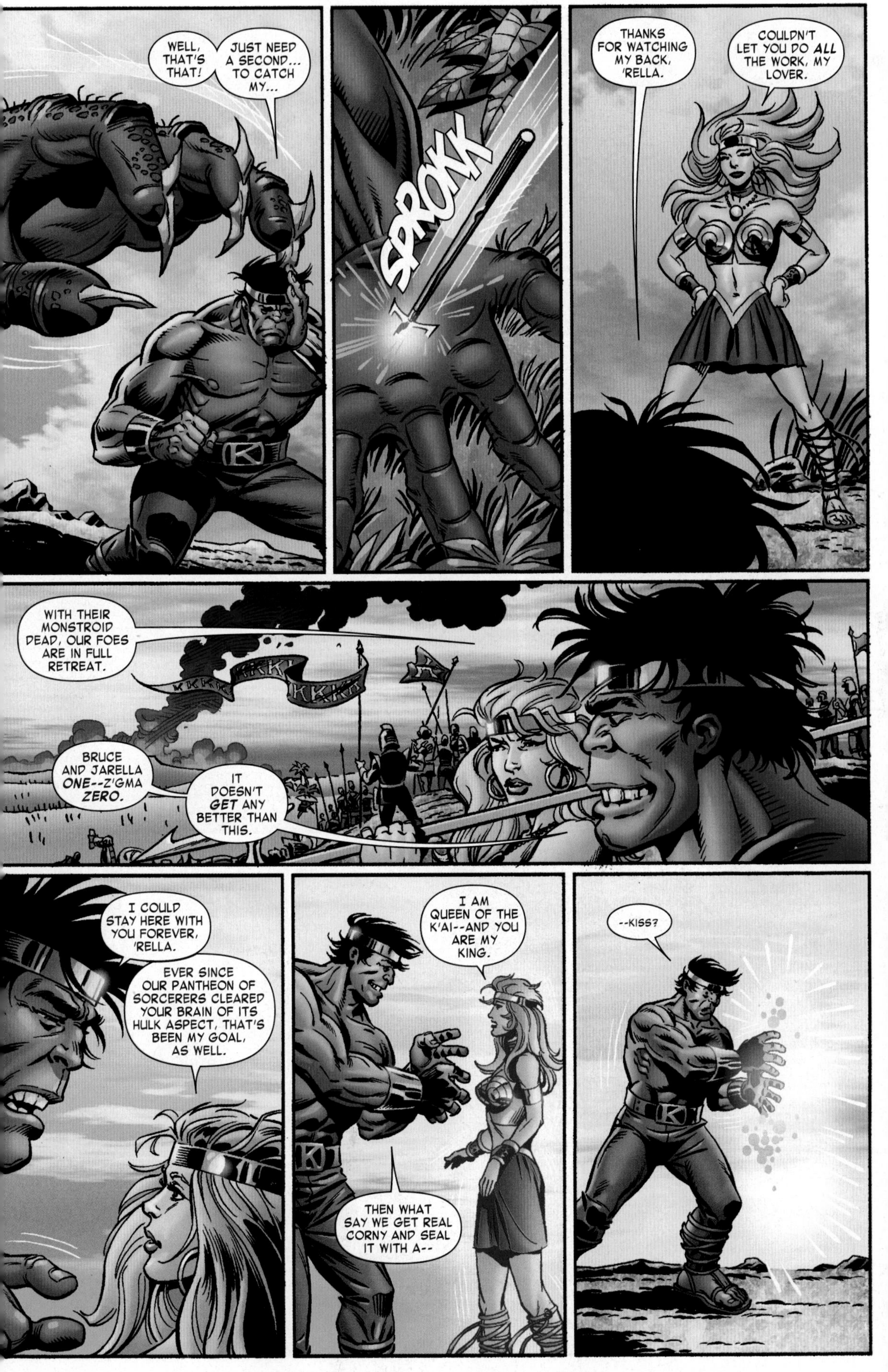
WELL, THAT'S THAT!
JUST NEED A SECOND... TO CATCH MY...
SPROKK
THANKS FOR WATCHING MY BACK, 'RELLA.
COULDN'T LET YOU DO ALL THE WORK, MY LOVER.
WITH THEIR MONSTROID DEAD, OUR FOES ARE IN FULL RETREAT.
BRUCE AND JARELLA ONE--Z'GMA ZERO.
IT DOESN'T GET ANY BETTER THAN THIS.
I COULD STAY HERE WITH YOU FOREVER, 'RELLA.
EVER SINCE OUR PANTHEON OF SORCERERS CLEARED YOUR BRAIN OF ITS HULK ASPECT, THAT'S BEEN MY GOAL, AS WELL.
I AM QUEEN OF THE K'AI--AND YOU ARE MY KING.
THEN WHAT SAY WE GET REAL CORNY AND SEAL IT WITH A--
--KISS?

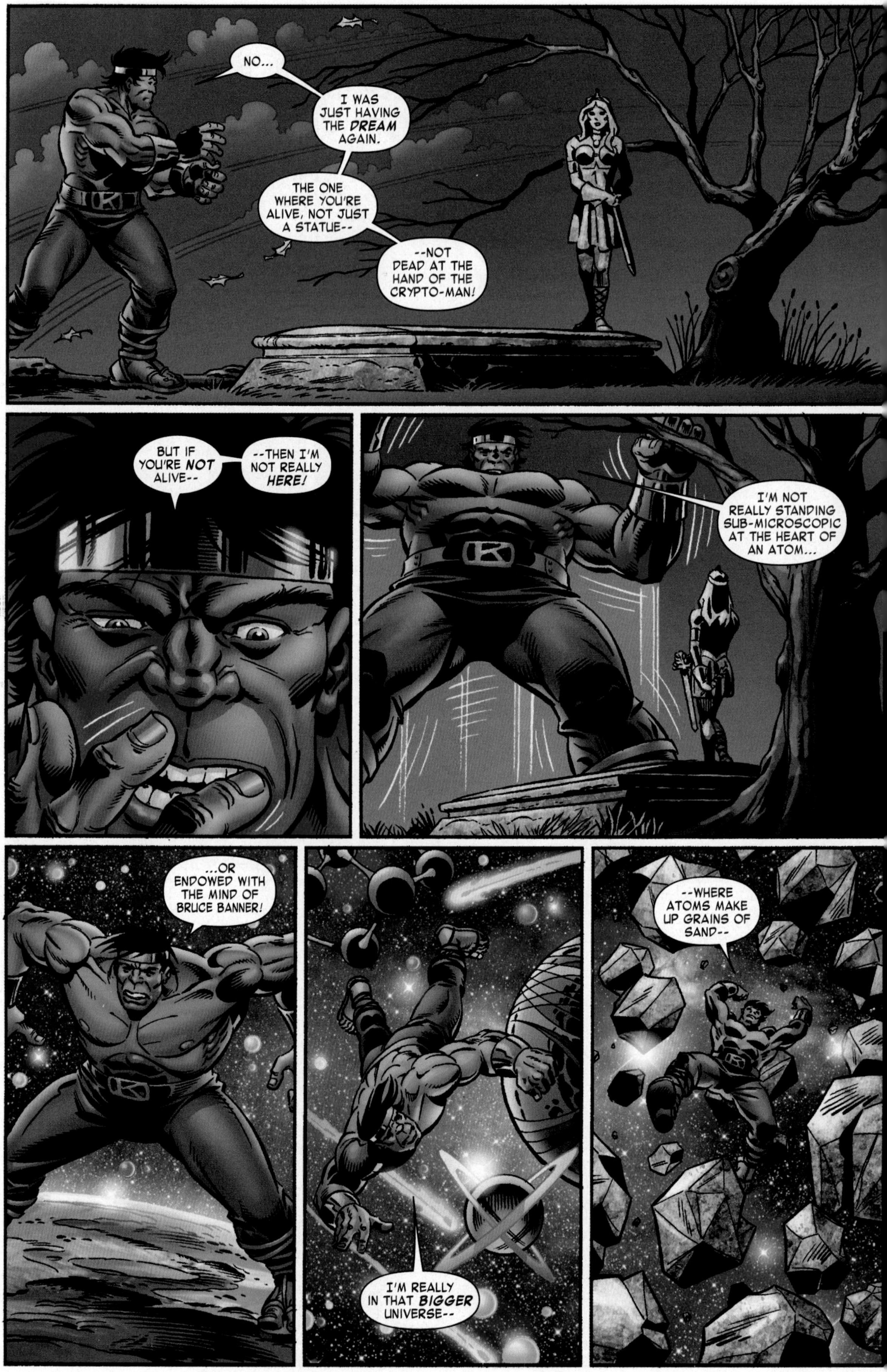
NO...
I WAS JUST HAVING THE DREAM AGAIN.
THE ONE WHERE YOU'RE ALIVE, NOT JUST A STATUE--
--NOT DEAD AT THE HAND OF THE CRYPTO-MAN!
BUT IF YOU'RE NOT ALIVE--
--THEN I'M NOT REALLY HERE!
I'M NOT REALLY STANDING SUB-MICROSCOPIC AT THE HEART OF AN ATOM...
...OR ENDOWED WITH THE MIND OF BRUCE BANNER!
I'M REALLY IN THAT BIGGER UNIVERSE--
--WHERE ATOMS MAKE UP GRAINS OF SAND--

--AND PLANES AND TANKS ROAR ABOVE THOSE SANDS--

--HUNTING FOR *THE HULK!*

HULK WILL SMASH!

WITH THAT FINAL REALIZATION, THE LAST VESTIGES OF HUMANITY-- OF DR. ROBERT BRUCE BANNER-- FADE LIKE MELTING FROST...

GRRRR

...LEAVING NOTHING, SO FAR AS HIS ARMY ATTACKERS CAN TELL, BUT THE BEAST.

YET, IF WE LOOKED CLOSER... WE WOULD SEE...

...THAT A SHARD OF THAT FORMER LIFE REMAINS...

...REFLECTED IN AN EMERALD EYE...

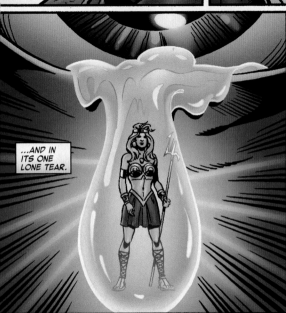

...AND IN ITS ONE LONE TEAR.

"BRUCE..."

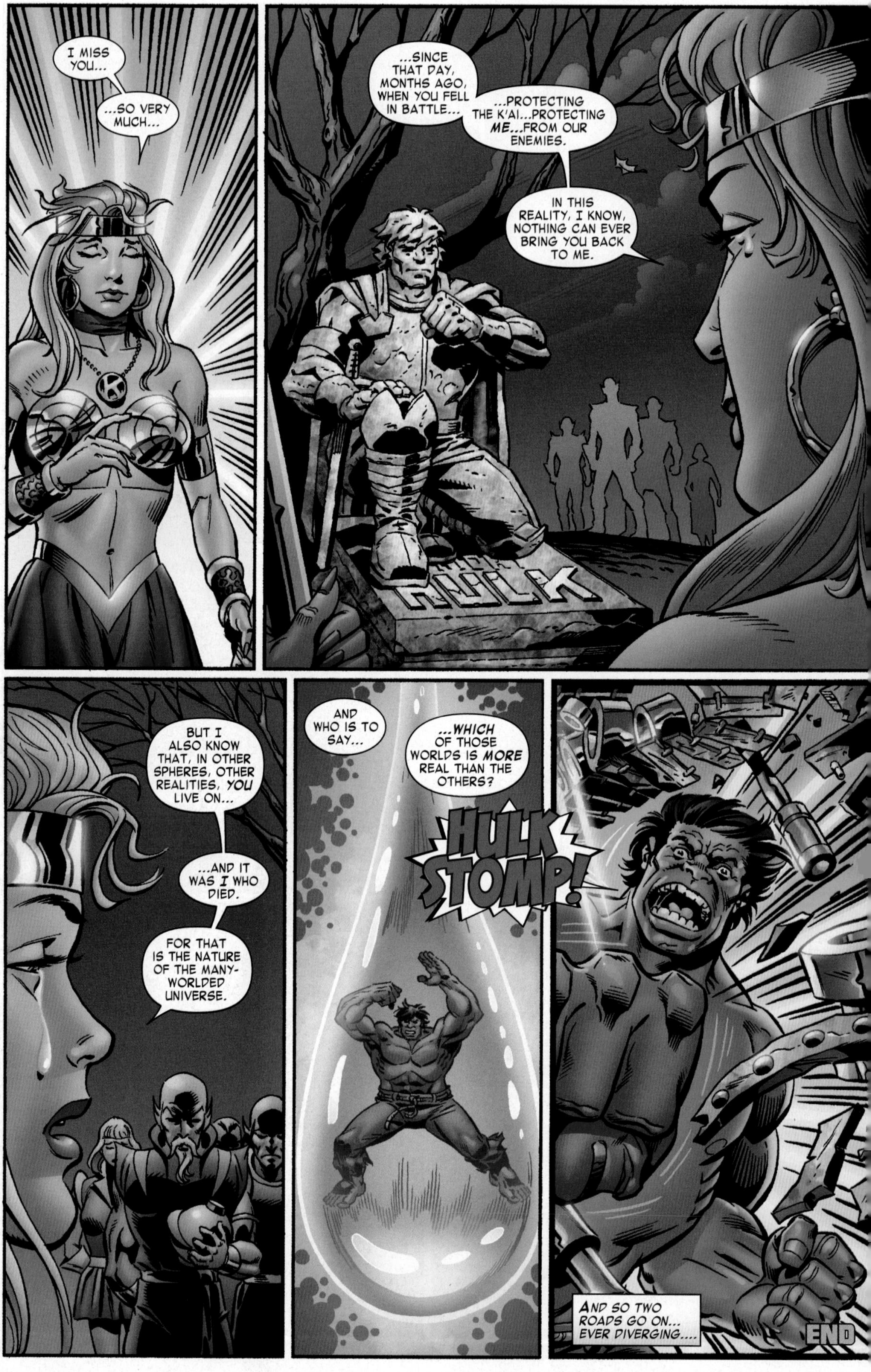
I MISS YOU...
...SO VERY MUCH...
...SINCE THAT DAY, MONTHS AGO, WHEN YOU FELL IN BATTLE...
...PROTECTING THE K'AI...PROTECTING ME...FROM OUR ENEMIES.
IN THIS REALITY, I KNOW, NOTHING CAN EVER BRING YOU BACK TO ME.
HULK
BUT I ALSO KNOW THAT, IN OTHER SPHERES, OTHER REALITIES, YOU LIVE ON...
...AND IT WAS I WHO DIED.
FOR THAT IS THE NATURE OF THE MANY-WORLDED UNIVERSE.
AND WHO IS TO SAY...
...WHICH OF THOSE WORLDS IS MORE REAL THAN THE OTHERS?
HULK STOMP!
AND SO TWO ROADS GO ON... EVER DIVERGING....
END

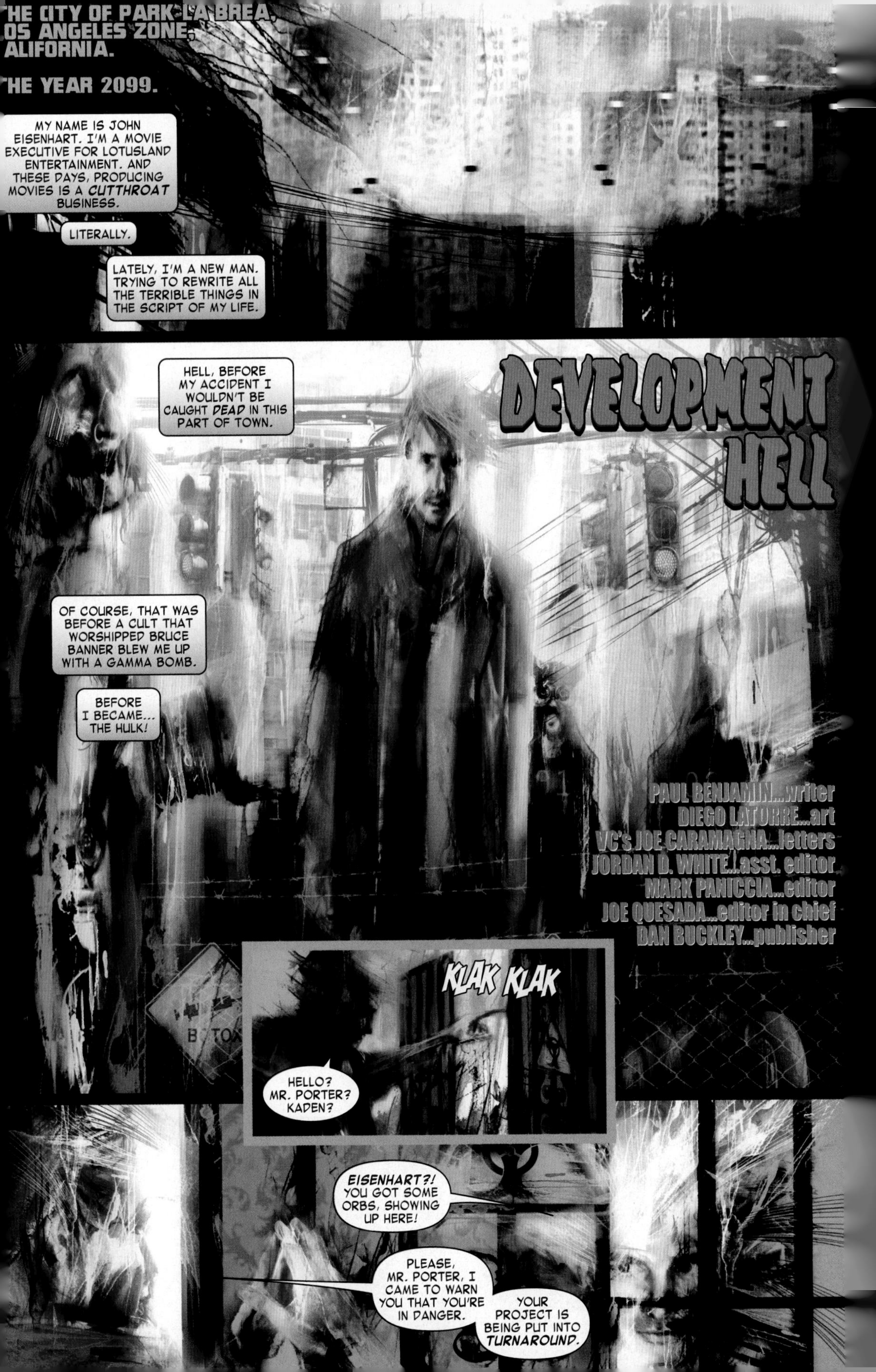

HE CITY OF PARK LA BREA,
OS ANGELES ZONE,
ALIFORNIA.
HE YEAR 2099.
MY NAME IS JOHN EISENHART. I'M A MOVIE EXECUTIVE FOR LOTUSLAND ENTERTAINMENT. AND THESE DAYS, PRODUCING MOVIES IS A CUTTHROAT BUSINESS.
LITERALLY.
LATELY, I'M A NEW MAN. TRYING TO REWRITE ALL THE TERRIBLE THINGS IN THE SCRIPT OF MY LIFE.
HELL, BEFORE MY ACCIDENT I WOULDN'T BE CAUGHT DEAD IN THIS PART OF TOWN.
DEVELOPMENT HELL
OF COURSE, THAT WAS BEFORE A CULT THAT WORSHIPPED BRUCE BANNER BLEW ME UP WITH A GAMMA BOMB.
BEFORE I BECAME... THE HULK!
PAUL BENJAMIN...writer
DIEGO LATORRE...art
VC's JOE CARAMAGNA...letters
JORDAN D. WHITE...asst. editor
MARK PANICCIA...editor
JOE QUESADA...editor in chief
DAN BUCKLEY...publisher
KLAK KLAK
HELLO? MR. PORTER? KADEN?
EISENHART?! YOU GOT SOME ORBS, SHOWING UP HERE!
PLEASE, MR. PORTER, I CAME TO WARN YOU THAT YOU'RE IN DANGER.
YOUR PROJECT IS BEING PUT INTO TURNAROUND.

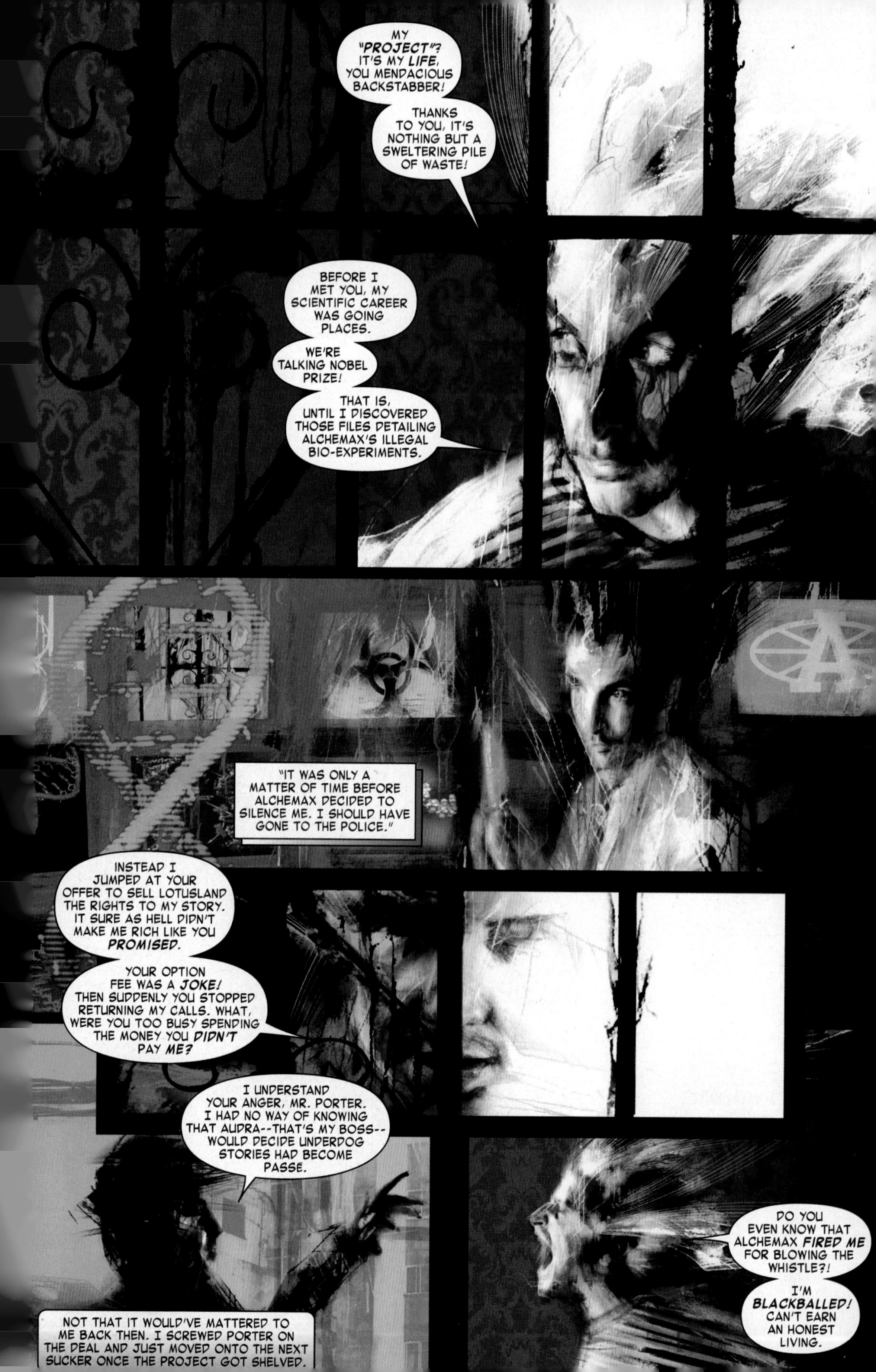
MY "PROJECT"? IT'S MY LIFE, YOU MENDACIOUS BACKSTABBER!
THANKS TO YOU, IT'S NOTHING BUT A SWELTERING PILE OF WASTE!
BEFORE I MET YOU, MY SCIENTIFIC CAREER WAS GOING PLACES.
WE'RE TALKING NOBEL PRIZE!
THAT IS, UNTIL I DISCOVERED THOSE FILES DETAILING ALCHEMAX'S ILLEGAL BIO-EXPERIMENTS.
"IT WAS ONLY A MATTER OF TIME BEFORE ALCHEMAX DECIDED TO SILENCE ME. I SHOULD HAVE GONE TO THE POLICE."
INSTEAD I JUMPED AT YOUR OFFER TO SELL LOTUSLAND THE RIGHTS TO MY STORY. IT SURE AS HELL DIDN'T MAKE ME RICH LIKE YOU PROMISED.
YOUR OPTION FEE WAS A JOKE! THEN SUDDENLY YOU STOPPED RETURNING MY CALLS. WHAT, WERE YOU TOO BUSY SPENDING THE MONEY YOU DIDN'T PAY ME?
I UNDERSTAND YOUR ANGER, MR. PORTER. I HAD NO WAY OF KNOWING THAT AUDRA--THAT'S MY BOSS--WOULD DECIDE UNDERDOG STORIES HAD BECOME PASSE.
DO YOU EVEN KNOW THAT ALCHEMAX FIRED ME FOR BLOWING THE WHISTLE?!
I'M BLACKBALLED! CAN'T EARN AN HONEST LIVING.
NOT THAT IT WOULD'VE MATTERED TO ME BACK THEN. I SCREWED PORTER ON THE DEAL AND JUST MOVED ONTO THE NEXT SUCKER ONCE THE PROJECT GOT SHELVED.

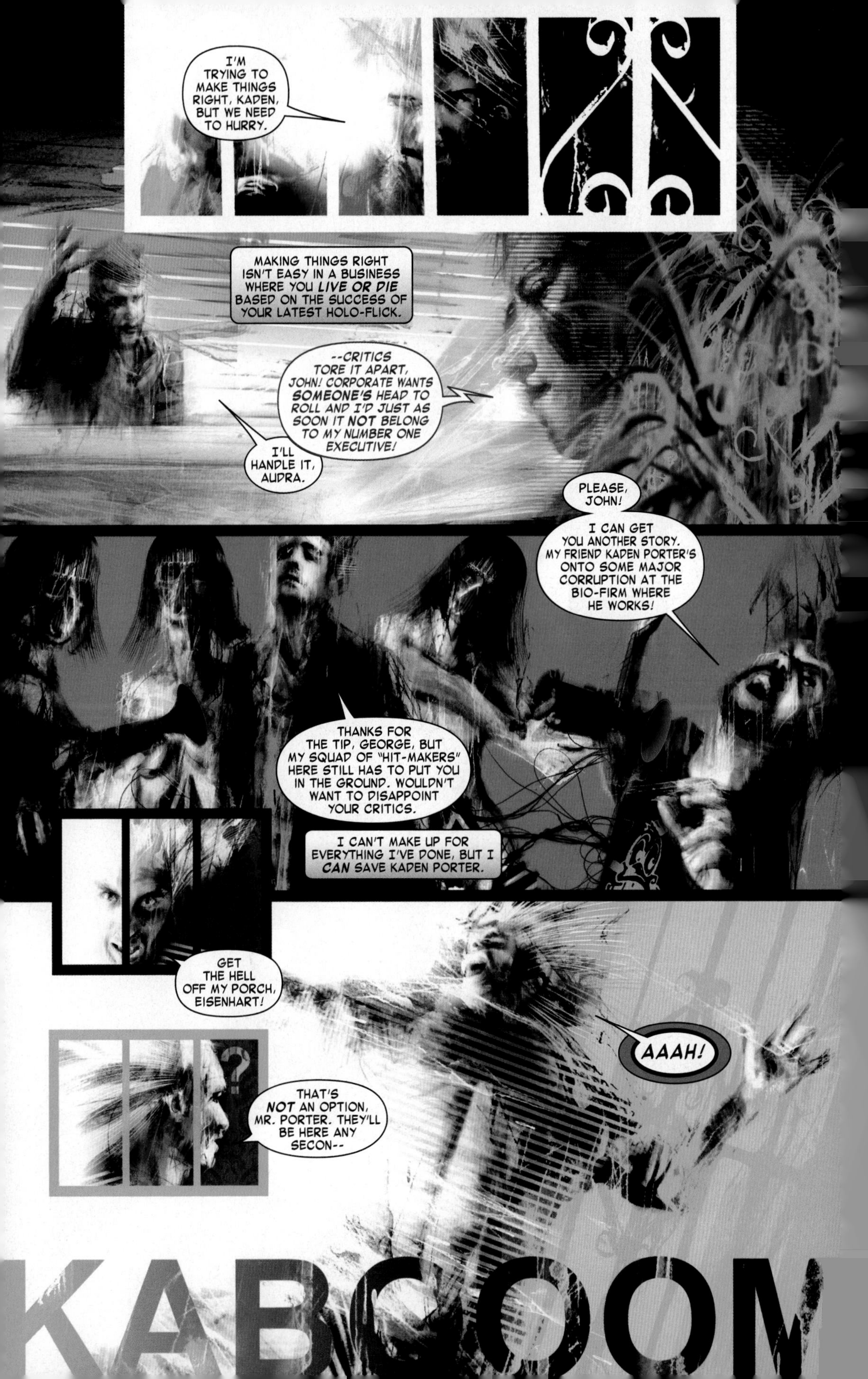
I'M TRYING TO MAKE THINGS RIGHT, KADEN, BUT WE NEED TO HURRY.
MAKING THINGS RIGHT ISN'T EASY IN A BUSINESS WHERE YOU LIVE OR DIE BASED ON THE SUCCESS OF YOUR LATEST HOLO-FLICK.
--CRITICS TORE IT APART, JOHN! CORPORATE WANTS SOMEONE'S HEAD TO ROLL AND I'D JUST AS SOON IT NOT BELONG TO MY NUMBER ONE EXECUTIVE!
I'LL HANDLE IT, AUDRA.
PLEASE, JOHN!
I CAN GET YOU ANOTHER STORY. MY FRIEND KADEN PORTER'S ONTO SOME MAJOR CORRUPTION AT THE BIO-FIRM WHERE HE WORKS!
THANKS FOR THE TIP, GEORGE, BUT MY SQUAD OF "HIT-MAKERS" HERE STILL HAS TO PUT YOU IN THE GROUND. WOULDN'T WANT TO DISAPPOINT YOUR CRITICS.
I CAN'T MAKE UP FOR EVERYTHING I'VE DONE, BUT I CAN SAVE KADEN PORTER.
GET THE HELL OFF MY PORCH, EISENHART!
AAAH!
THAT'S NOT AN OPTION, MR. PORTER. THEY'LL BE HERE ANY SECON--
KABOOOM

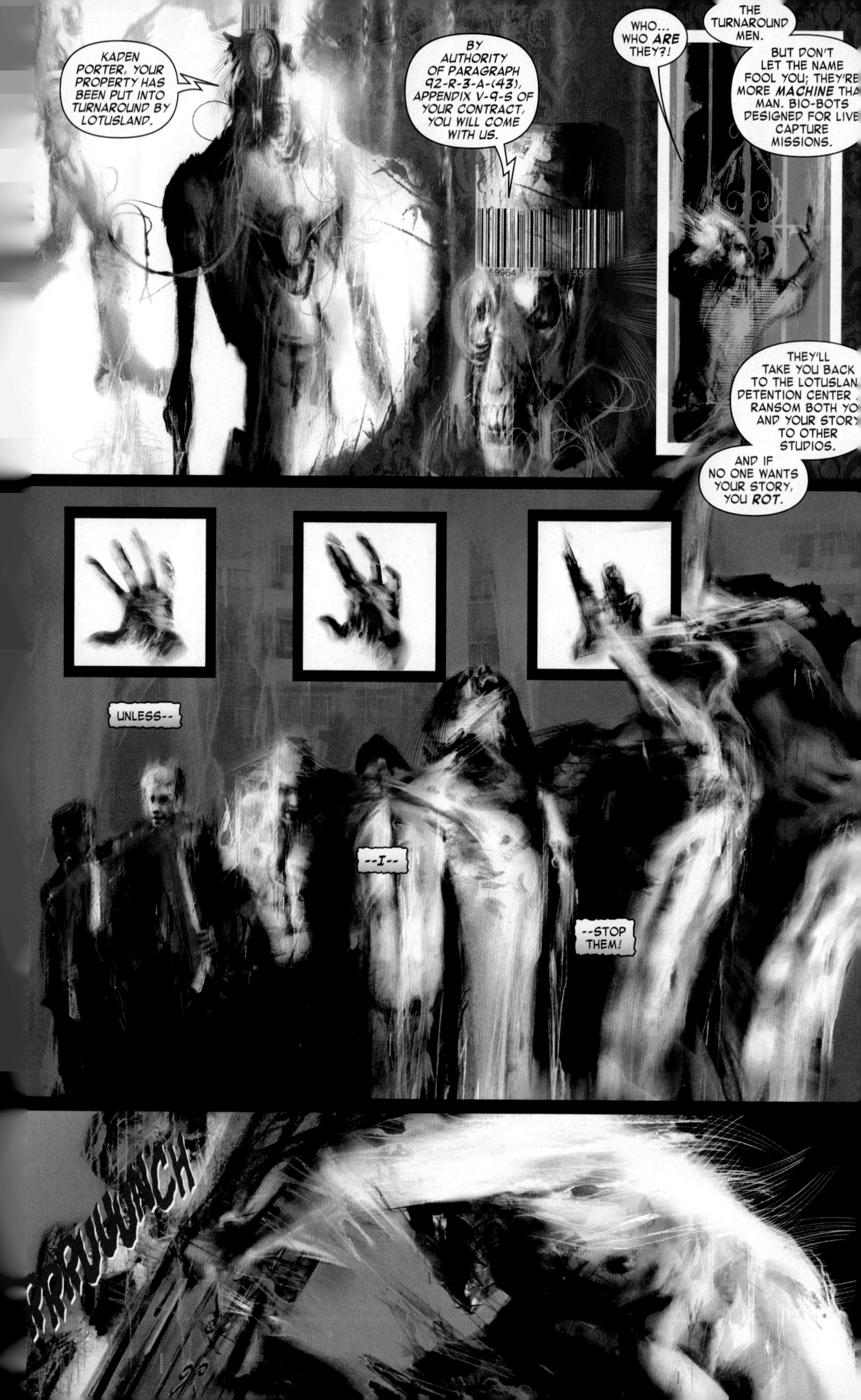

KADEN PORTER, YOUR PROPERTY HAS BEEN PUT INTO TURNAROUND BY LOTUSLAND.
BY AUTHORITY OF PARAGRAPH 92-R-3-A-(43), APPENDIX V-9-S OF YOUR CONTRACT, YOU WILL COME WITH US.
WHO... WHO ARE THEY?!
THE TURNAROUND MEN.
BUT DON'T LET THE NAME FOOL YOU; THEY'RE MORE MACHINE THAN MAN. BIO-BOTS DESIGNED FOR LIVE CAPTURE MISSIONS.
THEY'LL TAKE YOU BACK TO THE LOTUSLAND DETENTION CENTER AND RANSOM BOTH YOU AND YOUR STORY TO OTHER STUDIOS.
AND IF NO ONE WANTS YOUR STORY, YOU ROT.
UNLESS--
--I--
--STOP THEM!
KRRUUNCH

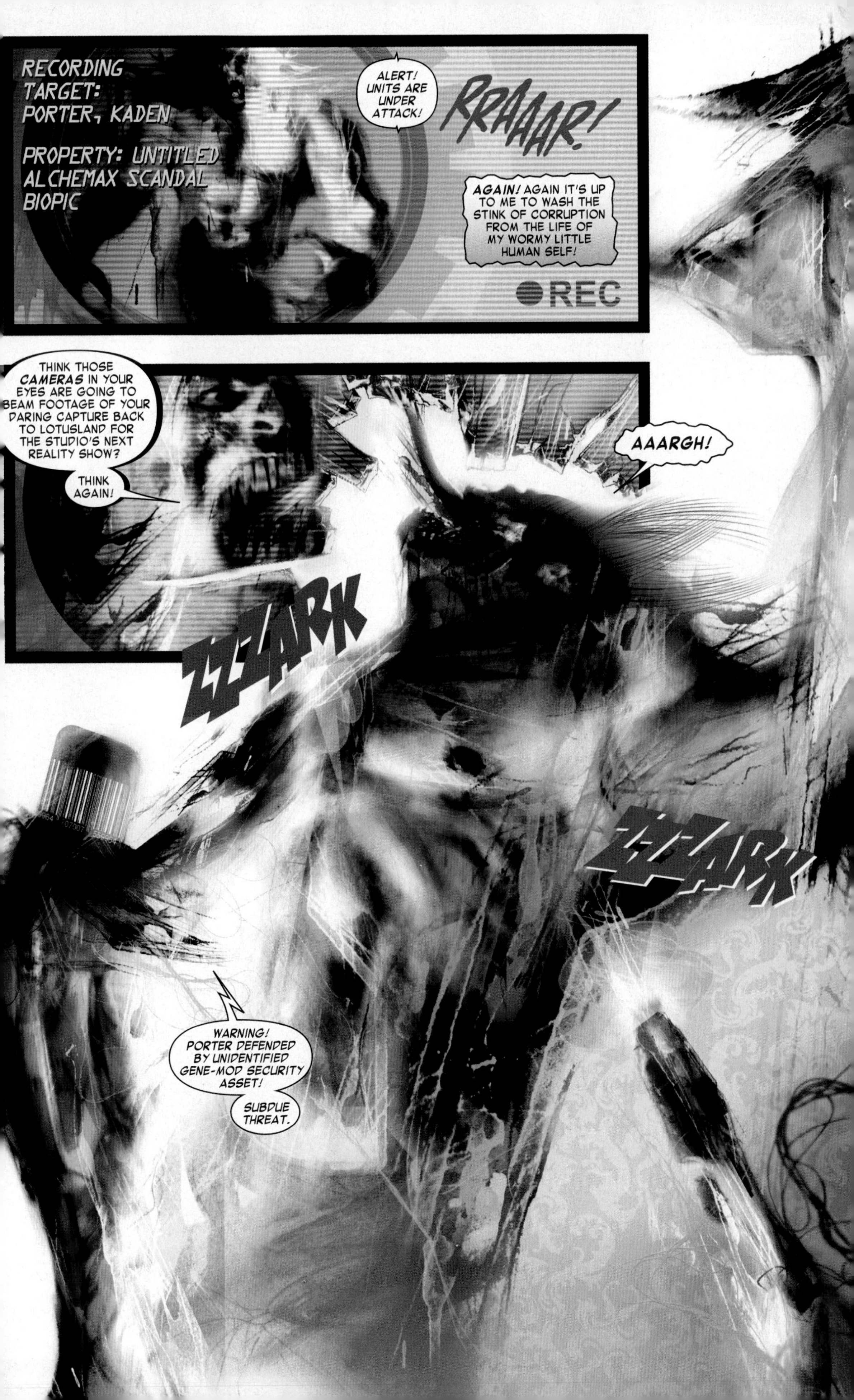

RECORDING TARGET: PORTER, KADEN
PROPERTY: UNTITLED ALCHEMAX SCANDAL BIOPIC
ALERT! UNITS ARE UNDER ATTACK!
RRAAAR!
AGAIN! AGAIN IT'S UP TO ME TO WASH THE STINK OF CORRUPTION FROM THE LIFE OF MY WORMY LITTLE HUMAN SELF!
REC
THINK THOSE CAMERAS IN YOUR EYES ARE GOING TO BEAM FOOTAGE OF YOUR DARING CAPTURE BACK TO LOTUSLAND FOR THE STUDIO'S NEXT REALITY SHOW?
THINK AGAIN!
AAARGH!
ZZZARK
ZZZARK
WARNING! PORTER DEFENDED BY UNIDENTIFIED GENE-MOD SECURITY ASSET!
SUBDUE THREAT.

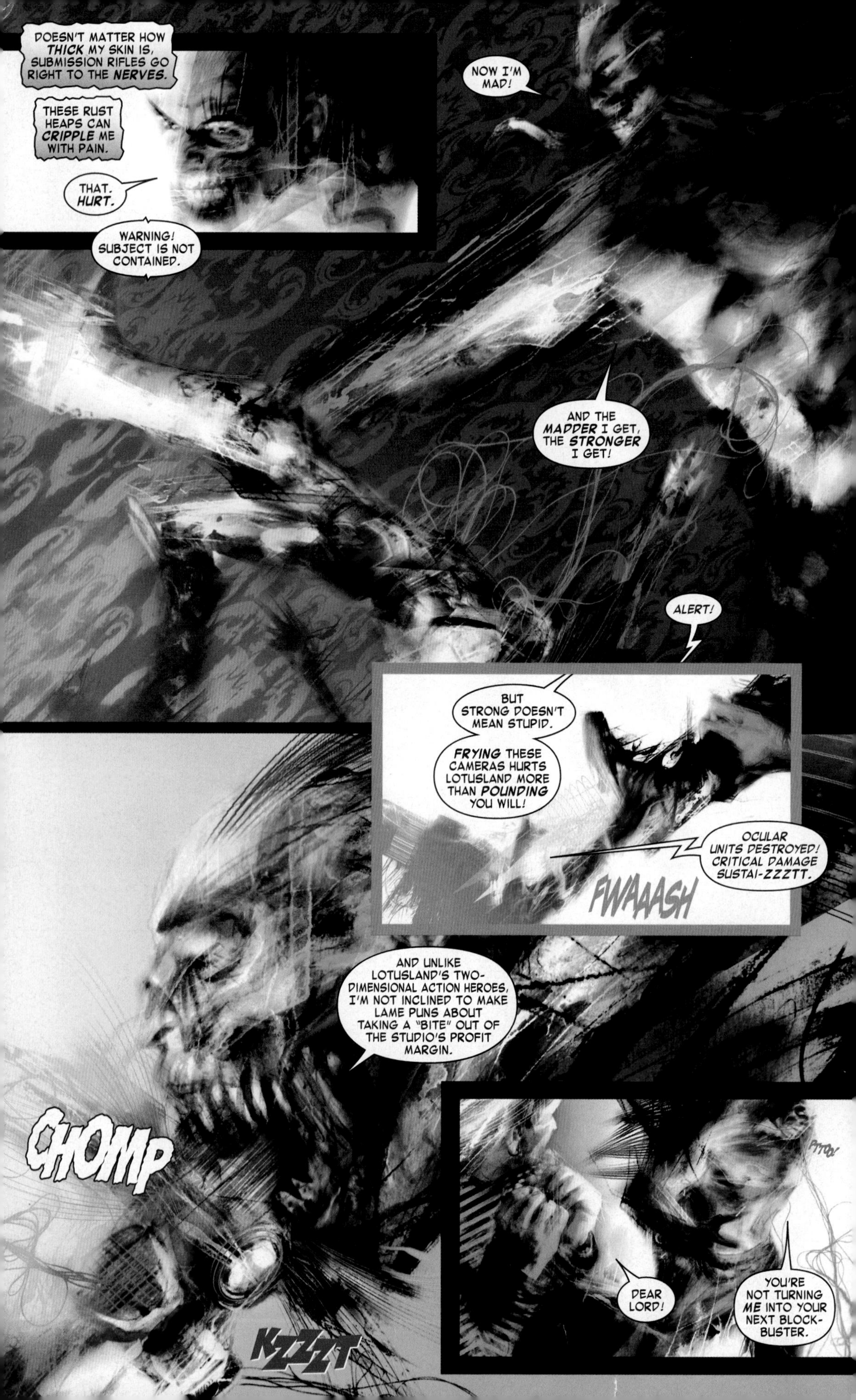

DOESN'T MATTER HOW THICK MY SKIN IS, SUBMISSION RIFLES GO RIGHT TO THE NERVES.
THESE RUST HEAPS CAN CRIPPLE ME WITH PAIN.
THAT. HURT.
WARNING! SUBJECT IS NOT CONTAINED.
NOW I'M MAD!
AND THE MADDER I GET, THE STRONGER I GET!
ALERT!
BUT STRONG DOESN'T MEAN STUPID.
FRYING THESE CAMERAS HURTS LOTUSLAND MORE THAN POUNDING YOU WILL!
OCULAR UNITS DESTROYED! CRITICAL DAMAGE SUSTAI-ZZZTT.
FWAAASH
AND UNLIKE LOTUSLAND'S TWO-DIMENSIONAL ACTION HEROES, I'M NOT INCLINED TO MAKE LAME PUNS ABOUT TAKING A "BITE" OUT OF THE STUDIO'S PROFIT MARGIN.
CHOMP
KZZZT
DEAR LORD!
YOU'RE NOT TURNING ME INTO YOUR NEXT BLOCK-BUSTER.

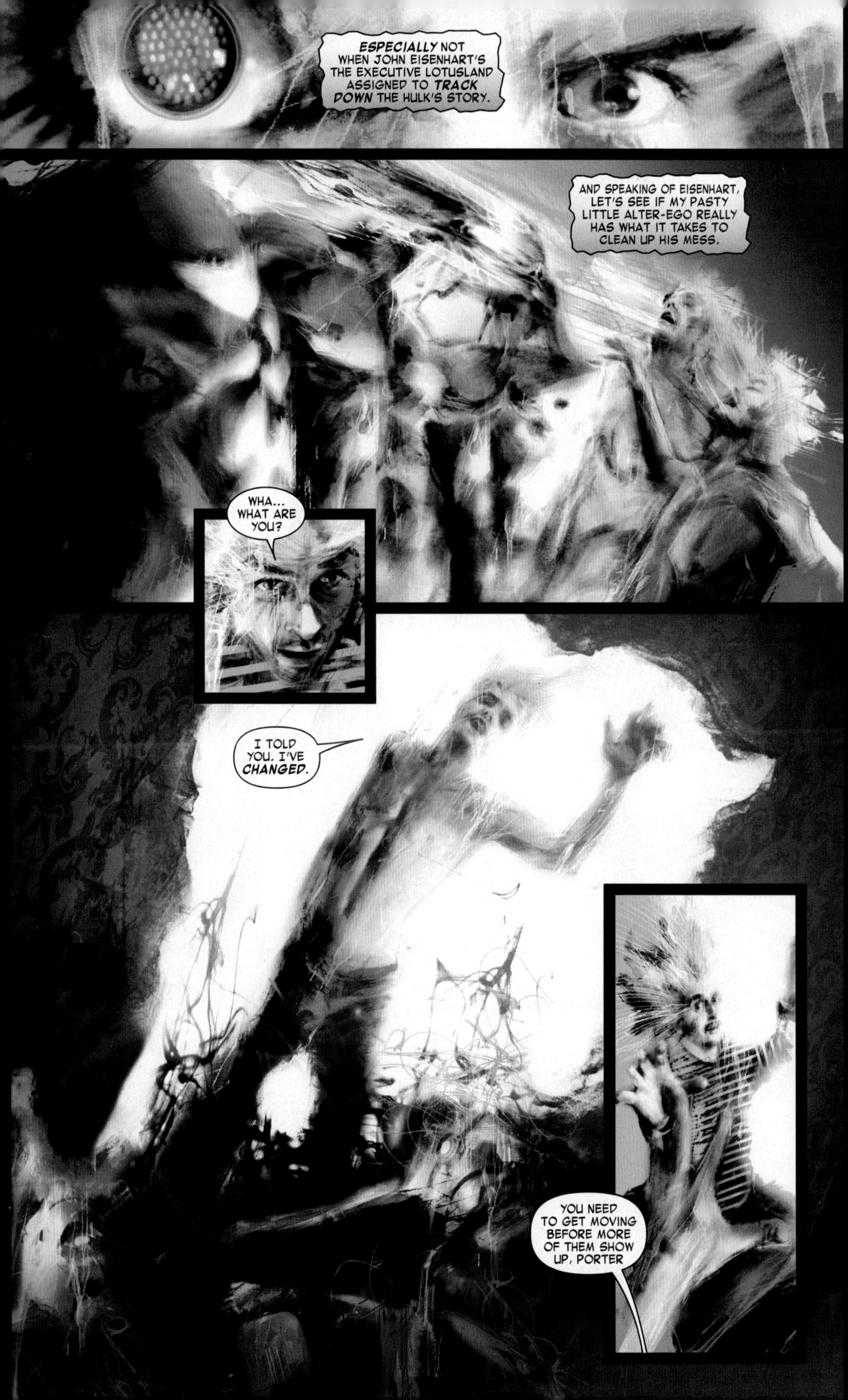
ESPECIALLY NOT WHEN JOHN EISENHART'S THE EXECUTIVE LOTUSLAND ASSIGNED TO TRACK DOWN THE HULK'S STORY.
AND SPEAKING OF EISENHART, LET'S SEE IF MY PASTY LITTLE ALTER-EGO REALLY HAS WHAT IT TAKES TO CLEAN UP HIS MESS.
WHA... WHAT ARE YOU?
I TOLD YOU. I'VE CHANGED.
YOU NEED TO GET MOVING BEFORE MORE OF THEM SHOW UP, PORTER

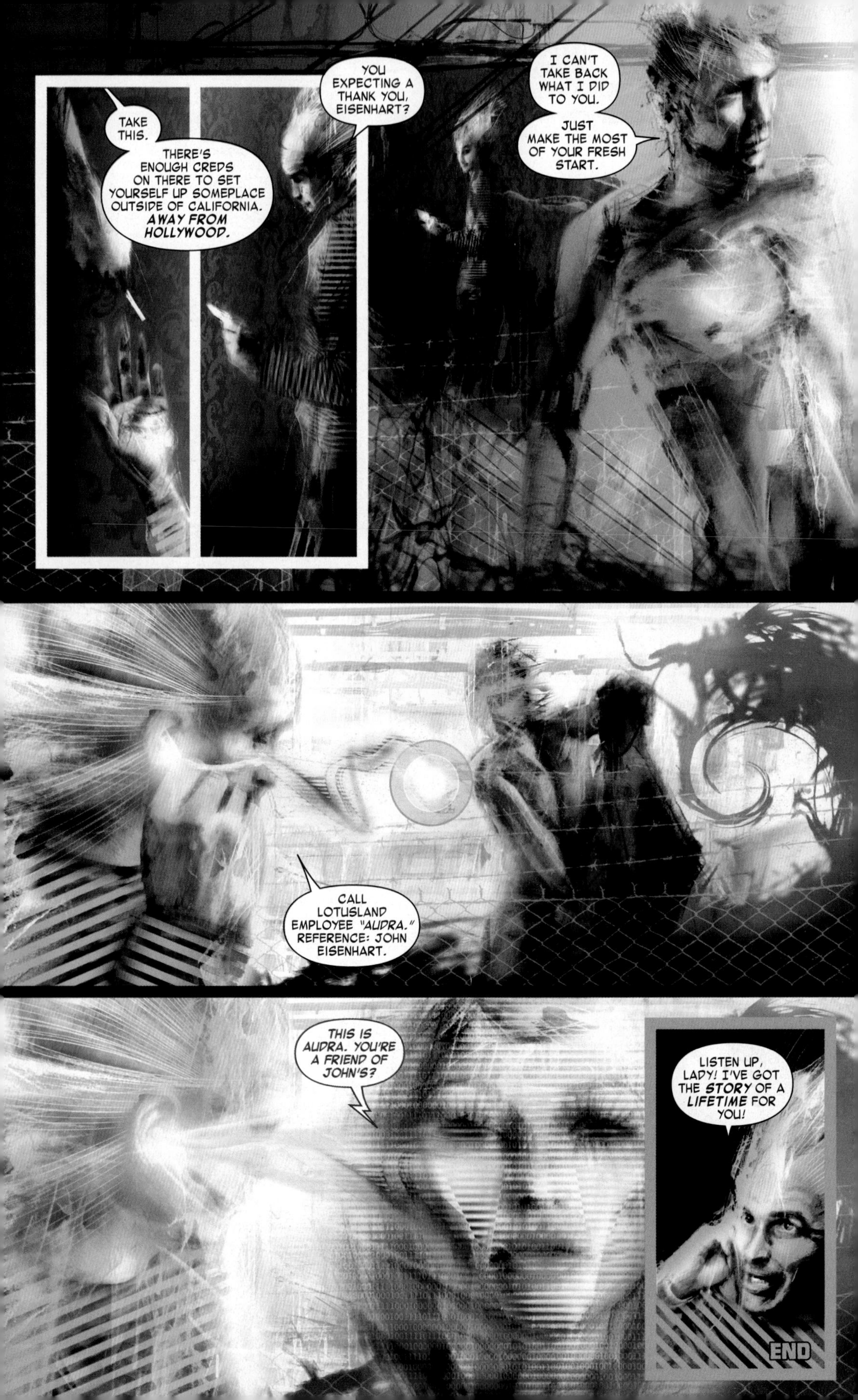
TAKE THIS.
THERE'S ENOUGH CREDS ON THERE TO SET YOURSELF UP SOMEPLACE OUTSIDE OF CALIFORNIA. AWAY FROM HOLLYWOOD.
YOU EXPECTING A THANK YOU, EISENHART?
I CAN'T TAKE BACK WHAT I DID TO YOU.
JUST MAKE THE MOST OF YOUR FRESH START.
CALL LOTUSLAND EMPLOYEE "AUDRA." REFERENCE: JOHN EISENHART.
THIS IS AUDRA. YOU'RE A FRIEND OF JOHN'S?
LISTEN UP, LADY! I'VE GOT THE STORY OF A LIFETIME FOR YOU!
END

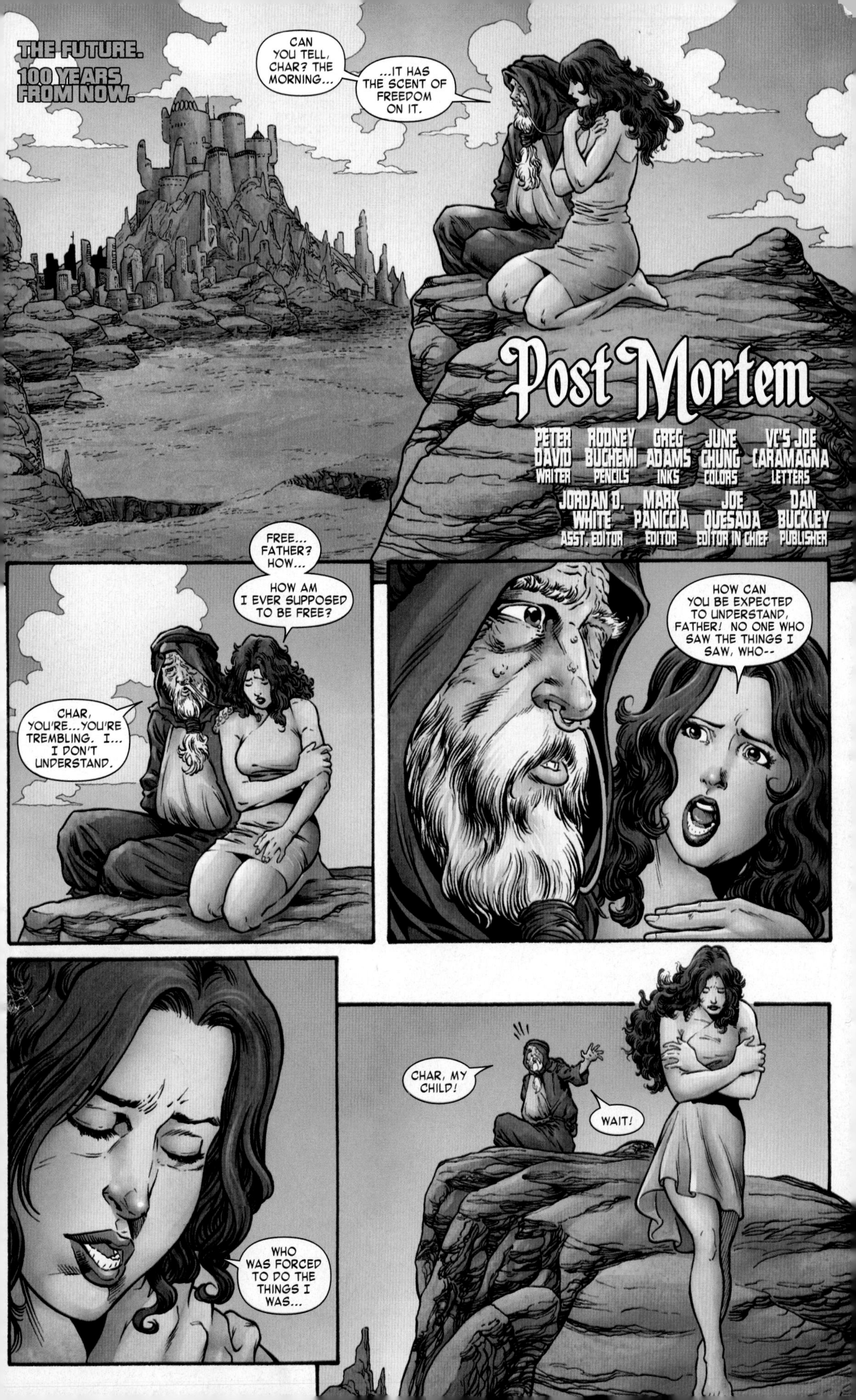
THE FUTURE.
100 YEARS FROM NOW.
CAN YOU TELL, CHAR? THE MORNING...
...IT HAS THE SCENT OF FREEDOM ON IT.
Post Mortem
PETER DAVID WRITER
RODNEY BUCHEMI PENCILS
GREG ADAMS INKS
JUNE CHUNG COLORS
VC'S JOE CARAMAGNA LETTERS
JORDAN D. WHITE ASST. EDITOR
MARK PANICCIA EDITOR
JOE QUESADA EDITOR IN CHIEF
DAN BUCKLEY PUBLISHER
FREE... FATHER? HOW...
HOW AM I EVER SUPPOSED TO BE FREE?
CHAR, YOU'RE...YOU'RE TREMBLING. I... I DON'T UNDERSTAND.
HOW CAN YOU BE EXPECTED TO UNDERSTAND, FATHER! NO ONE WHO SAW THE THINGS I SAW, WHO--
WHO WAS FORCED TO DO THE THINGS I WAS...
CHAR, MY CHILD!
WAIT!

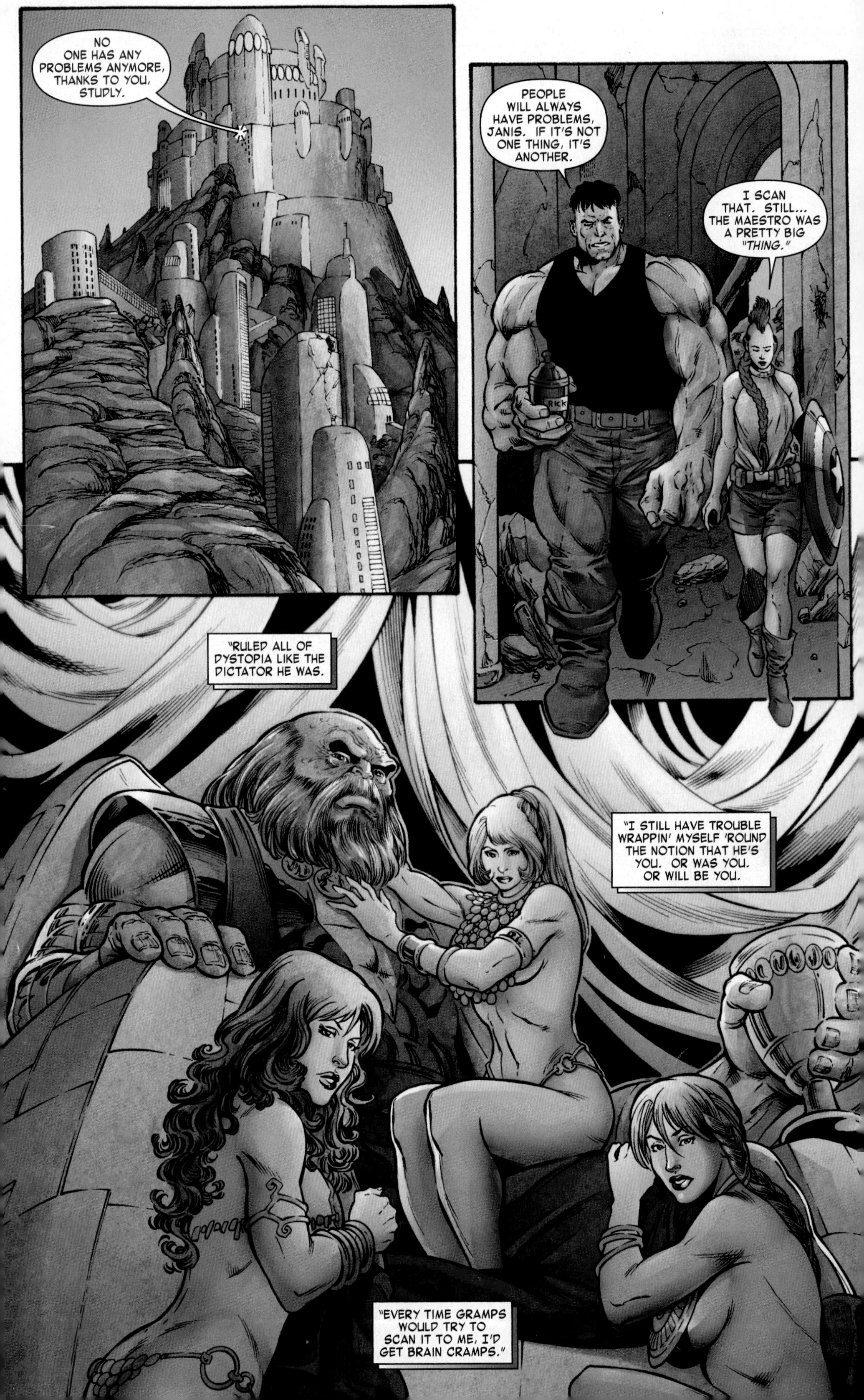
NO ONE HAS ANY PROBLEMS ANYMORE, THANKS TO YOU, STUDLY.
PEOPLE WILL ALWAYS HAVE PROBLEMS, JANIS. IF IT'S NOT ONE THING, IT'S ANOTHER.
I SCAN THAT. STILL... THE MAESTRO WAS A PRETTY BIG "THING."
"RULED ALL OF DYSTOPIA LIKE THE DICTATOR HE WAS.
"I STILL HAVE TROUBLE WRAPPIN' MYSELF 'ROUND THE NOTION THAT HE'S YOU. OR WAS YOU. OR WILL BE YOU.
"EVERY TIME GRAMPS WOULD TRY TO SCAN IT TO ME, I'D GET BRAIN CRAMPS."

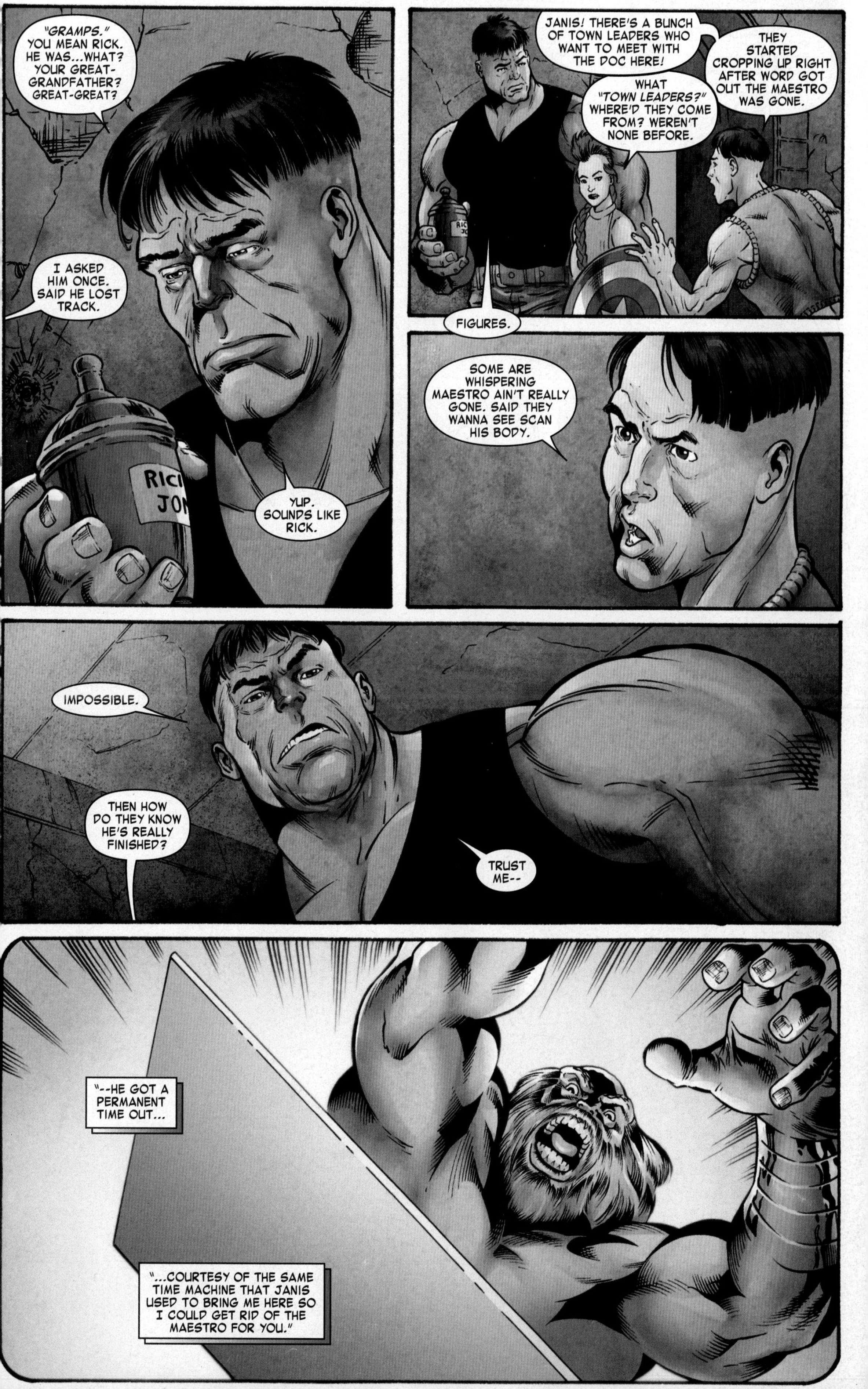
"GRAMPS." YOU MEAN RICK. HE WAS...WHAT? YOUR GREAT-GRANDFATHER? GREAT-GREAT?
I ASKED HIM ONCE. SAID HE LOST TRACK.
YUP. SOUNDS LIKE RICK.
JANIS! THERE'S A BUNCH OF TOWN LEADERS WHO WANT TO MEET WITH THE DOC HERE!
WHAT "TOWN LEADERS?" WHERE'D THEY COME FROM? WEREN'T NONE BEFORE.
THEY STARTED CROPPING UP RIGHT AFTER WORD GOT OUT THE MAESTRO WAS GONE.
FIGURES.
SOME ARE WHISPERING MAESTRO AIN'T REALLY GONE. SAID THEY WANNA SEE SCAN HIS BODY.
IMPOSSIBLE.
THEN HOW DO THEY KNOW HE'S REALLY FINISHED?
TRUST ME--
"--HE GOT A PERMANENT TIME OUT...
"...COURTESY OF THE SAME TIME MACHINE THAT JANIS USED TO BRING ME HERE SO I COULD GET RID OF THE MAESTRO FOR YOU."

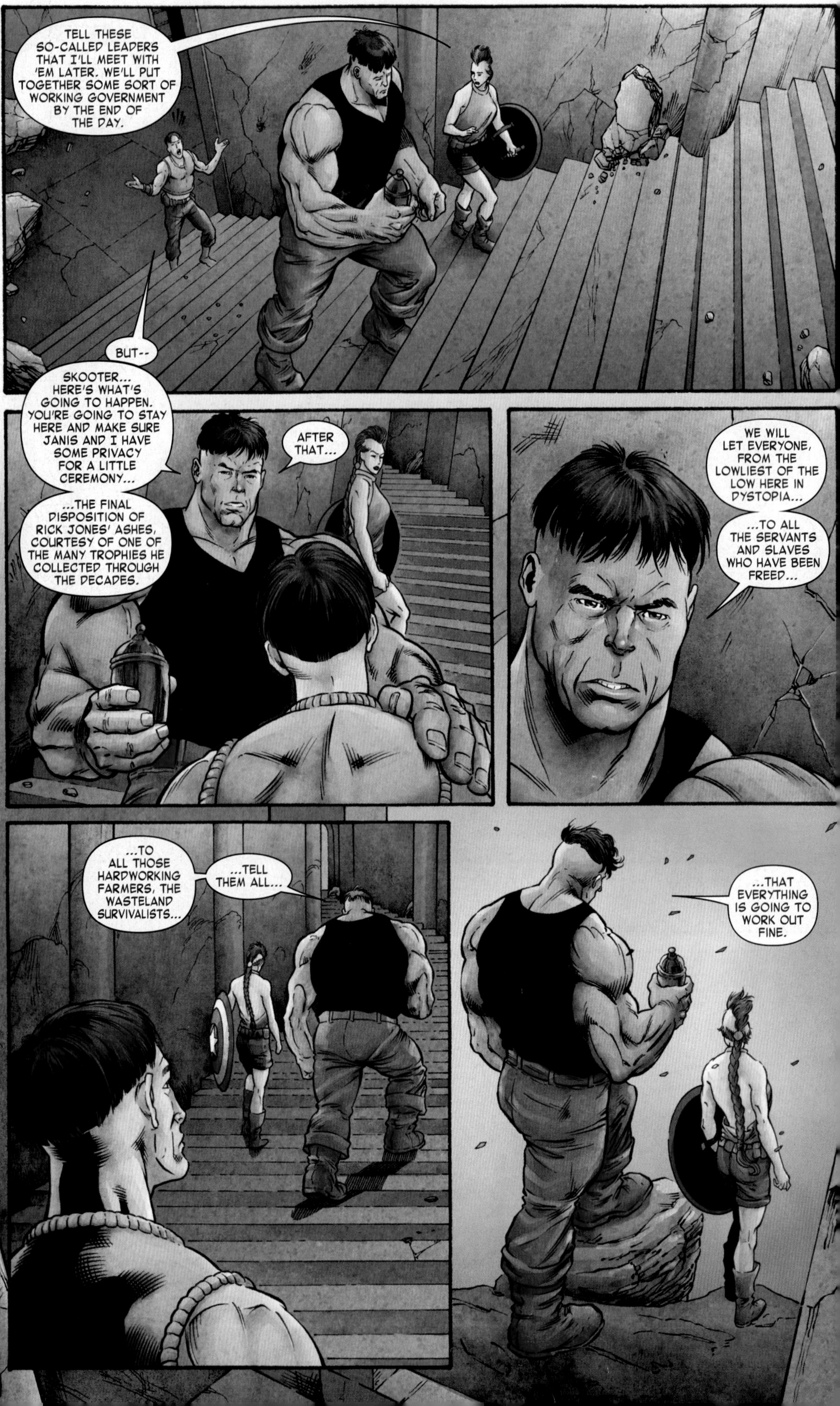
TELL THESE SO-CALLED LEADERS THAT I'LL MEET WITH 'EM LATER. WE'LL PUT TOGETHER SOME SORT OF WORKING GOVERNMENT BY THE END OF THE DAY.
BUT--
SKOOTER... HERE'S WHAT'S GOING TO HAPPEN. YOU'RE GOING TO STAY HERE AND MAKE SURE JANIS AND I HAVE SOME PRIVACY FOR A LITTLE CEREMONY...
...THE FINAL DISPOSITION OF RICK JONES' ASHES, COURTESY OF ONE OF THE MANY TROPHIES HE COLLECTED THROUGH THE DECADES.
AFTER THAT...
WE WILL LET EVERYONE, FROM THE LOWLIEST OF THE LOW HERE IN DYSTOPIA...
...TO ALL THE SERVANTS AND SLAVES WHO HAVE BEEN FREED...
...TO ALL THOSE HARDWORKING FARMERS, THE WASTELAND SURVIVALISTS...
...TELL THEM ALL...
...THAT EVERYTHING IS GOING TO WORK OUT FINE.

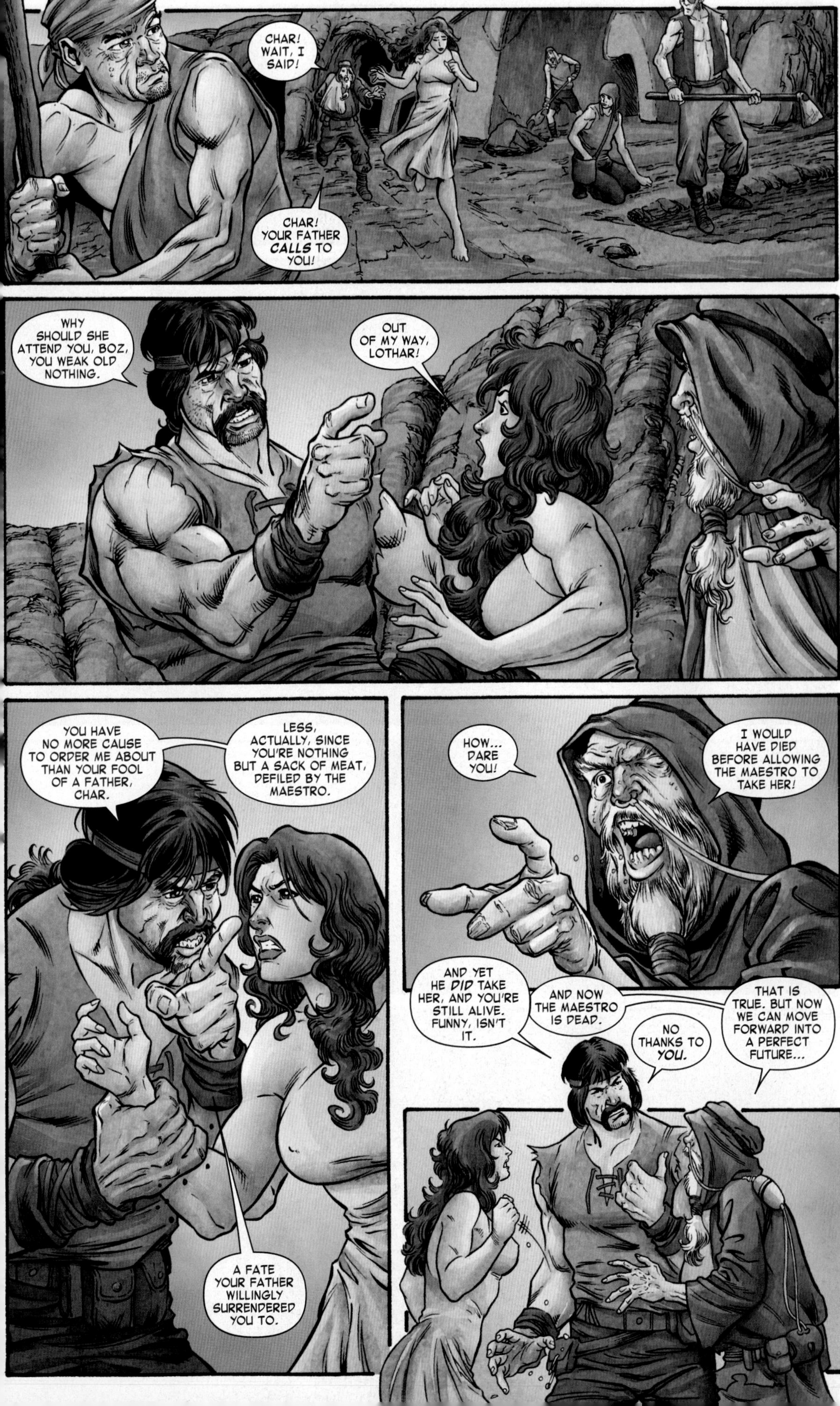
CHAR! WAIT, I SAID!
CHAR! YOUR FATHER CALLS TO YOU!
WHY SHOULD SHE ATTEND YOU, BOZ, YOU WEAK OLD NOTHING.
OUT OF MY WAY, LOTHAR!
YOU HAVE NO MORE CAUSE TO ORDER ME ABOUT THAN YOUR FOOL OF A FATHER, CHAR.
LESS, ACTUALLY, SINCE YOU'RE NOTHING BUT A SACK OF MEAT, DEFILED BY THE MAESTRO.
A FATE YOUR FATHER WILLINGLY SURRENDERED YOU TO.
HOW... DARE YOU!
I WOULD HAVE DIED BEFORE ALLOWING THE MAESTRO TO TAKE HER!
AND YET HE DID TAKE HER, AND YOU'RE STILL ALIVE. FUNNY, ISN'T IT.
AND NOW THE MAESTRO IS DEAD.
NO THANKS TO YOU.
THAT IS TRUE. BUT NOW WE CAN MOVE FORWARD INTO A PERFECT FUTURE...

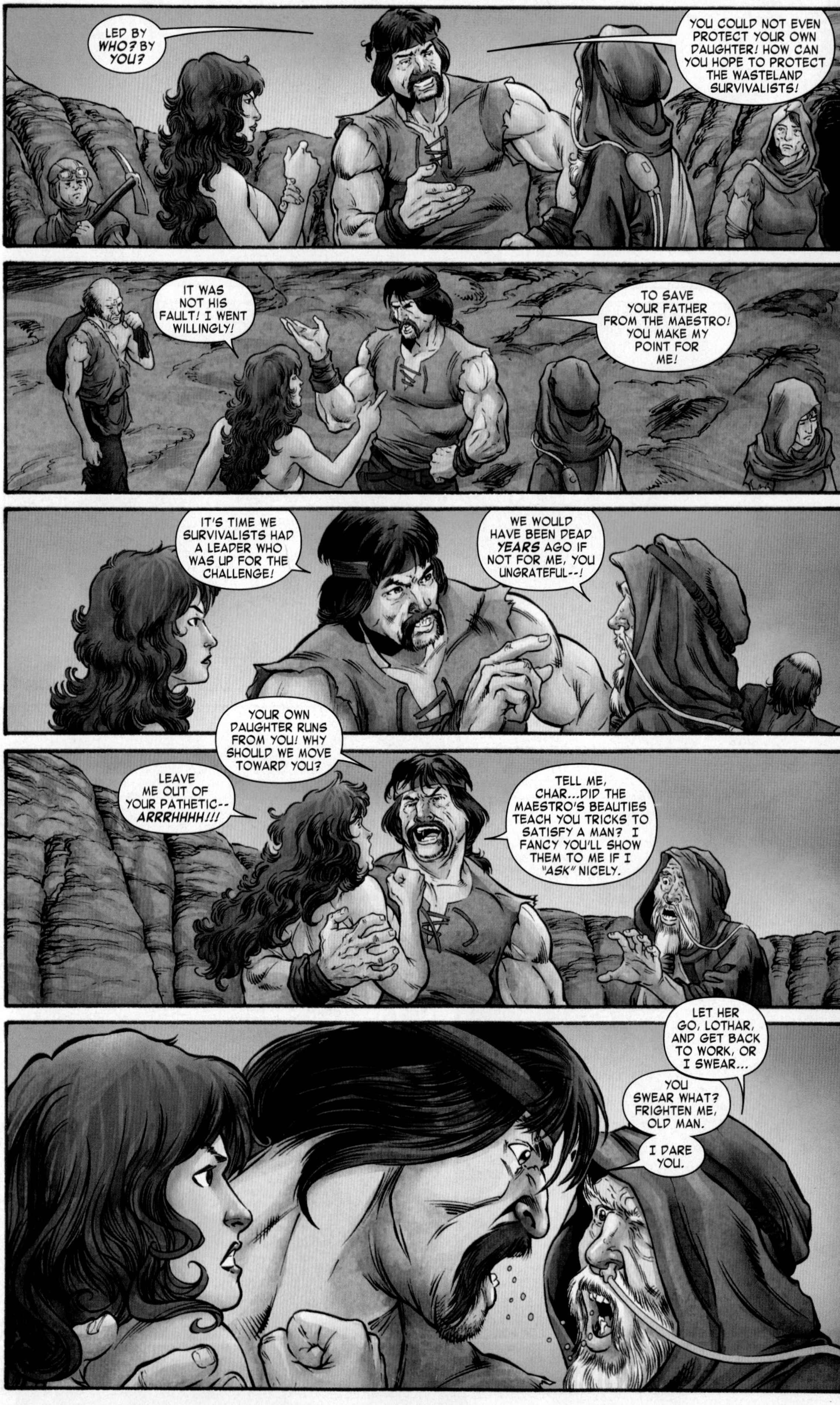
LED BY WHO? BY YOU?
YOU COULD NOT EVEN PROTECT YOUR OWN DAUGHTER! HOW CAN YOU HOPE TO PROTECT THE WASTELAND SURVIVALISTS!
IT WAS NOT HIS FAULT! I WENT WILLINGLY!
TO SAVE YOUR FATHER FROM THE MAESTRO! YOU MAKE MY POINT FOR ME!
IT'S TIME WE SURVIVALISTS HAD A LEADER WHO WAS UP FOR THE CHALLENGE!
WE WOULD HAVE BEEN DEAD YEARS AGO IF NOT FOR ME, YOU UNGRATEFUL--!
YOUR OWN DAUGHTER RUNS FROM YOU! WHY SHOULD WE MOVE TOWARD YOU?
LEAVE ME OUT OF YOUR PATHETIC-- ARRRHHHH!!!
TELL ME, CHAR...DID THE MAESTRO'S BEAUTIES TEACH YOU TRICKS TO SATISFY A MAN? I FANCY YOU'LL SHOW THEM TO ME IF I "ASK" NICELY.
LET HER GO, LOTHAR, AND GET BACK TO WORK, OR I SWEAR...
YOU SWEAR WHAT? FRIGHTEN ME, OLD MAN.
I DARE YOU.

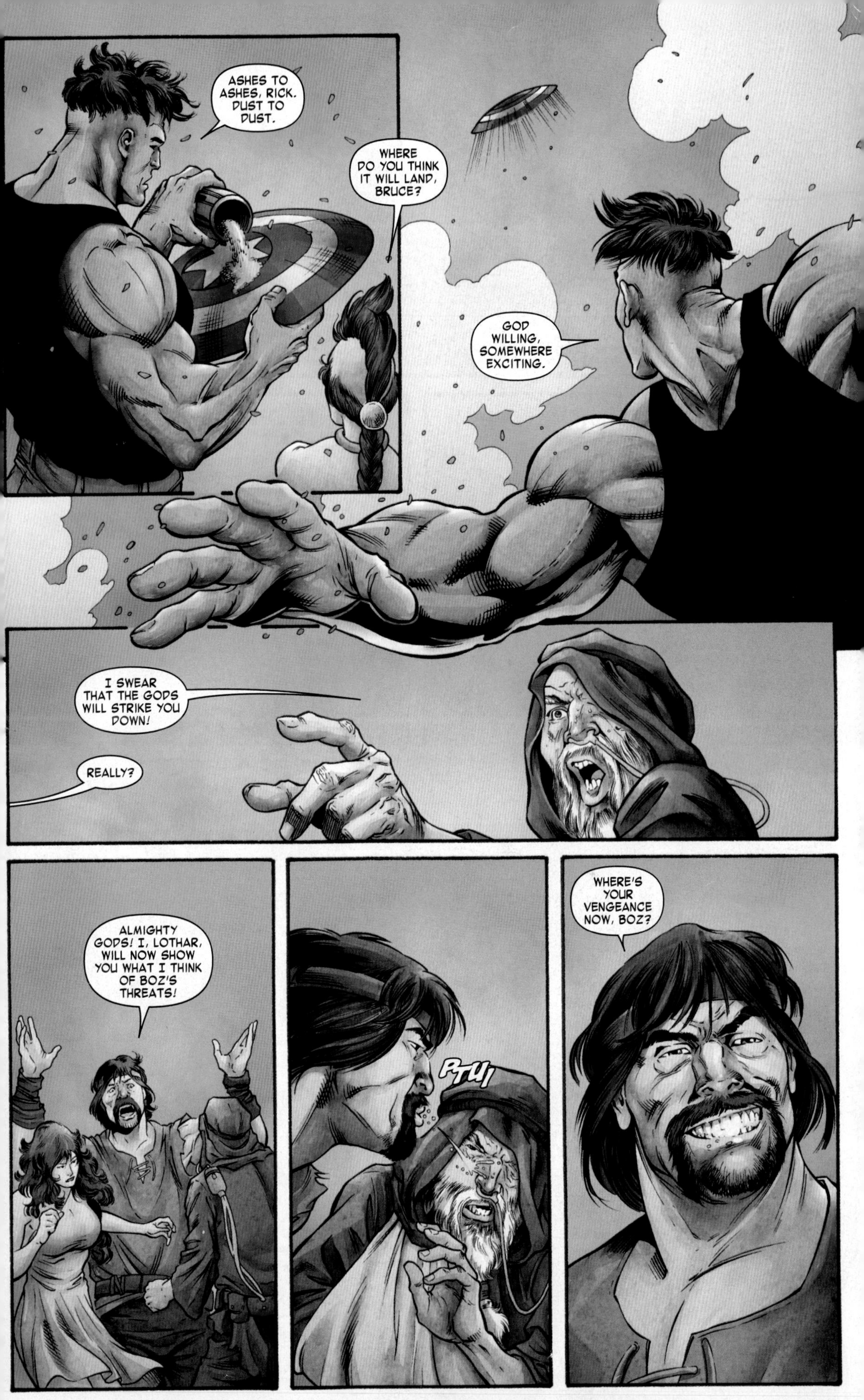
ASHES TO ASHES, RICK. DUST TO DUST.
WHERE DO YOU THINK IT WILL LAND, BRUCE?
GOD WILLING, SOMEWHERE EXCITING.
I SWEAR THAT THE GODS WILL STRIKE YOU DOWN!
REALLY?
ALMIGHTY GODS! I, LOTHAR, WILL NOW SHOW YOU WHAT I THINK OF BOZ'S THREATS!
PTUI
WHERE'S YOUR VENGEANCE NOW, BOZ?

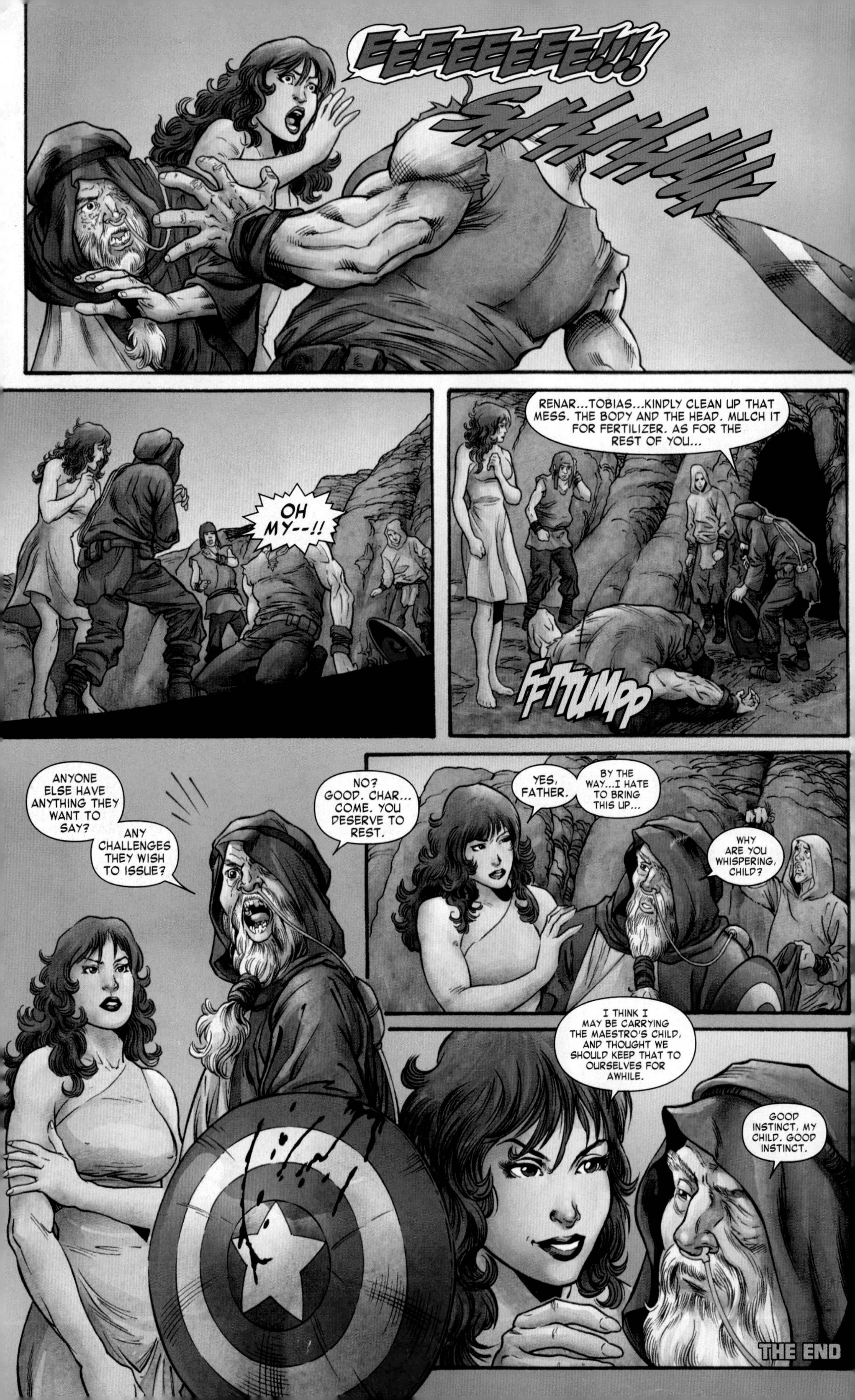
EEEEEEEE!!!
SHHHHHUNK
OH MY--!!
RENAR...TOBIAS...KINDLY CLEAN UP THAT MESS. THE BODY AND THE HEAD. MULCH IT FOR FERTILIZER. AS FOR THE REST OF YOU...
FFTTUMPP
ANYONE ELSE HAVE ANYTHING THEY WANT TO SAY?
ANY CHALLENGES THEY WISH TO ISSUE?
NO? GOOD. CHAR... COME. YOU DESERVE TO REST.
YES, FATHER.
BY THE WAY...I HATE TO BRING THIS UP...
WHY ARE YOU WHISPERING, CHILD?
I THINK I MAY BE CARRYING THE MAESTRO'S CHILD, AND THOUGHT WE SHOULD KEEP THAT TO OURSELVES FOR AWHILE.
GOOD INSTINCT, MY CHILD. GOOD INSTINCT.
THE END

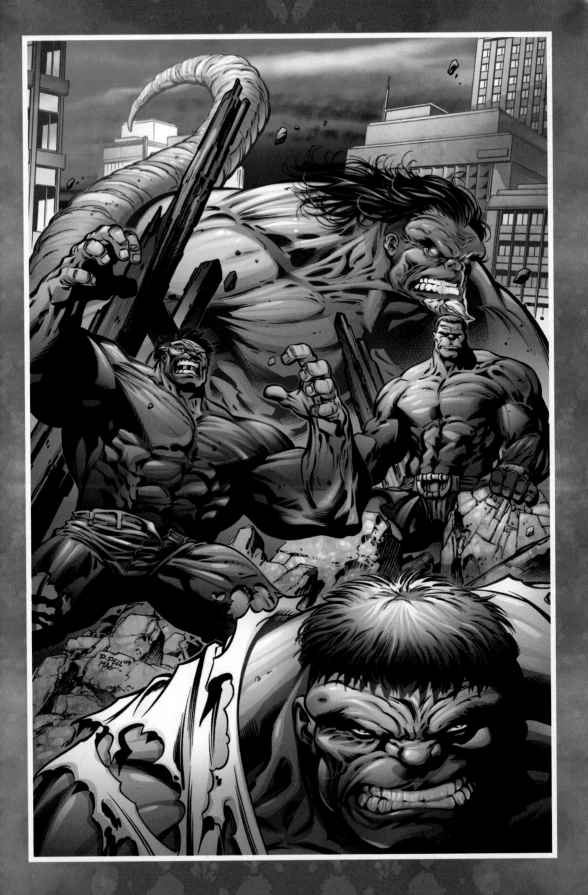

BROKEN WORLDS: BOOK TWO

HULK
BROKEN WORLDS

HULK:

CAUGHT IN A BLAST OF GAMMA-RADIATION, BRILLIANT SCIENTIST BRUCE BANNER NOW FINDS HIMSELF CURSED TO TRANSFORM IN TIMES OF STRESS INTO THE LIVING ENGINE OF DESTRUCTION KNOWN AS **THE INCREDIBLE HULK**...OR SO IT IS ON THE EARTH WE KNOW. BUT WHAT OF OTHER WORLDS?

AGE OF APOCALYPSE:

A WORLD WHERE THE MEGALOMANIACAL APOCALYPSE ROSE TO POWER AND MUTANTS RULE MERCILESSLY WHILE HUMANS ARE TREATED LIKE CATTLE. BRUCE BANNER ORIGINALLY BETRAYED MANKIND, BUT AFTER HIS EXPERIMENTS TRANSFORMED HIM, HE TURNED TO THE SIDE OF HUMANITY.

MANGAVERSE:

IN A WORLD OF ANCIENT MAGIC, MARTIAL ARTS, AND HIGH TECHNOLOGY, THE HULK WAS A SEVENTY-FOOT TALL MYTHOLOGICAL MONSTER SUMMONED BY BRUCE BANNER. ON EARTH, HULK TOWERED OVER THE CITY, RAINING DESTRUCTION WITH EVERY STEP... BUT LITTLE IS KNOWN FROM WHENCE HE CAME.

1602:

IN A WORLD WHERE THE AGE OF MARVELS BEGAN IN 1602, SIR DAVID BANNER WAS TRANSFORMED INTO AN IRRADIATED MONSTER IN THE AMERICAN COLONIES. TURNING HIS BACK ON KING AND COUNTRY, BANNER BECAME A FUGITIVE BY HELPING THE REBELLIOUS COLONISTS DEFEAT THEIR OPPRESSORS.

DAYS OF FUTURE PAST:

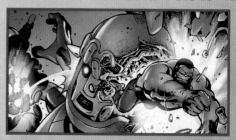

AN ALTERNATE FUTURE IN WHICH MUTANT HYSTERIA ROSE TO ITS ULTIMATE HEIGHTS. THE X-MEN HAVE BEEN WIPED OUT AND MUTANTS HAVE BEEN FORCED INTO INTERNMENT CAMPS BY THE RUTHLESS SENTINELS. THE HEROES OF THE WORLD HAVE ALL BEEN KILLED OR IMPRISONED, BRUCE BANNER AMONG THEM.

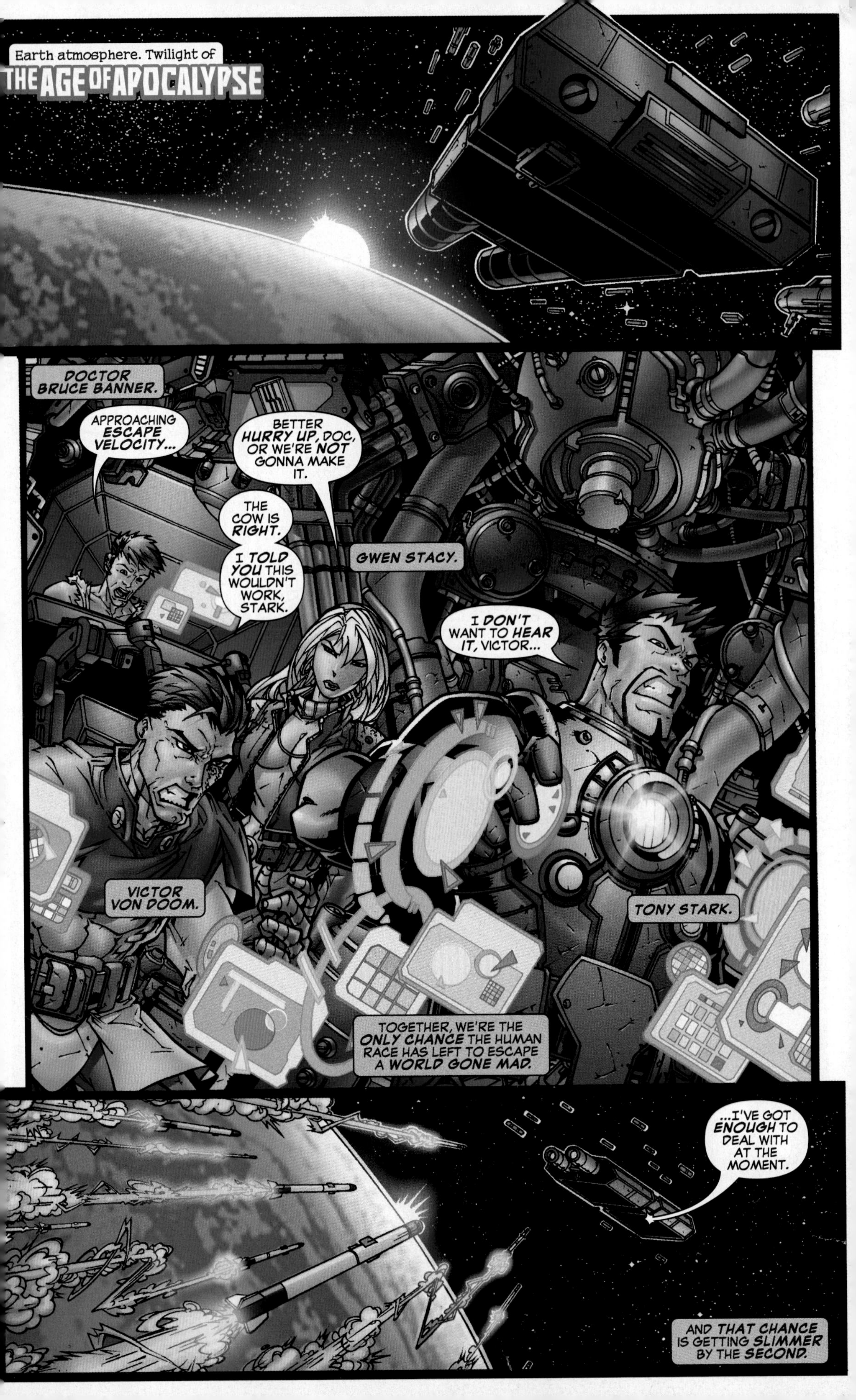
Earth atmosphere. Twilight of
THE AGE OF APOCALYPSE
DOCTOR BRUCE BANNER.
APPROACHING ESCAPE VELOCITY...
BETTER HURRY UP, DOC, OR WE'RE NOT GONNA MAKE IT.
THE COW IS RIGHT.
I TOLD YOU THIS WOULDN'T WORK, STARK.
GWEN STACY.
I DON'T WANT TO HEAR IT, VICTOR...
VICTOR VON DOOM.
TONY STARK.
TOGETHER, WE'RE THE ONLY CHANCE THE HUMAN RACE HAS LEFT TO ESCAPE A WORLD GONE MAD.
...I'VE GOT ENOUGH TO DEAL WITH AT THE MOMENT.
AND THAT CHANCE IS GETTING SLIMMER BY THE SECOND.

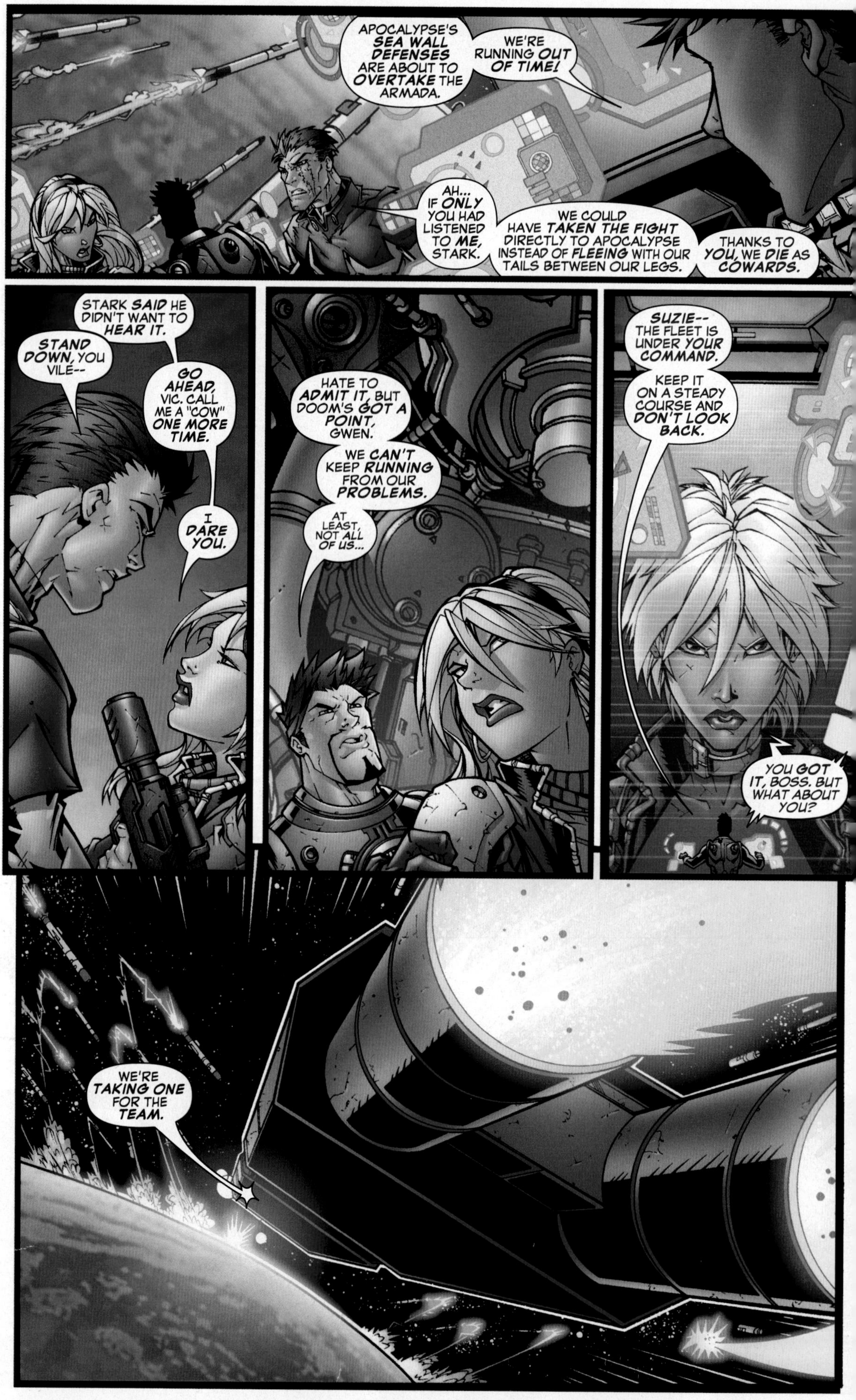
APOCALYPSE'S SEA WALL DEFENSES ARE ABOUT TO OVERTAKE THE ARMADA.
WE'RE RUNNING OUT OF TIME!
AH... IF ONLY YOU HAD LISTENED TO ME, STARK.
WE COULD HAVE TAKEN THE FIGHT DIRECTLY TO APOCALYPSE INSTEAD OF FLEEING WITH OUR TAILS BETWEEN OUR LEGS.
THANKS TO YOU, WE DIE AS COWARDS.
STAND DOWN, YOU VILE--
STARK SAID HE DIDN'T WANT TO HEAR IT.
GO AHEAD, VIC. CALL ME A "COW" ONE MORE TIME.
I DARE YOU.
HATE TO ADMIT IT, BUT DOOM'S GOT A POINT, GWEN.
WE CAN'T KEEP RUNNING FROM OUR PROBLEMS.
AT LEAST, NOT ALL OF US...
SUZIE-- THE FLEET IS UNDER YOUR COMMAND.
KEEP IT ON A STEADY COURSE AND DON'T LOOK BACK.
YOU GOT IT, BOSS. BUT WHAT ABOUT YOU?
WE'RE TAKING ONE FOR THE TEAM.

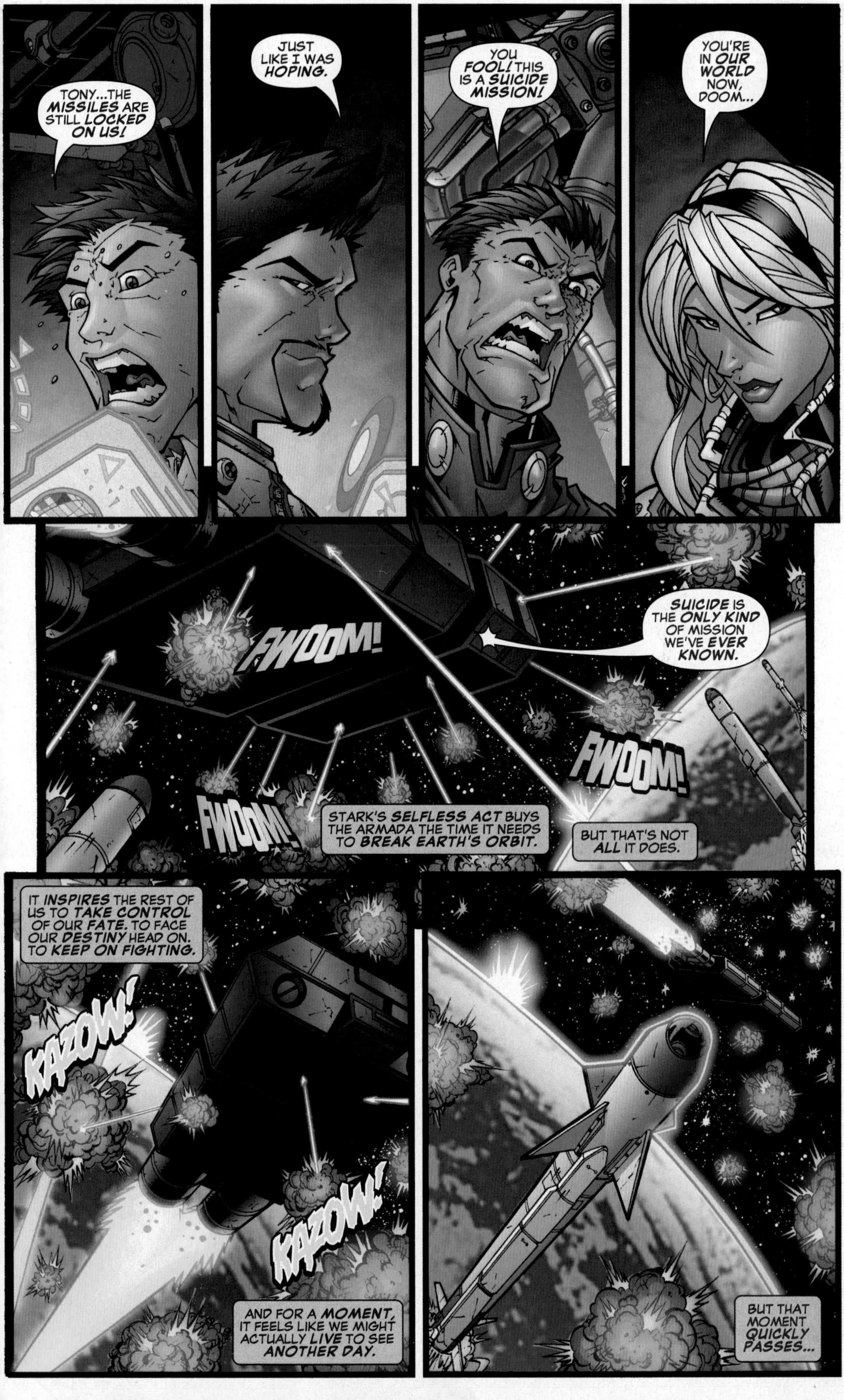
TONY...THE MISSILES ARE STILL LOCKED ON US!
JUST LIKE I WAS HOPING.
YOU FOOL! THIS IS A SUICIDE MISSION!
YOU'RE IN OUR WORLD NOW, DOOM...
SUICIDE IS THE ONLY KIND OF MISSION WE'VE EVER KNOWN.
FWOOM!
FWOOM!
FWOOM!
STARK'S SELFLESS ACT BUYS THE ARMADA THE TIME IT NEEDS TO BREAK EARTH'S ORBIT.
BUT THAT'S NOT ALL IT DOES.
IT INSPIRES THE REST OF US TO TAKE CONTROL OF OUR FATE. TO FACE OUR DESTINY HEAD ON. TO KEEP ON FIGHTING.
KAZOW!
KAZOW!
AND FOR A MOMENT, IT FEELS LIKE WE MIGHT ACTUALLY LIVE TO SEE ANOTHER DAY.
BUT THAT MOMENT QUICKLY PASSES...

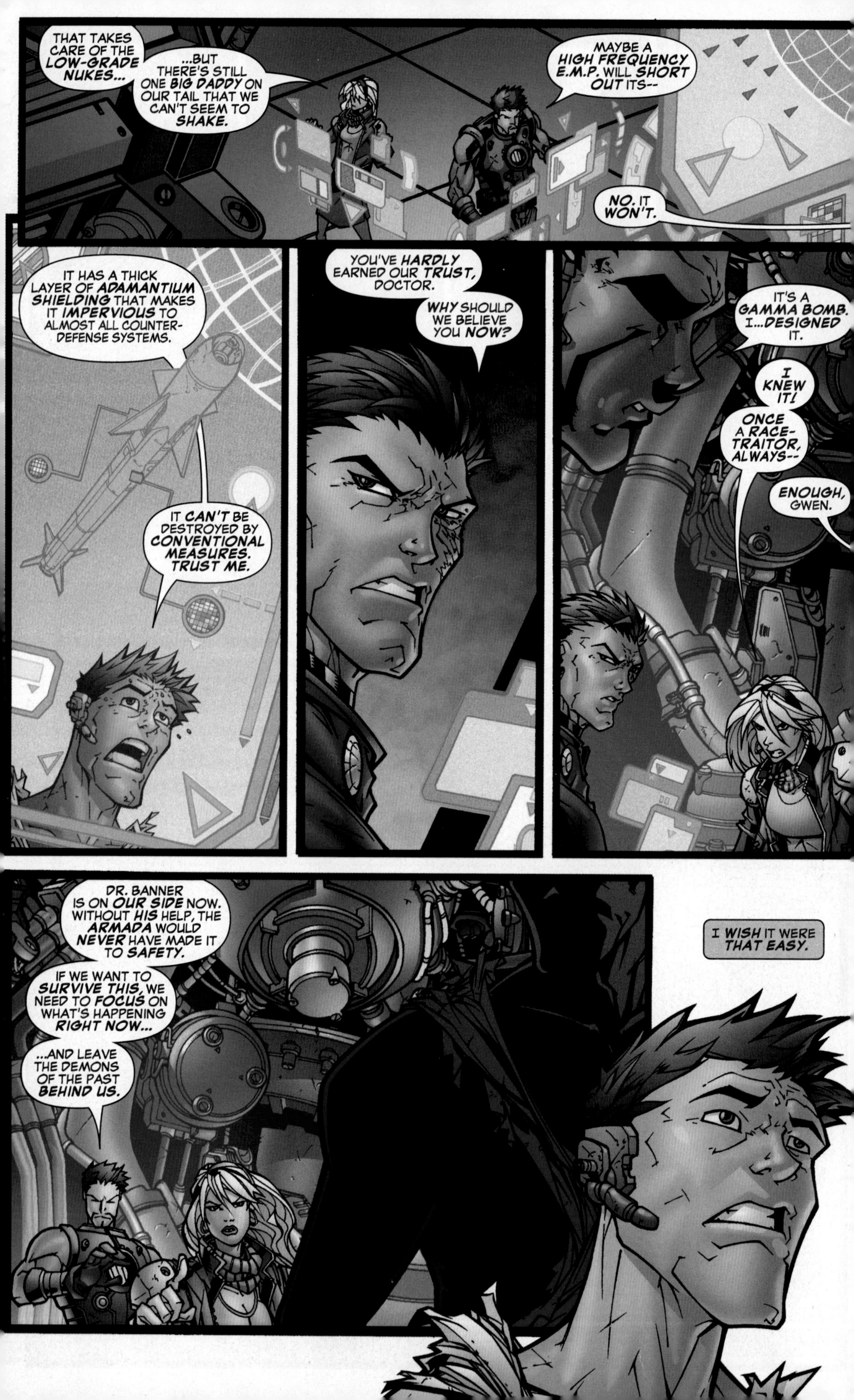
THAT TAKES CARE OF THE LOW-GRADE NUKES...
...BUT THERE'S STILL ONE BIG DADDY ON OUR TAIL THAT WE CAN'T SEEM TO SHAKE.
MAYBE A HIGH FREQUENCY E.M.P. WILL SHORT OUT ITS--
NO. IT WON'T.
IT HAS A THICK LAYER OF ADAMANTIUM SHIELDING THAT MAKES IT IMPERVIOUS TO ALMOST ALL COUNTER-DEFENSE SYSTEMS.
IT CAN'T BE DESTROYED BY CONVENTIONAL MEASURES. TRUST ME.
YOU'VE HARDLY EARNED OUR TRUST, DOCTOR.
WHY SHOULD WE BELIEVE YOU NOW?
IT'S A GAMMA BOMB. I...DESIGNED IT.
I KNEW IT!
ONCE A RACE-TRAITOR, ALWAYS--
ENOUGH, GWEN.
DR. BANNER IS ON OUR SIDE NOW. WITHOUT HIS HELP, THE ARMADA WOULD NEVER HAVE MADE IT TO SAFETY.
IF WE WANT TO SURVIVE THIS, WE NEED TO FOCUS ON WHAT'S HAPPENING RIGHT NOW...
...AND LEAVE THE DEMONS OF THE PAST BEHIND US.
I WISH IT WERE THAT EASY.

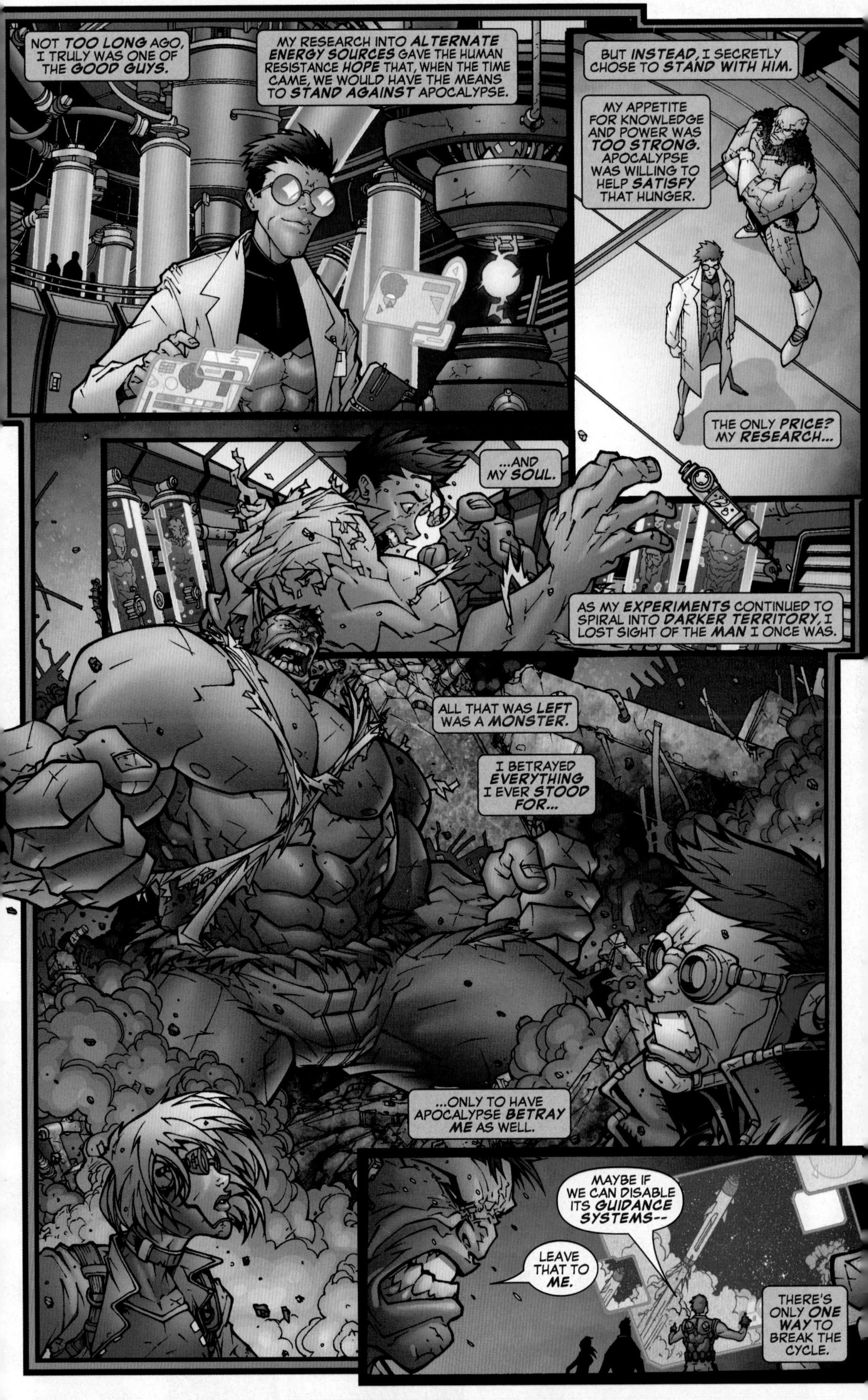

NOT TOO LONG AGO, I TRULY WAS ONE OF THE GOOD GUYS.
MY RESEARCH INTO ALTERNATE ENERGY SOURCES GAVE THE HUMAN RESISTANCE HOPE THAT, WHEN THE TIME CAME, WE WOULD HAVE THE MEANS TO STAND AGAINST APOCALYPSE.
BUT INSTEAD, I SECRETLY CHOSE TO STAND WITH HIM.
MY APPETITE FOR KNOWLEDGE AND POWER WAS TOO STRONG. APOCALYPSE WAS WILLING TO HELP SATISFY THAT HUNGER.
THE ONLY PRICE? MY RESEARCH...
...AND MY SOUL.
AS MY EXPERIMENTS CONTINUED TO SPIRAL INTO DARKER TERRITORY, I LOST SIGHT OF THE MAN I ONCE WAS.
ALL THAT WAS LEFT WAS A MONSTER.
I BETRAYED EVERYTHING I EVER STOOD FOR...
...ONLY TO HAVE APOCALYPSE BETRAY ME AS WELL.
MAYBE IF WE CAN DISABLE ITS GUIDANCE SYSTEMS--
LEAVE THAT TO ME.
THERE'S ONLY ONE WAY TO BREAK THE CYCLE.

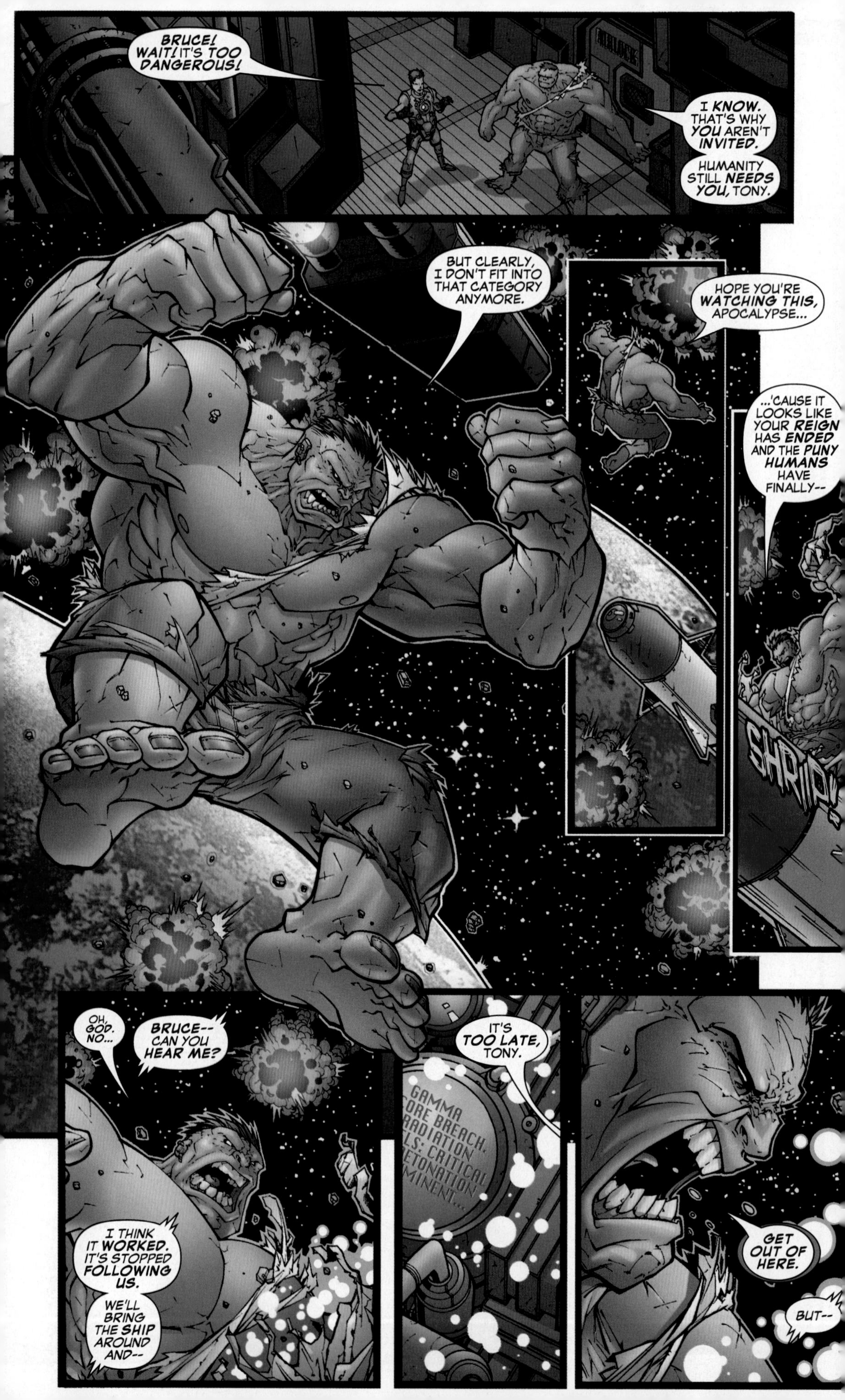

BRUCE! WAIT! IT'S TOO DANGEROUS!
I KNOW. THAT'S WHY YOU AREN'T INVITED.
HUMANITY STILL NEEDS YOU, TONY.
BUT CLEARLY, I DON'T FIT INTO THAT CATEGORY ANYMORE.
HOPE YOU'RE WATCHING THIS, APOCALYPSE...
...'CAUSE IT LOOKS LIKE YOUR REIGN HAS ENDED AND THE PUNY HUMANS HAVE FINALLY--
SHRIP!
I THINK IT WORKED. IT'S STOPPED FOLLOWING US.
WE'LL BRING THE SHIP AROUND AND--
OH, GOD. NO...
BRUCE-- CAN YOU HEAR ME?
IT'S TOO LATE, TONY.
GAMMA
ORE BREACH.
RADIATION
LS. CRITICAL
ETONATION
MINENT...
GET OUT OF HERE.
BUT--

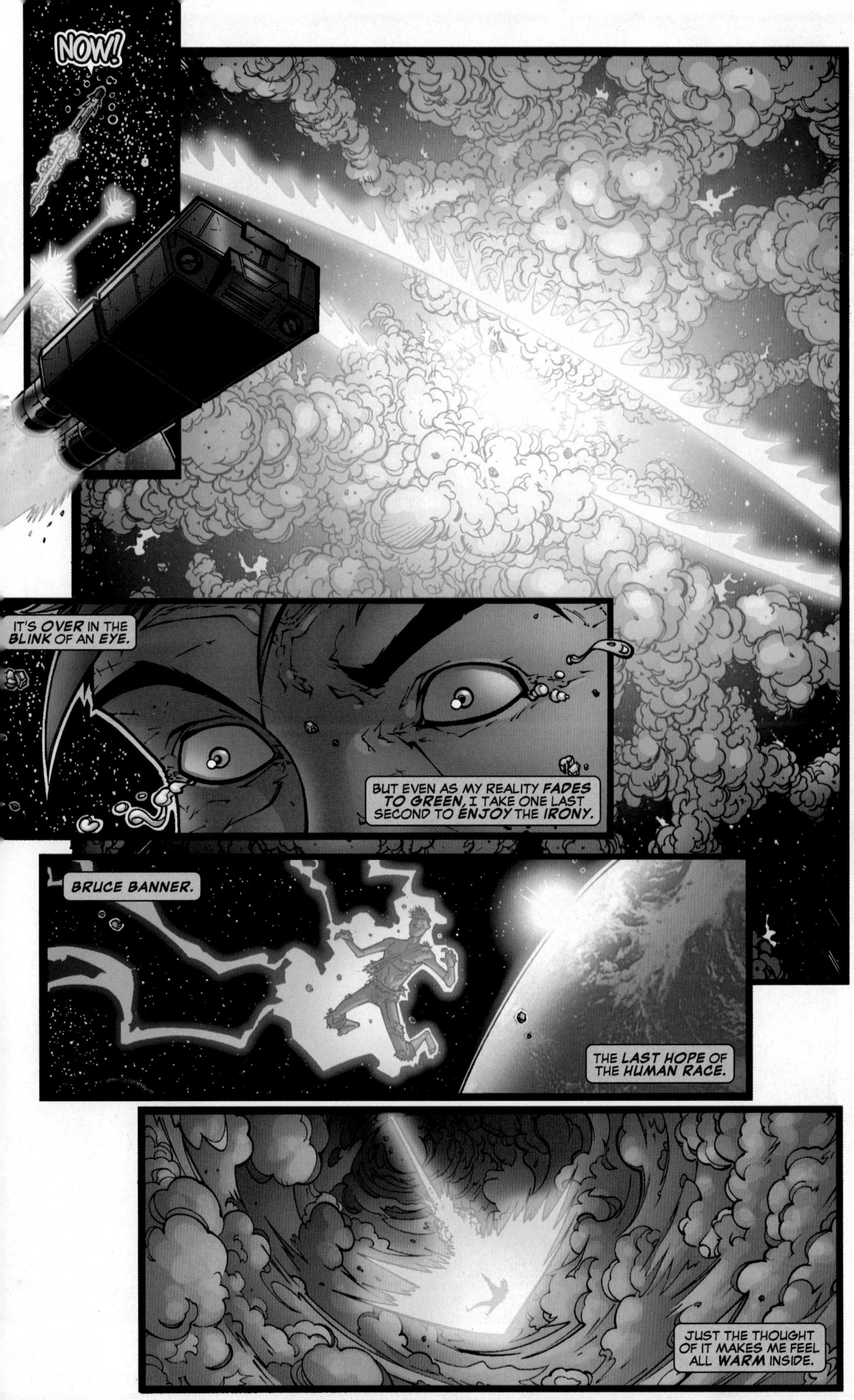
NOW!
IT'S OVER IN THE BLINK OF AN EYE.
BUT EVEN AS MY REALITY FADES TO GREEN, I TAKE ONE LAST SECOND TO ENJOY THE IRONY.
BRUCE BANNER.
THE LAST HOPE OF THE HUMAN RACE.
JUST THE THOUGHT OF IT MAKES ME FEEL ALL WARM INSIDE.

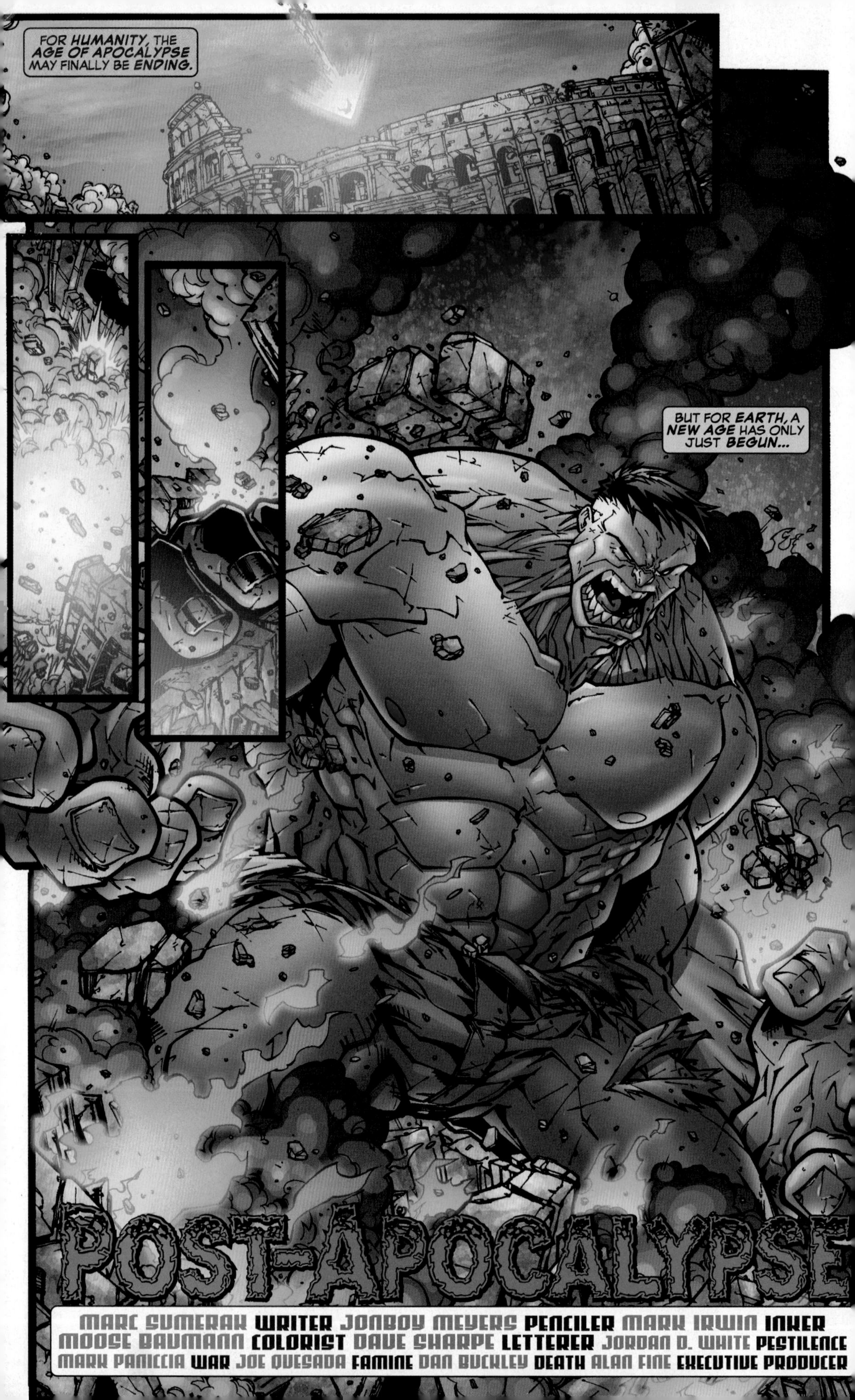
FOR HUMANITY, THE AGE OF APOCALYPSE MAY FINALLY BE ENDING.
BUT FOR EARTH, A NEW AGE HAS ONLY JUST BEGUN...
POST-APOCALYPSE
MARC SUMERAK WRITER JONBOY MEYERS PENCILER MARK IRWIN INKER
MOOSE BAUMANN COLORIST DAVE SHARPE LETTERER JORDAN D. WHITE PESTILENCE
MARK PANICCIA WAR JOE QUESADA FAMINE DAN BUCKLEY DEATH ALAN FINE EXECUTIVE PRODUCER

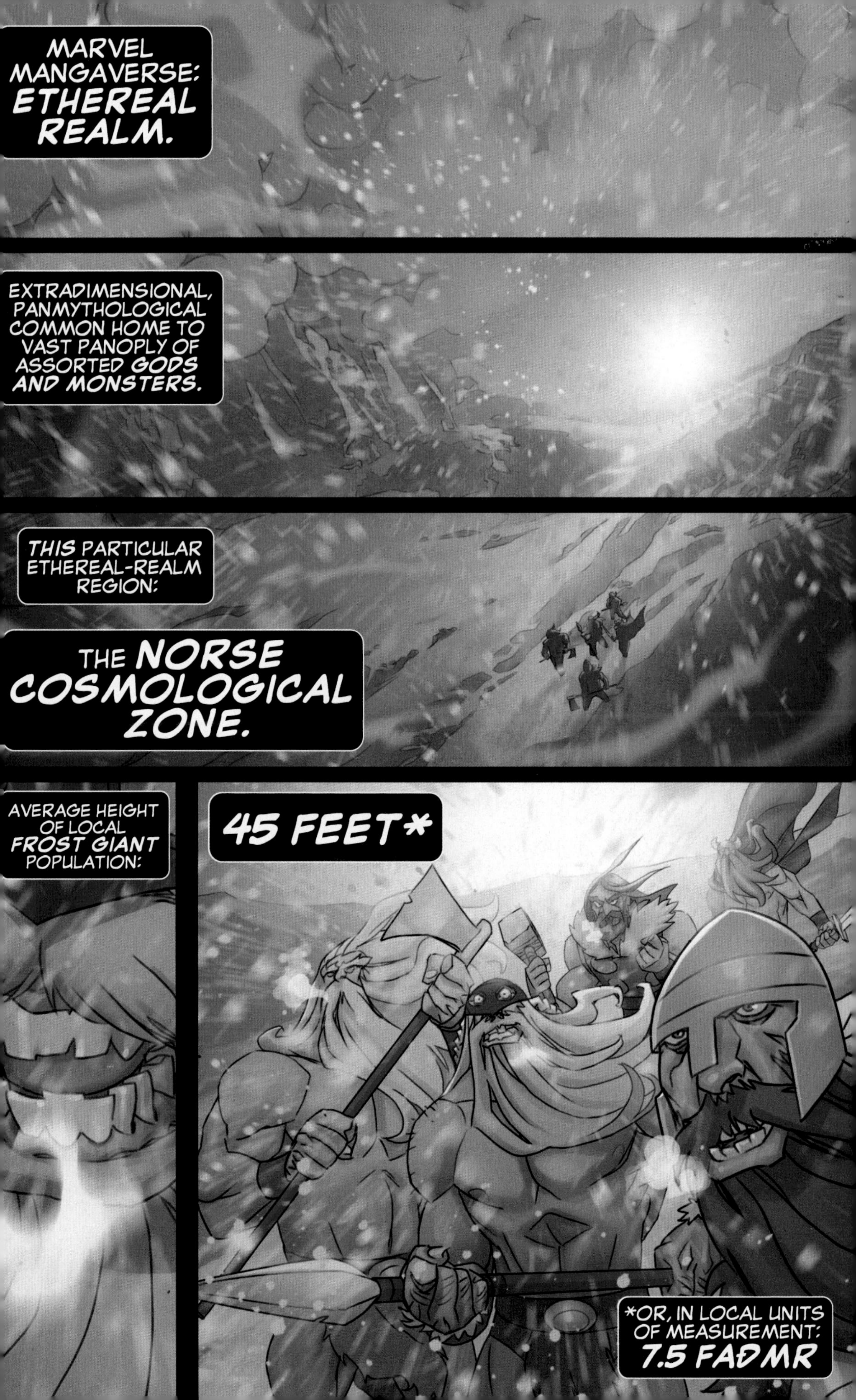
MARVEL MANGAVERSE: ETHEREAL REALM.
EXTRADIMENSIONAL, PANMYTHOLOGICAL COMMON HOME TO VAST PANOPLY OF ASSORTED GODS AND MONSTERS.
THIS PARTICULAR ETHEREAL-REALM REGION:
THE NORSE COSMOLOGICAL ZONE.
AVERAGE HEIGHT OF LOCAL FROST GIANT POPULATION:
45 FEET*
*OR, IN LOCAL UNITS OF MEASUREMENT: 7.5 FAÐMR

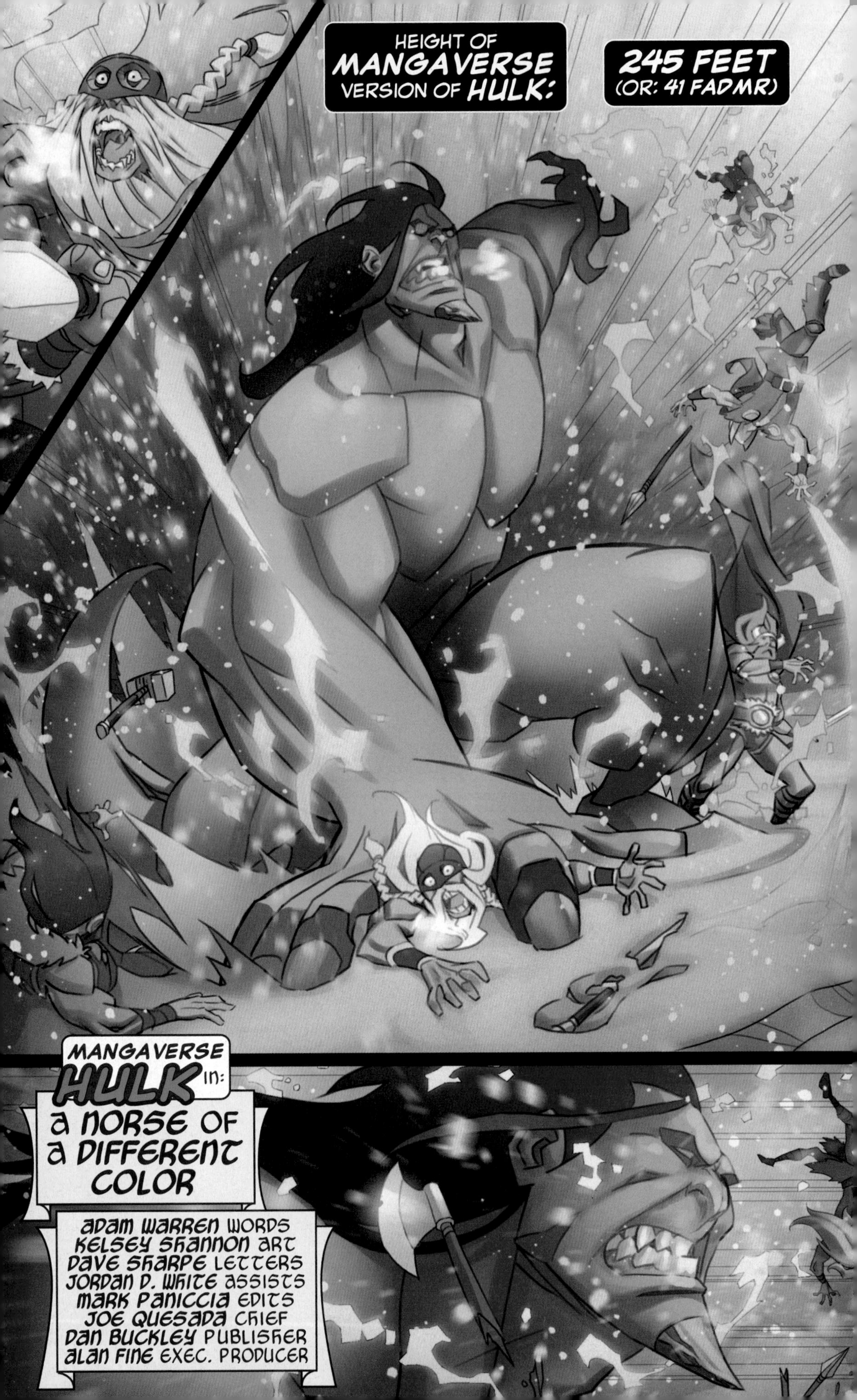
HEIGHT OF MANGAVERSE VERSION OF HULK:
245 FEET (OR: 41 FADMR)
MANGAVERSE HULK in:
A NORSE OF A DIFFERENT COLOR
ADAM WARREN WORDS
KELSEY SHANNON ART
DAVE SHARPE LETTERS
JORDAN D. WHITE ASSISTS
MARK PANICCIA EDITS
JOE QUESADA CHIEF
DAN BUCKLEY PUBLISHER
ALAN FINE EXEC. PRODUCER

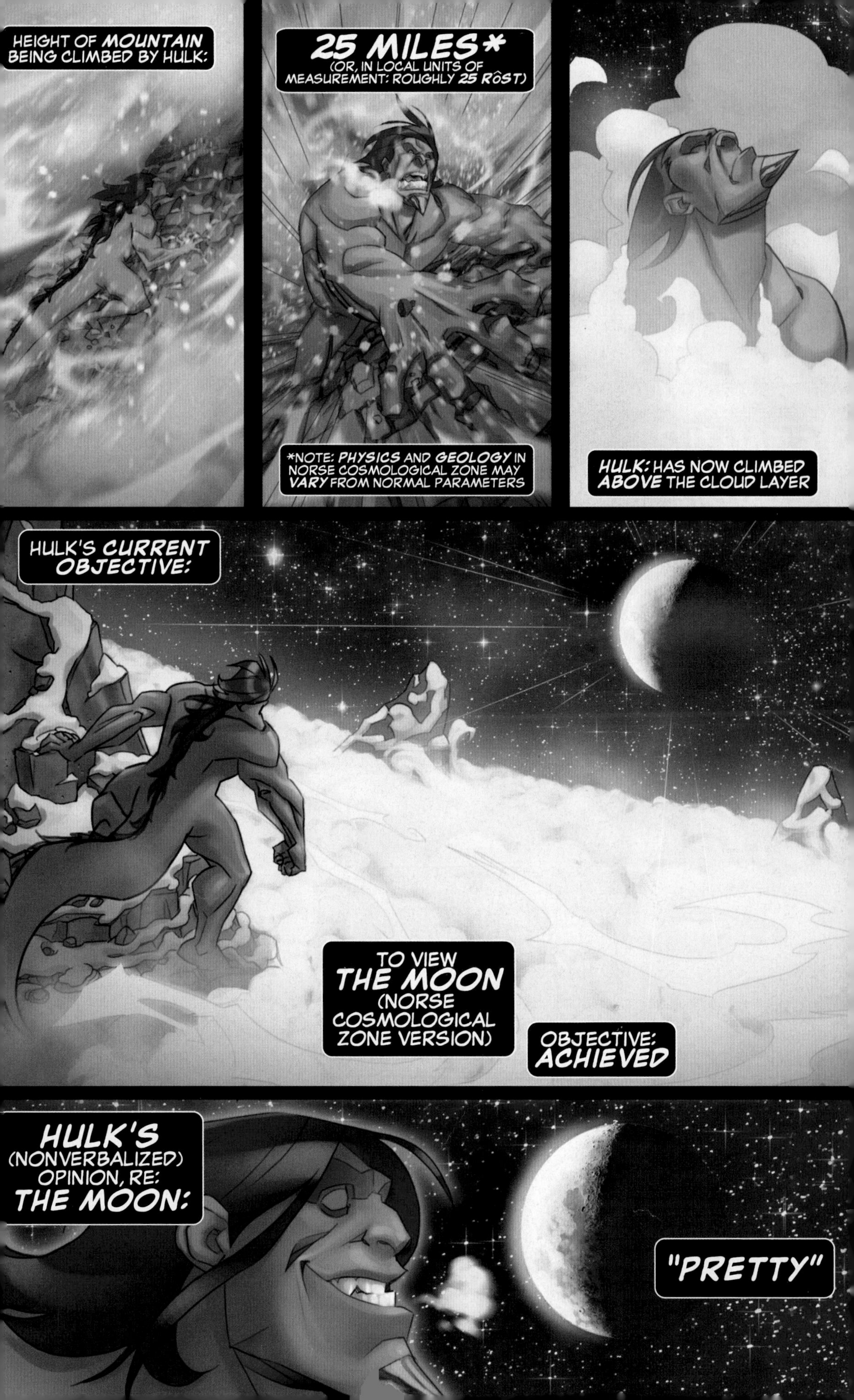
HEIGHT OF MOUNTAIN BEING CLIMBED BY HULK:
25 MILES* (OR, IN LOCAL UNITS OF MEASUREMENT: ROUGHLY 25 RÔST)
*NOTE: PHYSICS AND GEOLOGY IN NORSE COSMOLOGICAL ZONE MAY VARY FROM NORMAL PARAMETERS
HULK: HAS NOW CLIMBED ABOVE THE CLOUD LAYER
HULK'S CURRENT OBJECTIVE:
TO VIEW THE MOON (NORSE COSMOLOGICAL ZONE VERSION)
OBJECTIVE: ACHIEVED
HULK'S (NONVERBALIZED) OPINION, RE: THE MOON:
"PRETTY"

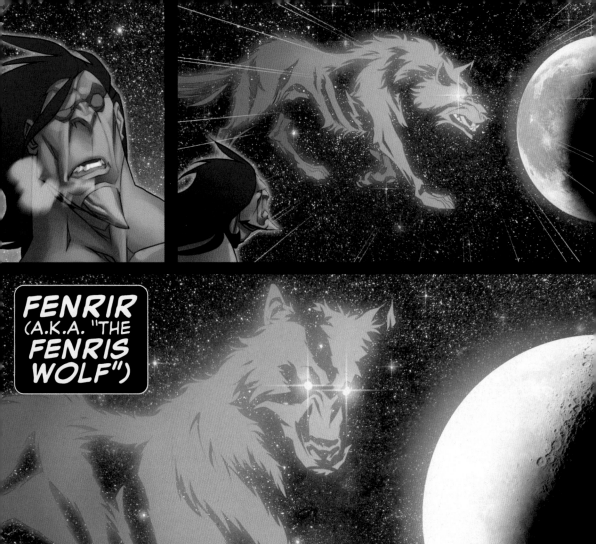

FENRIR (A.K.A. "THE FENRIS WOLF")

EXTREMELY LARGE CANINE, DESTINED TO EAT THE MOON AND SUN* (AND **ODIN**) DURING THE FUTURE APOCALYPSE OF **RAGNAROK**

*NOTE: MANGAVERSE MYTHOLOGICAL CONTINUITY MAY **VARY** FROM NORMAL NORSE-MYTHOS PARAMETERS

FENRIR: LIKE **MOST** CANINES, PRONE TO SNEAKING NIBBLES FROM **FORBIDDEN** FOOD ITEMS WHEN NOT BEING OBSERVED

HULK: **DISMAYED**

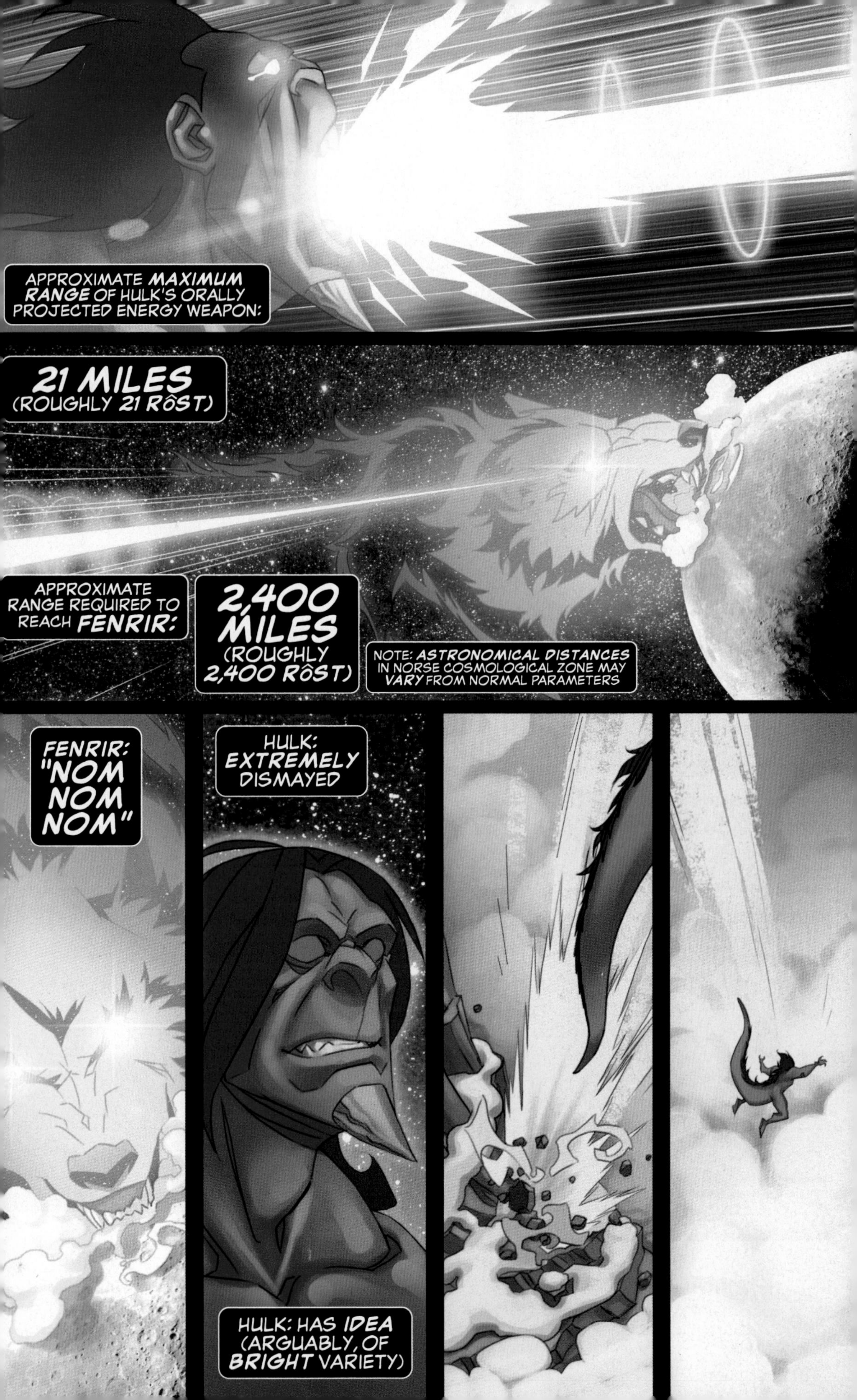
APPROXIMATE MAXIMUM RANGE OF HULK'S ORALLY PROJECTED ENERGY WEAPON:
21 MILES (ROUGHLY 21 RÔST)
APPROXIMATE RANGE REQUIRED TO REACH FENRIR:
2,400 MILES (ROUGHLY 2,400 RÔST)
NOTE: ASTRONOMICAL DISTANCES IN NORSE COSMOLOGICAL ZONE MAY VARY FROM NORMAL PARAMETERS
FENRIR: "NOM NOM NOM"
HULK: EXTREMELY DISMAYED
HULK: HAS IDEA (ARGUABLY, OF BRIGHT VARIETY)

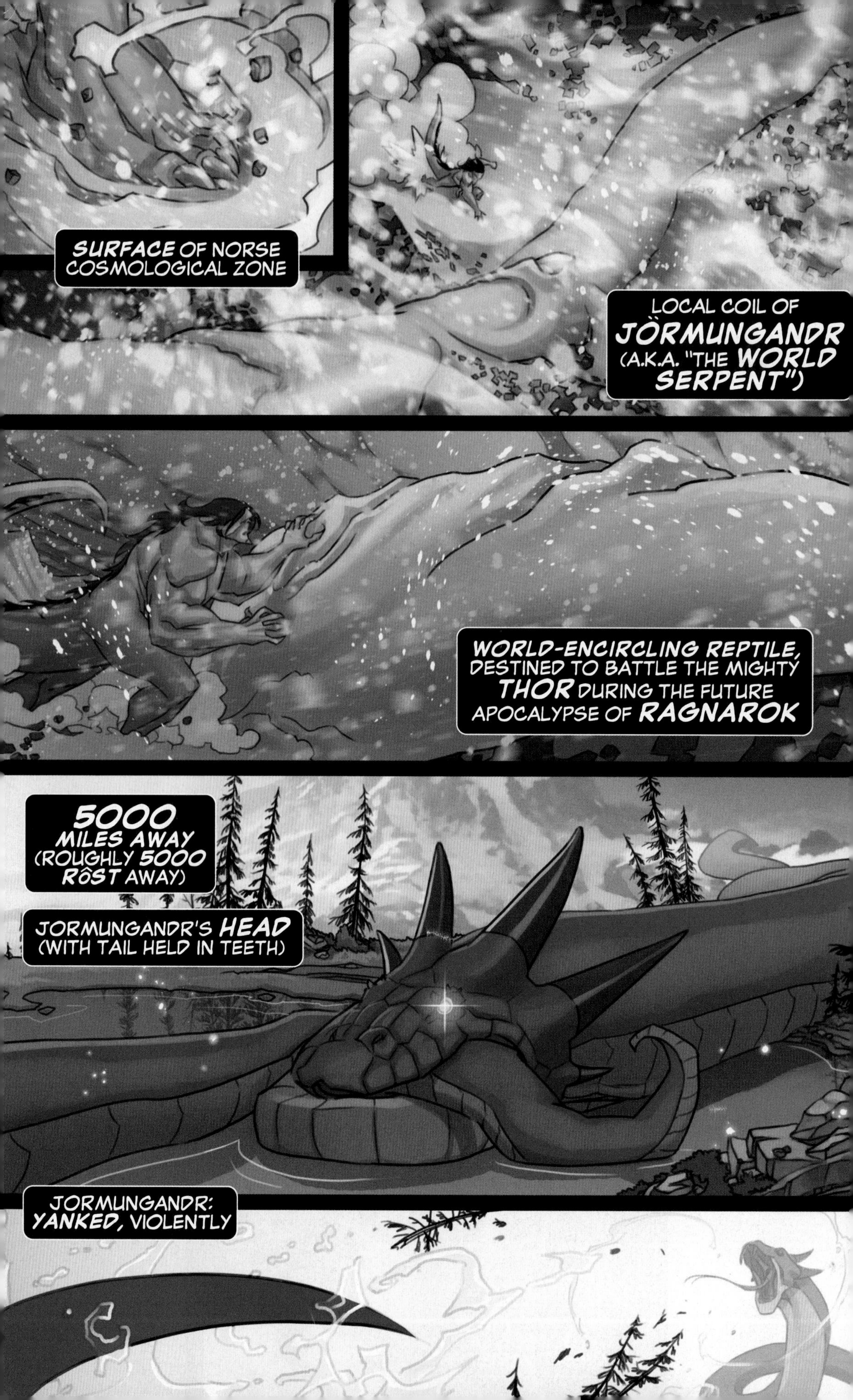
SURFACE OF NORSE COSMOLOGICAL ZONE
LOCAL COIL OF JÒRMUNGANDR (A.K.A. "THE WORLD SERPENT")
WORLD-ENCIRCLING REPTILE, DESTINED TO BATTLE THE MIGHTY THOR DURING THE FUTURE APOCALYPSE OF RAGNAROK
5000 MILES AWAY (ROUGHLY 5000 RÔST AWAY)
JORMUNGANDR'S HEAD (WITH TAIL HELD IN TEETH)
JORMUNGANDR: YANKED, VIOLENTLY

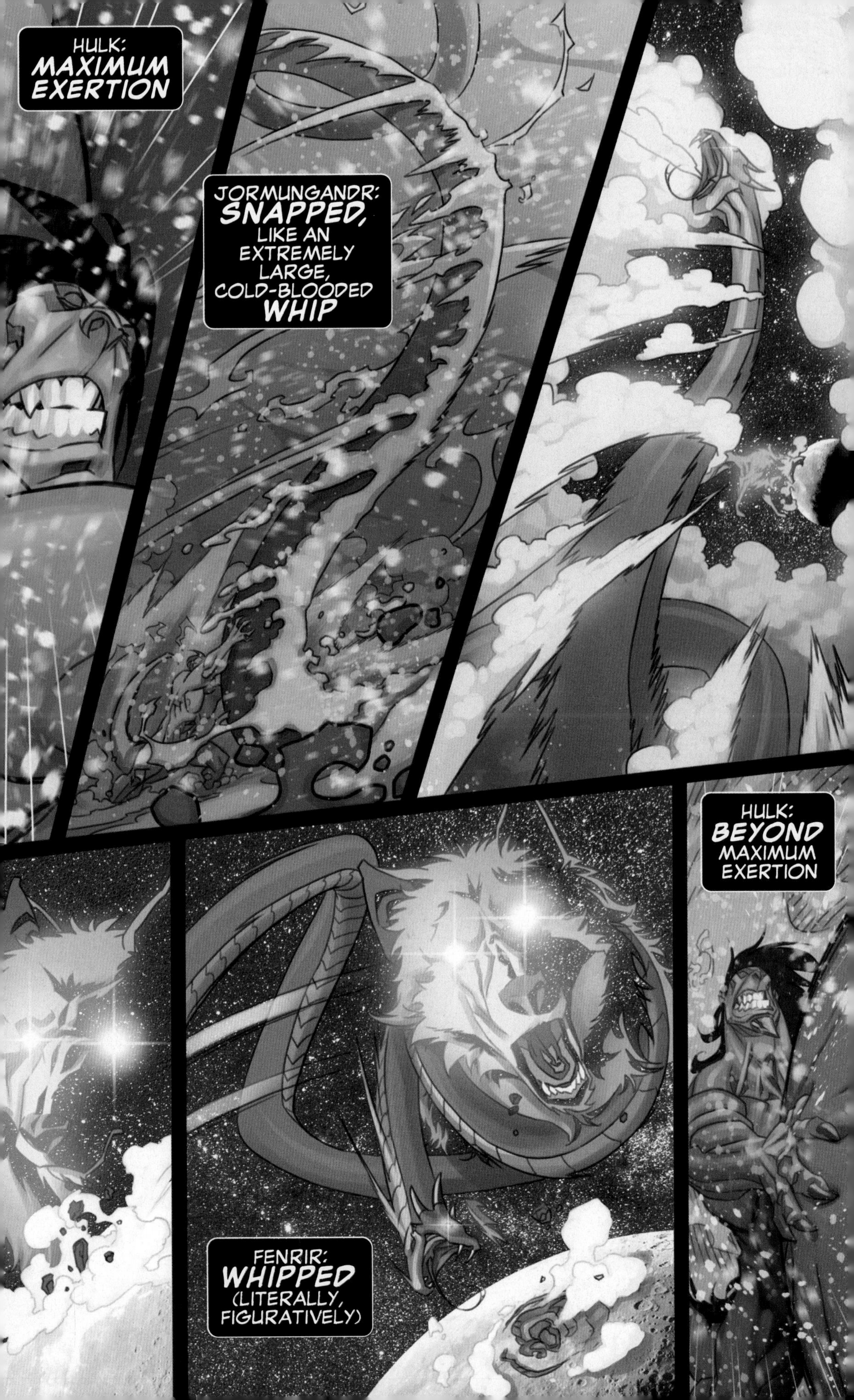
HULK: MAXIMUM EXERTION
JORMUNGANDR: SNAPPED, LIKE AN EXTREMELY LARGE, COLD-BLOODED WHIP
HULK: BEYOND MAXIMUM EXERTION
FENRIR: WHIPPED (LITERALLY, FIGURATIVELY)

JORMUNGANDR **AND** FENRIR:

YANKED BACK DOWN TO **SURFACE** OF NORSE COSMOLOGICAL ZONE

HULK: DECIDES TO **ALTER DESTINY** OF JORMUNGANDR AND FENRIR BY BEATING **ONE** TO DEATH WITH THE **OTHER***

*NOTE: MANGAVERSE MYTHOLOGICAL CONTINUITY MAY VARY **CONSIDERABLY** FROM NORMAL NORSE-MYTHOS PARAMETERS

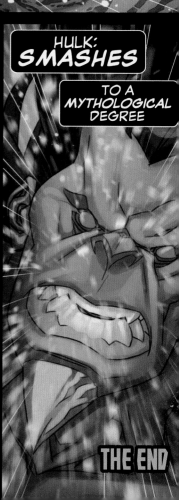

HULK: **SMASHES**

TO A **MYTHOLOGICAL DEGREE**

THE END

1602. CHINA.

ONCE, I WAS KNOWN AS *MASTER DAVID BANNER*...

...BUT THAT WAS BEFORE THE *BEASTIE INSIDE* TOOK AWAY EVERYTHING I HELD DEAR.

MY KING.

MY COUNTRY.

E'EN MY *GOD*.

'TWAS THE *NEW WORLD* THAT BESTOWED THE *CURSE* OF THE *WITCHBREED* UPON ME.

'TIS STRANGELY FITTING, THEN, THAT THIS *ANCIENT LAND* HAS FINALLY TAUGHT ME TO KEEP IT *SUBDUED*.

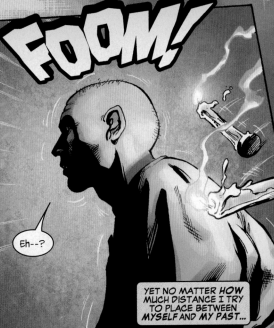

FOOM!

EH--?

YET NO MATTER *HOW* MUCH DISTANCE I TRY TO PLACE BETWEEN MYSELF AND MY PAST...

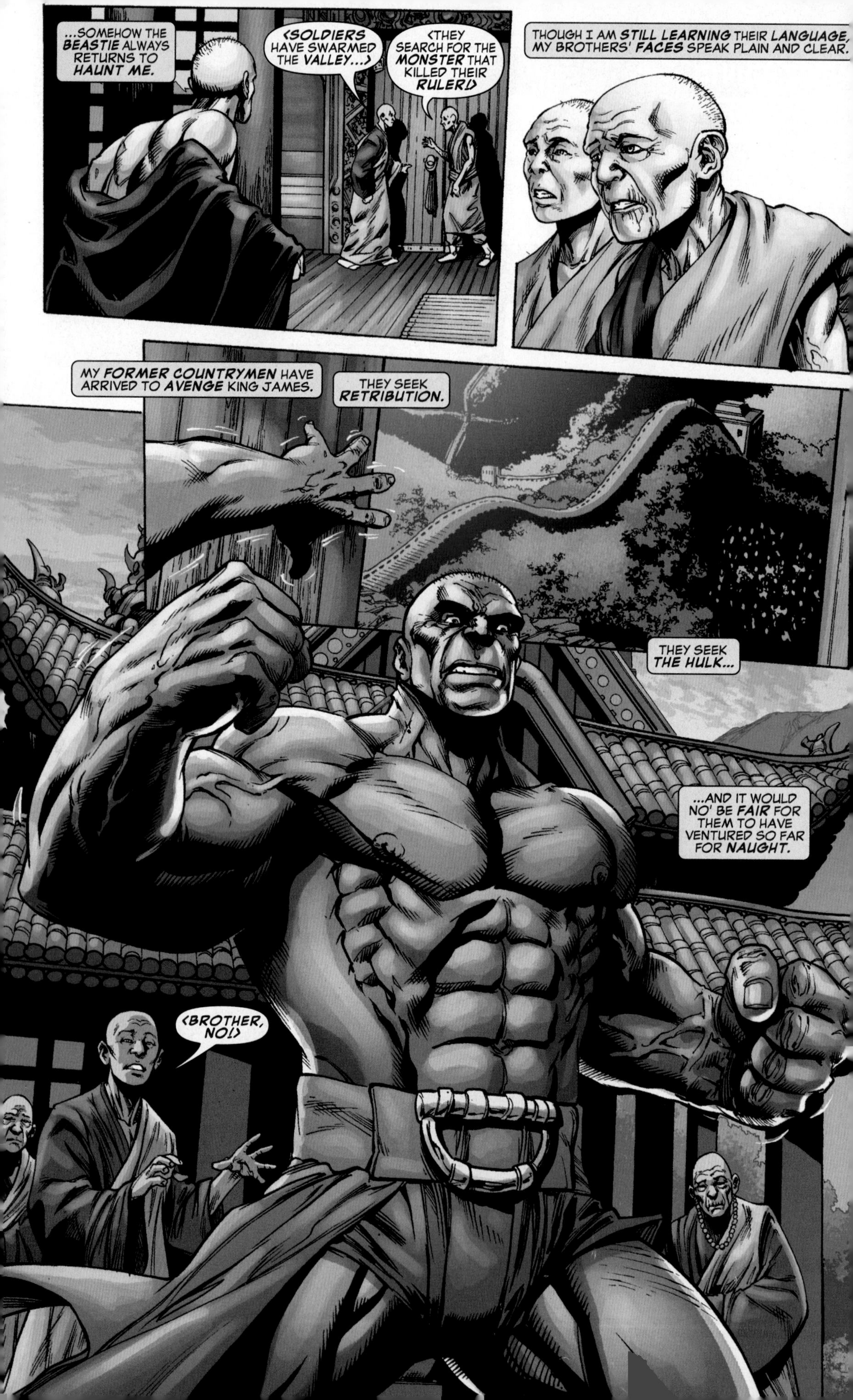

...SOMEHOW THE BEASTIE ALWAYS RETURNS TO HAUNT ME.
<SOLDIERS HAVE SWARMED THE VALLEY...>
<THEY SEARCH FOR THE MONSTER THAT KILLED THEIR RULER!>
THOUGH I AM STILL LEARNING THEIR LANGUAGE, MY BROTHERS' FACES SPEAK PLAIN AND CLEAR.
MY FORMER COUNTRYMEN HAVE ARRIVED TO AVENGE KING JAMES.
THEY SEEK RETRIBUTION.
THEY SEEK THE HULK...
...AND IT WOULD NO' BE FAIR FOR THEM TO HAVE VENTURED SO FAR FOR NAUGHT.
<BROTHER, NO!>

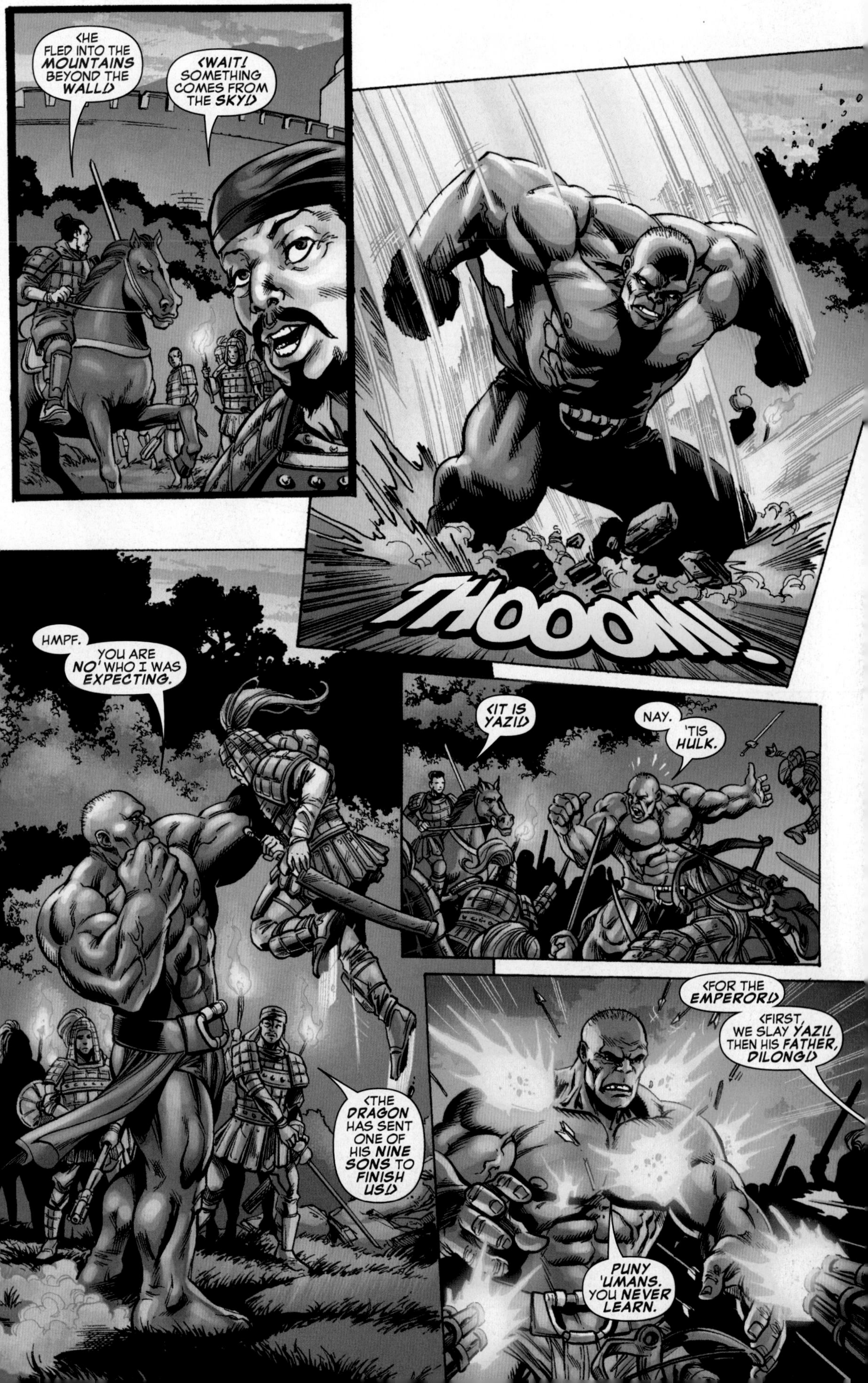

<HE FLED INTO THE MOUNTAINS BEYOND THE WALL!>
<WAIT! SOMETHING COMES FROM THE SKY!>
THOOOM!
HMPF.
YOU ARE NO' WHO I WAS EXPECTING.
<THE DRAGON HAS SENT ONE OF HIS NINE SONS TO FINISH US!>
<IT IS YAZI!>
NAY.
'TIS HULK.
<FOR THE EMPEROR!>
<FIRST, WE SLAY YAZI! THEN HIS FATHER, DILONG!>
PUNY 'UMANS. YOU NEVER LEARN.

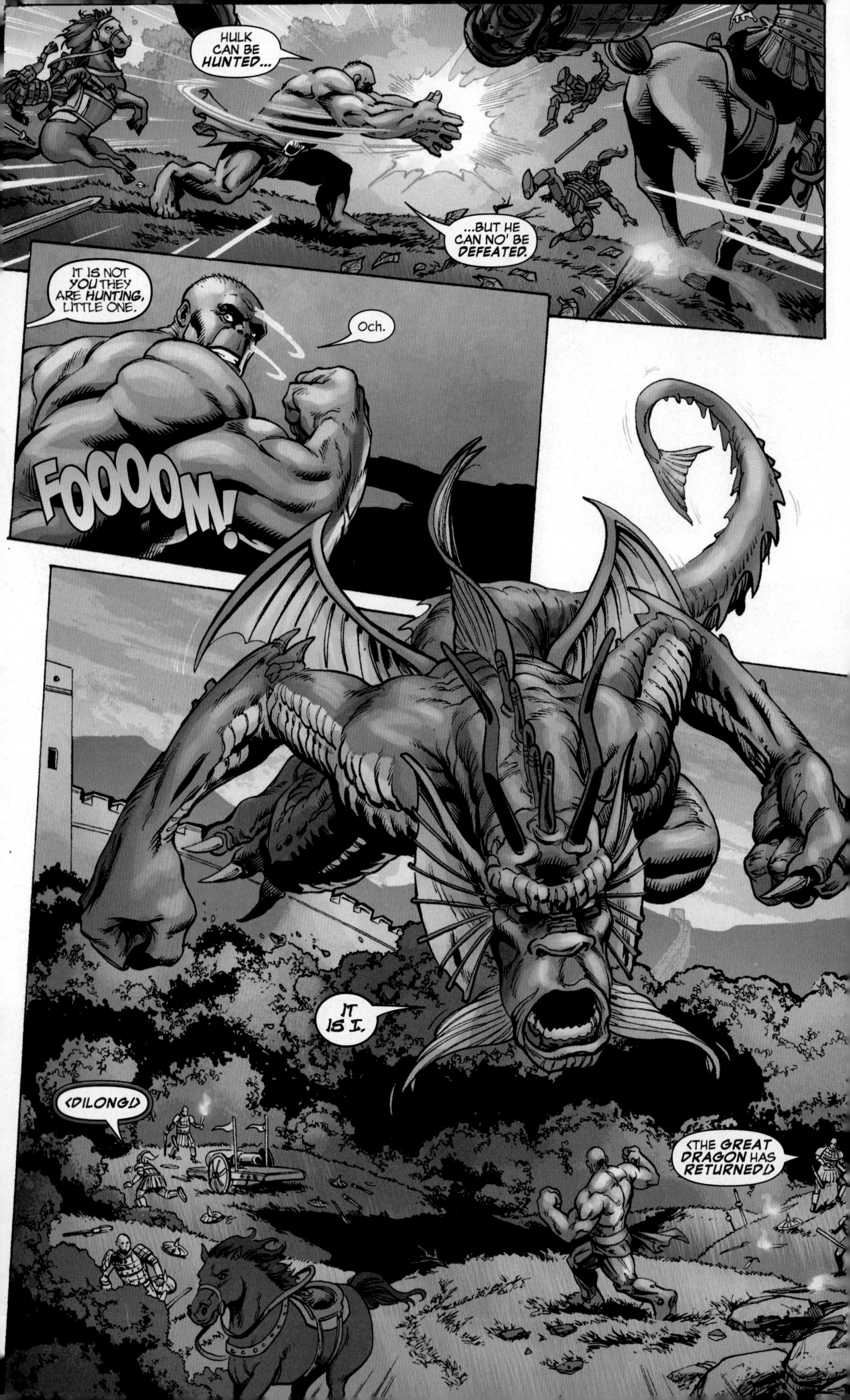
HULK CAN BE HUNTED...
...BUT HE CAN NO' BE DEFEATED.
IT IS NOT YOU THEY ARE HUNTING, LITTLE ONE.
Och.
FOOOOM!
IT IS I.
<DILONG!>
<THE GREAT DRAGON HAS RETURNED!>

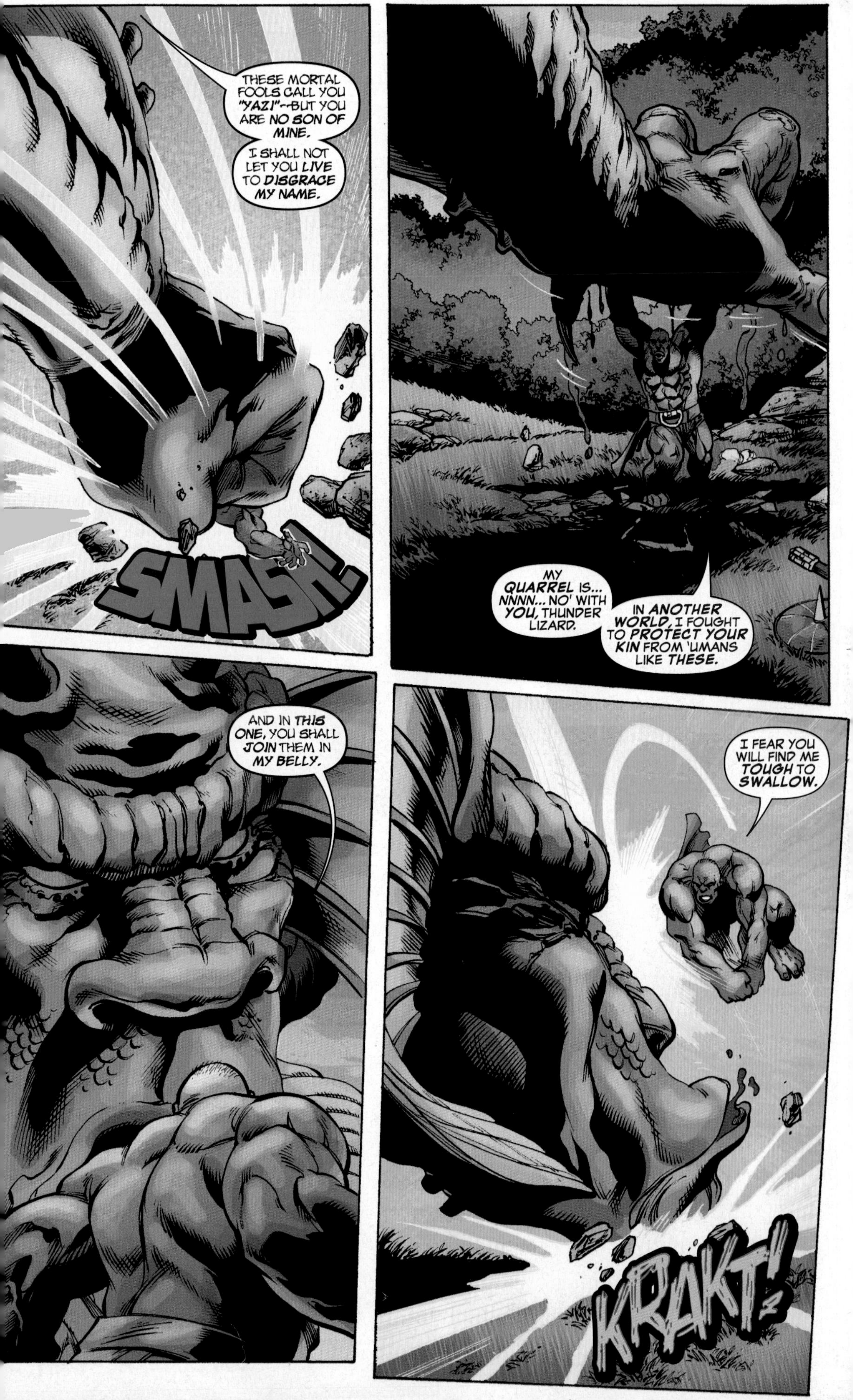
THESE MORTAL FOOLS CALL YOU "YAZI"--BUT YOU ARE NO SON OF MINE.
I SHALL NOT LET YOU LIVE TO DISGRACE MY NAME.
SMASH!
MY QUARREL IS... NNNN... NO' WITH YOU, THUNDER LIZARD.
IN ANOTHER WORLD, I FOUGHT TO PROTECT YOUR KIN FROM 'UMANS LIKE THESE.
AND IN THIS ONE, YOU SHALL JOIN THEM IN MY BELLY.
I FEAR YOU WILL FIND ME TOUGH TO SWALLOW.
KRAKT!

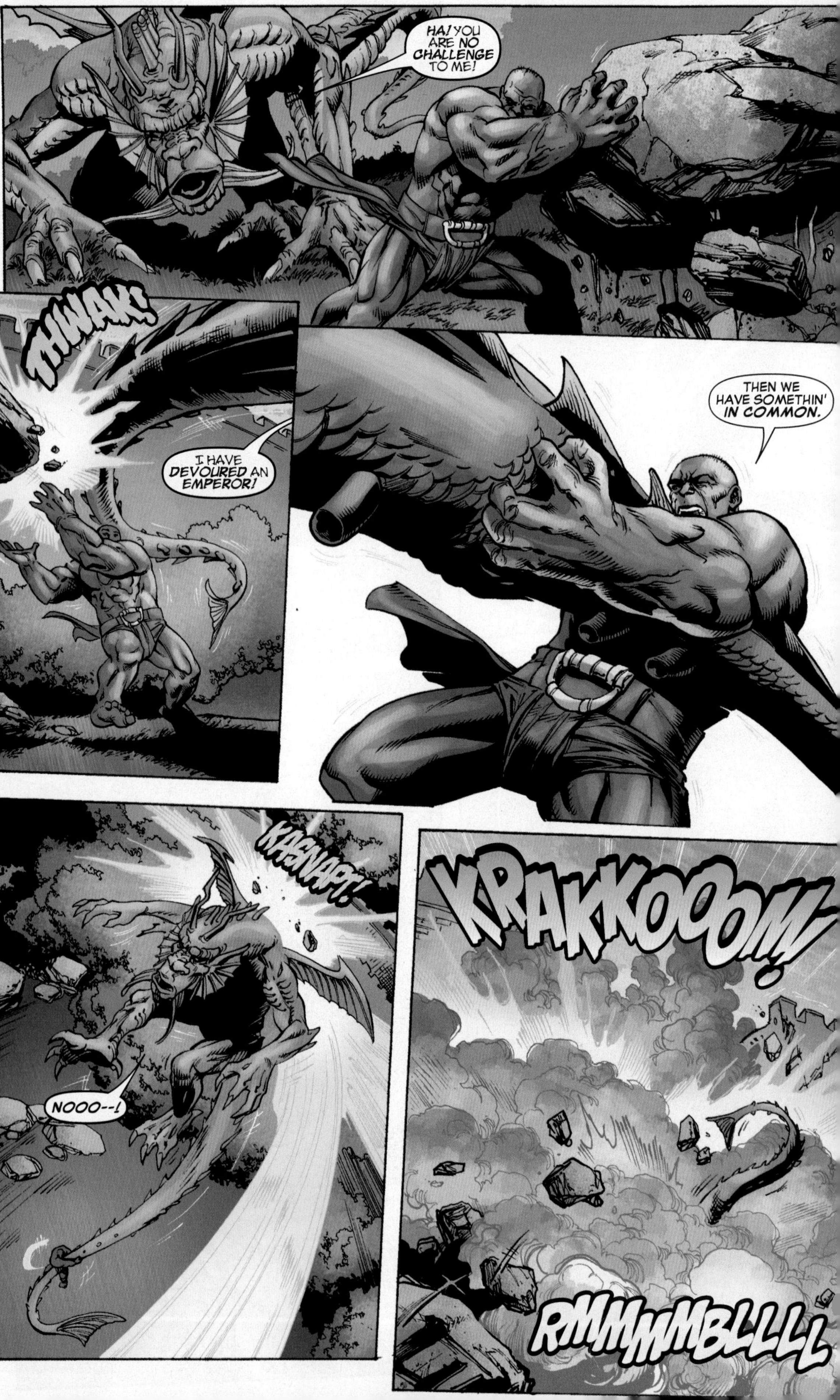
HA! YOU ARE NO CHALLENGE TO ME!
THWAK!
I HAVE DEVOURED AN EMPEROR!
THEN WE HAVE SOMETHIN' IN COMMON.
KASNAPT!
NOOO--!
KRAKKOOOM!
RMMMMMBLLLL

KRNKK!

WELL, THEN...

...WHO IS NEXT?

<SHOW US MERCY, SON OF HEAVEN!>

<OUR LAND IS FOREVER IN YOUR DEBT!>

<OUR FATE IS IN YOUR HANDS!>

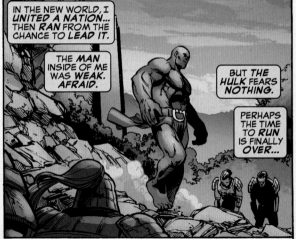

IN THE NEW WORLD, I UNITED A NATION... THEN RAN FROM THE CHANCE TO LEAD IT.

THE MAN INSIDE OF ME WAS WEAK. AFRAID.

BUT THE HULK FEARS NOTHING.

PERHAPS THE TIME TO RUN IS FINALLY OVER...

EPILOGUE.

ONCE, I WAS KNOWN AS MASTER DAVID BANNER...

...BUT THAT WAS BEFORE THE BEASTIE INSIDE GAVE ME BACK THAT WHICH I MOST DESIRED:

A COUNTRY TO CALL *MY* OWN.

AS FOR A KING AND A GOD?

I NO LONGER HAVE NEED FOR EITHER OF *THOSE*...

...NOW THAT I HAVE *BECOME* THEM BOTH.

‹LONG LIVE THE SON OF HEAVEN›

‹LONG LIVE THE NEW EMPEROR›

‹LONG LIVE THE HULK!›

SON OF THE DRAGON

MARC SUMERAK WRITER   STEVE SCOTT ARTIST   LEE LOUGHRIDGE COLORIST   DAVE SHARPE LETTERER

JORDAN D. WHITE ASSISTANT EDITOR MARK PANICCIA EDITOR JOE QUESADA EDITOR IN CHIEF DAN BUCKLEY PUBLISHER ALAN FINE EXECUTIVE PRODUCER

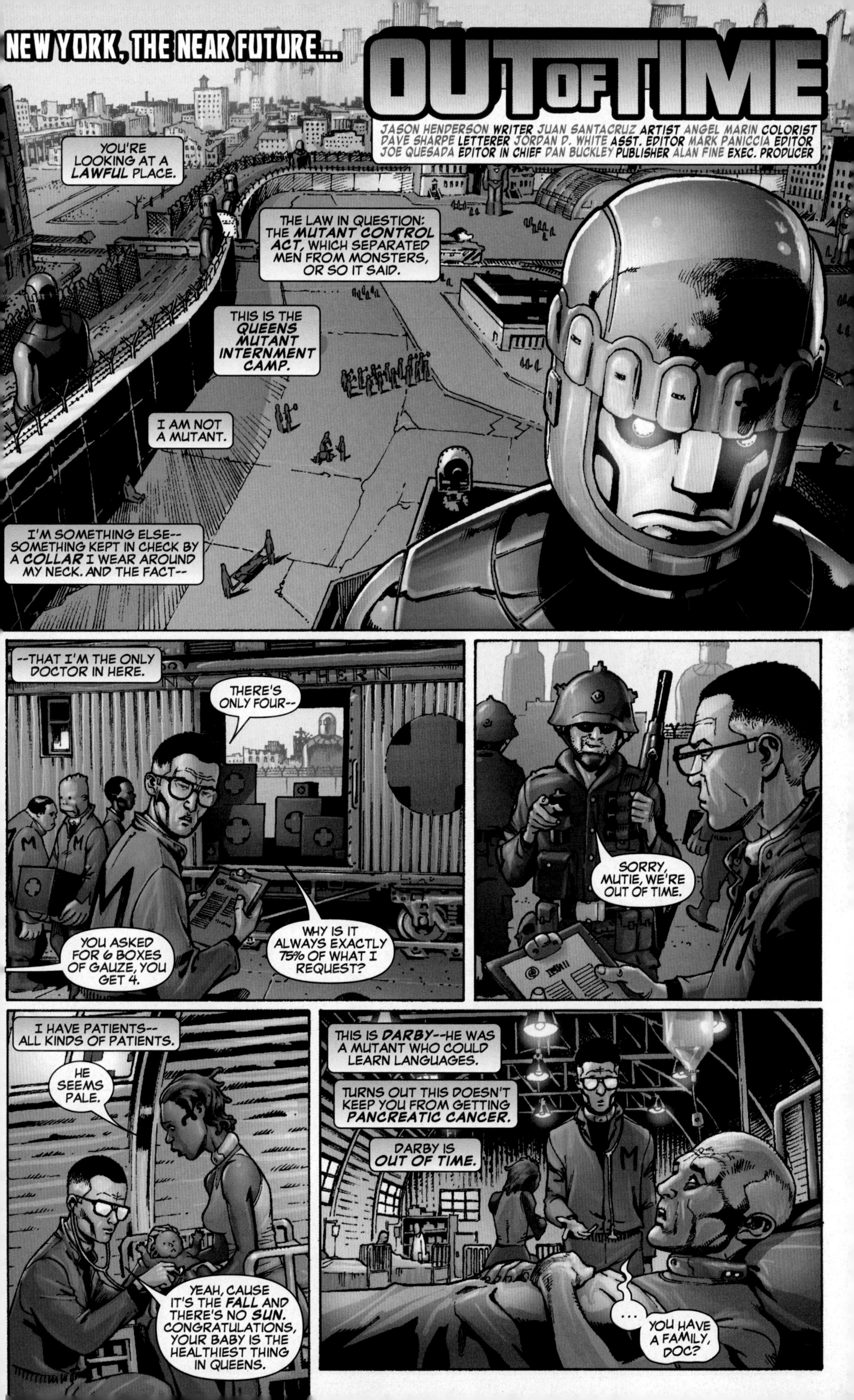

NEW YORK, THE NEAR FUTURE...
OUT OF TIME
JASON HENDERSON WRITER JUAN SANTACRUZ ARTIST ANGEL MARIN COLORIST
DAVE SHARPE LETTERER JORDAN D. WHITE ASST. EDITOR MARK PANICCIA EDITOR
JOE QUESADA EDITOR IN CHIEF DAN BUCKLEY PUBLISHER ALAN FINE EXEC. PRODUCER
YOU'RE LOOKING AT A LAWFUL PLACE.
THE LAW IN QUESTION: THE MUTANT CONTROL ACT, WHICH SEPARATED MEN FROM MONSTERS, OR SO IT SAID.
THIS IS THE QUEENS MUTANT INTERNMENT CAMP.
I AM NOT A MUTANT.
I'M SOMETHING ELSE-- SOMETHING KEPT IN CHECK BY A COLLAR I WEAR AROUND MY NECK. AND THE FACT--
--THAT I'M THE ONLY DOCTOR IN HERE.
THERE'S ONLY FOUR--
YOU ASKED FOR 6 BOXES OF GAUZE, YOU GET 4.
WHY IS IT ALWAYS EXACTLY 75% OF WHAT I REQUEST?
SORRY, MUTIE, WE'RE OUT OF TIME.
I HAVE PATIENTS-- ALL KINDS OF PATIENTS.
HE SEEMS PALE.
YEAH, CAUSE IT'S THE FALL AND THERE'S NO SUN. CONGRATULATIONS, YOUR BABY IS THE HEALTHIEST THING IN QUEENS.
THIS IS DARBY--HE WAS A MUTANT WHO COULD LEARN LANGUAGES.
TURNS OUT THIS DOESN'T KEEP YOU FROM GETTING PANCREATIC CANCER.
DARBY IS OUT OF TIME.
...
YOU HAVE A FAMILY, DOC?

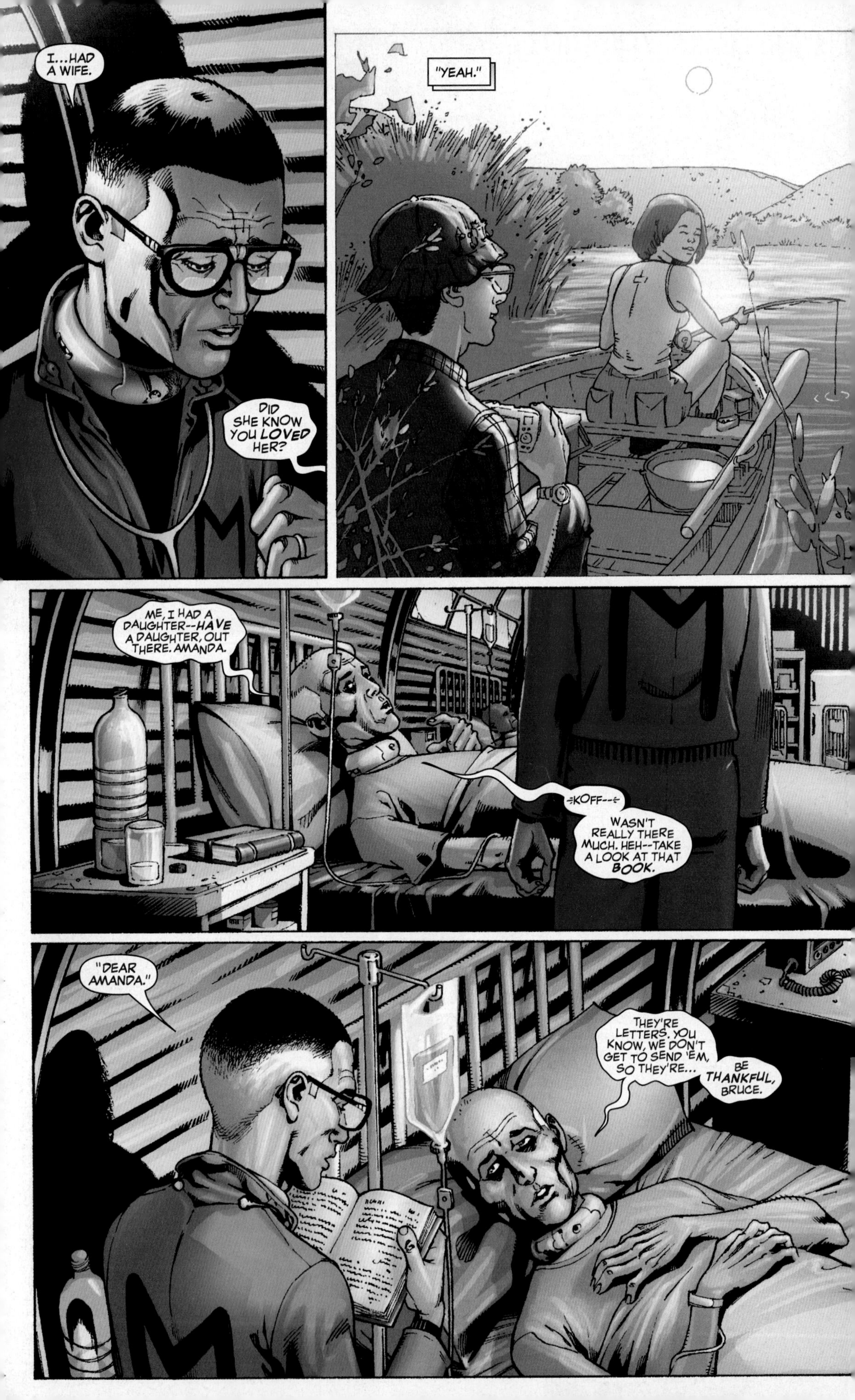
I...HAD A WIFE.
"YEAH."
DID SHE KNOW YOU LOVED HER?
ME, I HAD A DAUGHTER--HAVE A DAUGHTER, OUT THERE. AMANDA.
=KOFF--=
WASN'T REALLY THERE MUCH. HEH--TAKE A LOOK AT THAT BOOK.
"DEAR AMANDA."
THEY'RE LETTERS. YOU KNOW, WE DON'T GET TO SEND 'EM, SO THEY'RE...
BE THANKFUL, BRUCE.

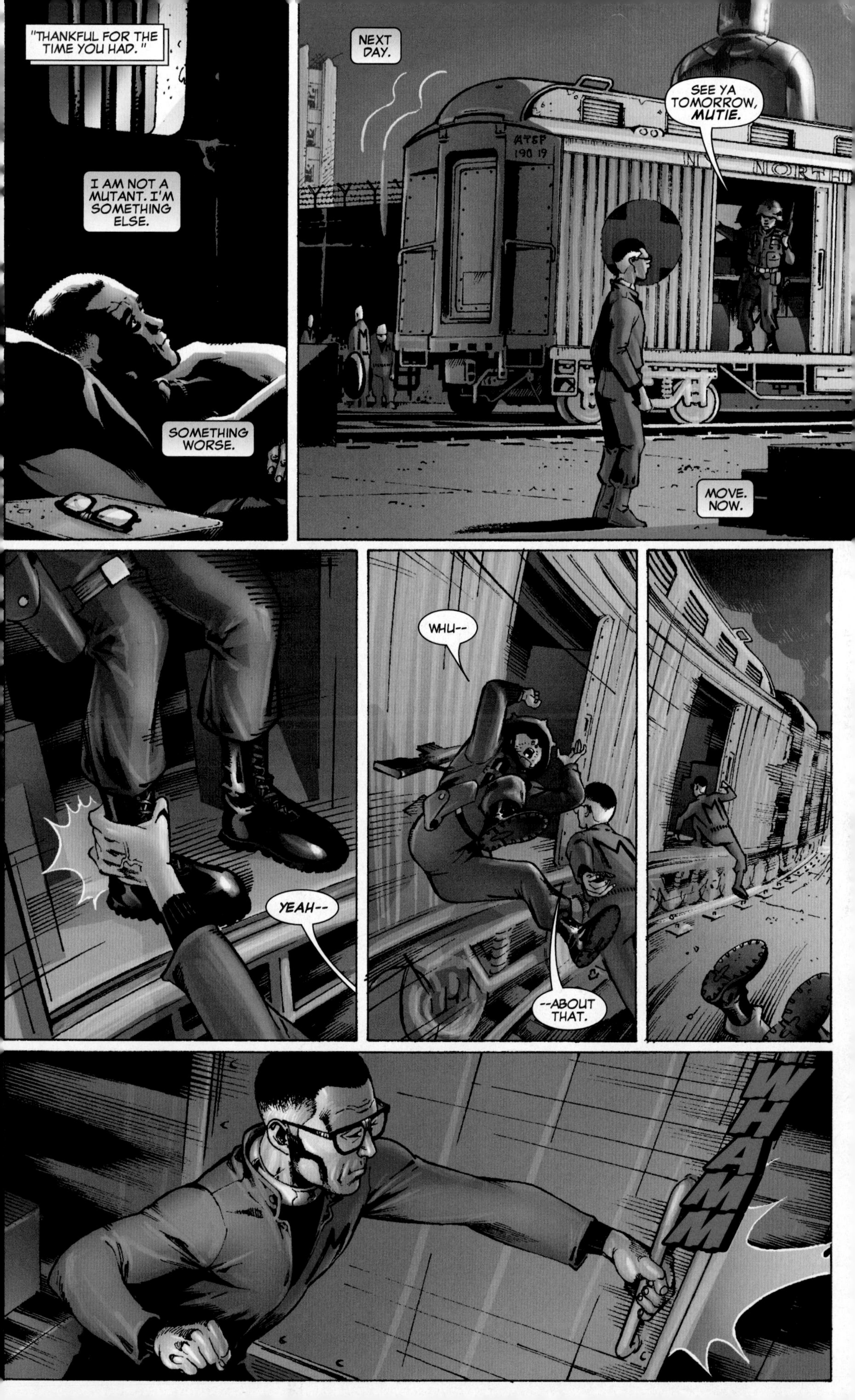
"THANKFUL FOR THE TIME YOU HAD."
I AM NOT A MUTANT. I'M SOMETHING ELSE.
SOMETHING WORSE.
NEXT DAY.
SEE YA TOMORROW, MUTIE.
MOVE. NOW.
YEAH--
WHU--
--ABOUT THAT.
WHAMM

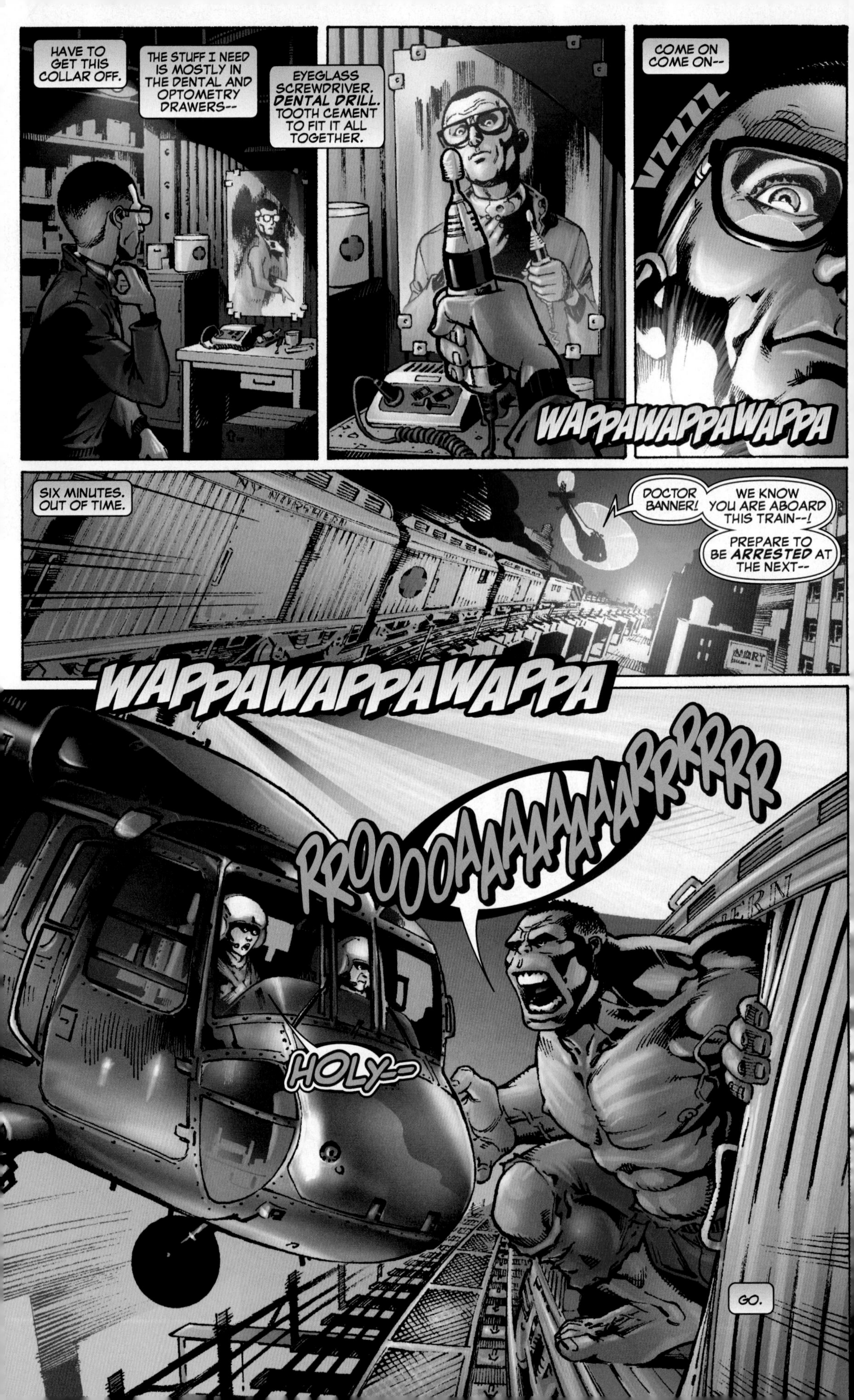
HAVE TO GET THIS COLLAR OFF.
THE STUFF I NEED IS MOSTLY IN THE DENTAL AND OPTOMETRY DRAWERS--
EYEGLASS SCREWDRIVER. DENTAL DRILL. TOOTH CEMENT TO FIT IT ALL TOGETHER.
COME ON COME ON--
VZZZZZ
WAPPAWAPPAWAPPA
SIX MINUTES. OUT OF TIME.
DOCTOR BANNER!
WE KNOW YOU ARE ABOARD THIS TRAIN--!
PREPARE TO BE ARRESTED AT THE NEXT--
WAPPAWAPPAWAPPA
RROOOOAAAAAAARRRRRR
HOLY--
GO.

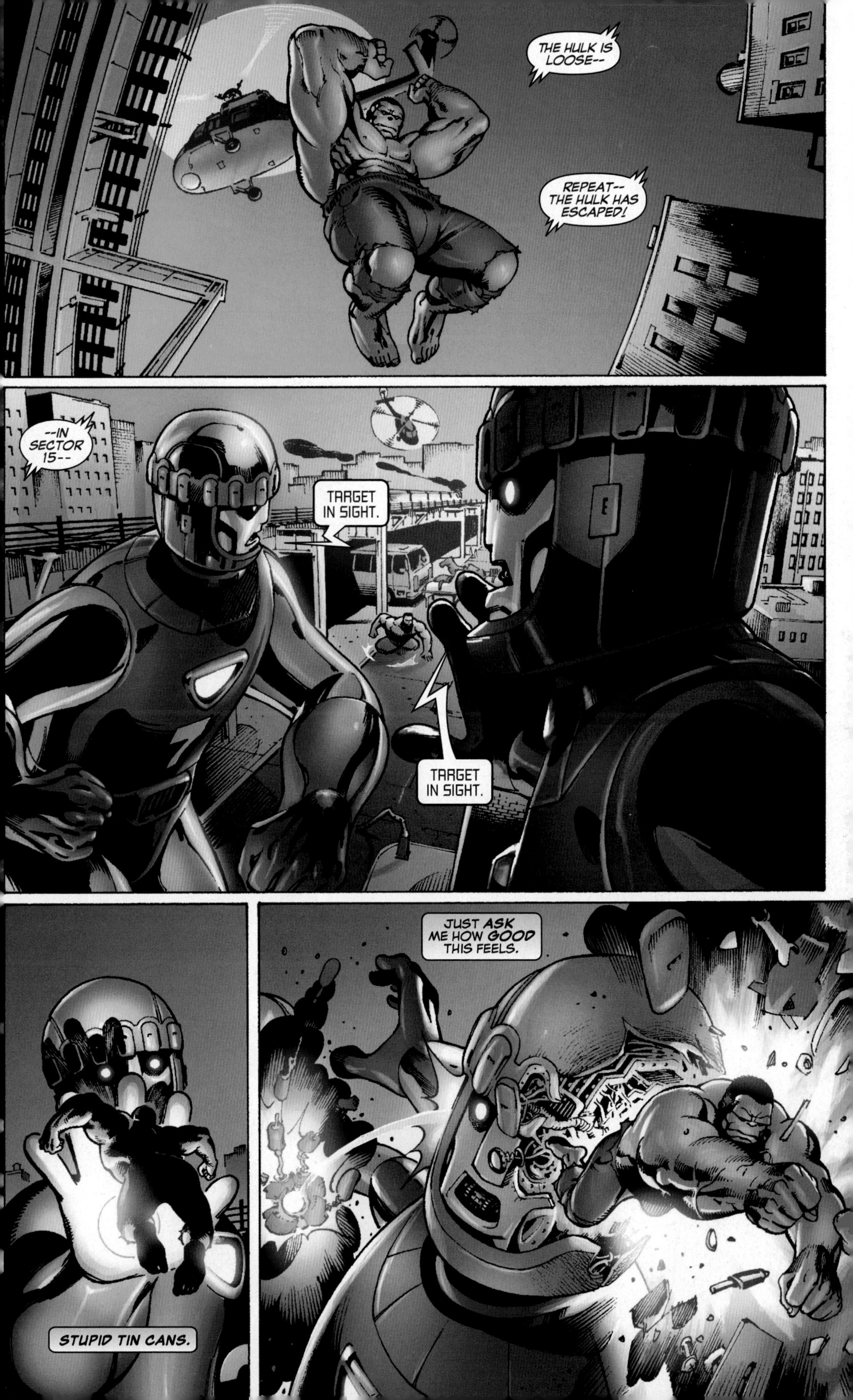
THE HULK IS LOOSE--
REPEAT-- THE HULK HAS ESCAPED!
--IN SECTOR 15--
TARGET IN SIGHT.
TARGET IN SIGHT.
STUPID TIN CANS.
JUST ASK ME HOW GOOD THIS FEELS.

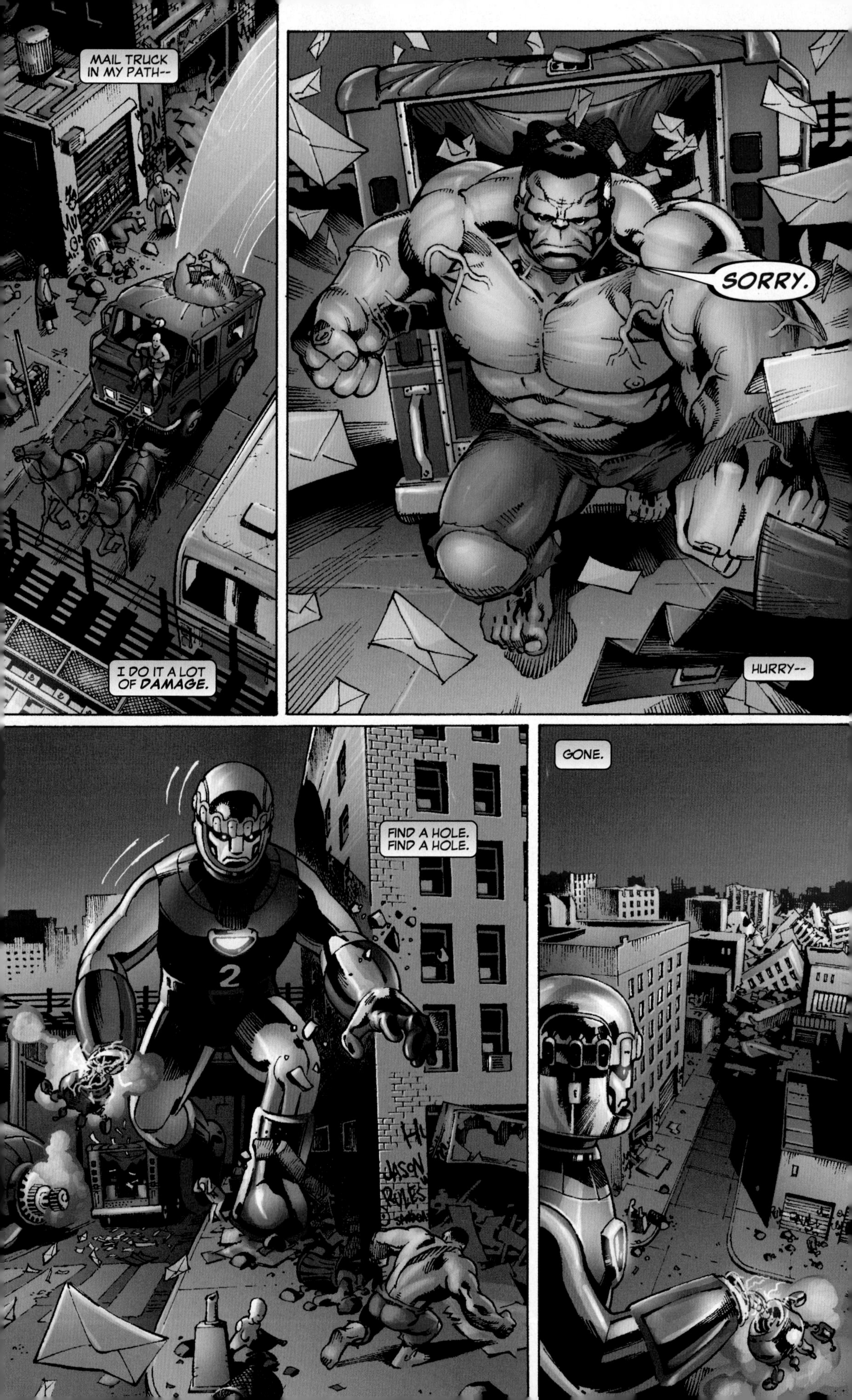
MAIL TRUCK IN MY PATH--
I DO IT A LOT OF DAMAGE.
SORRY.
HURRY--
FIND A HOLE. FIND A HOLE.
GONE.

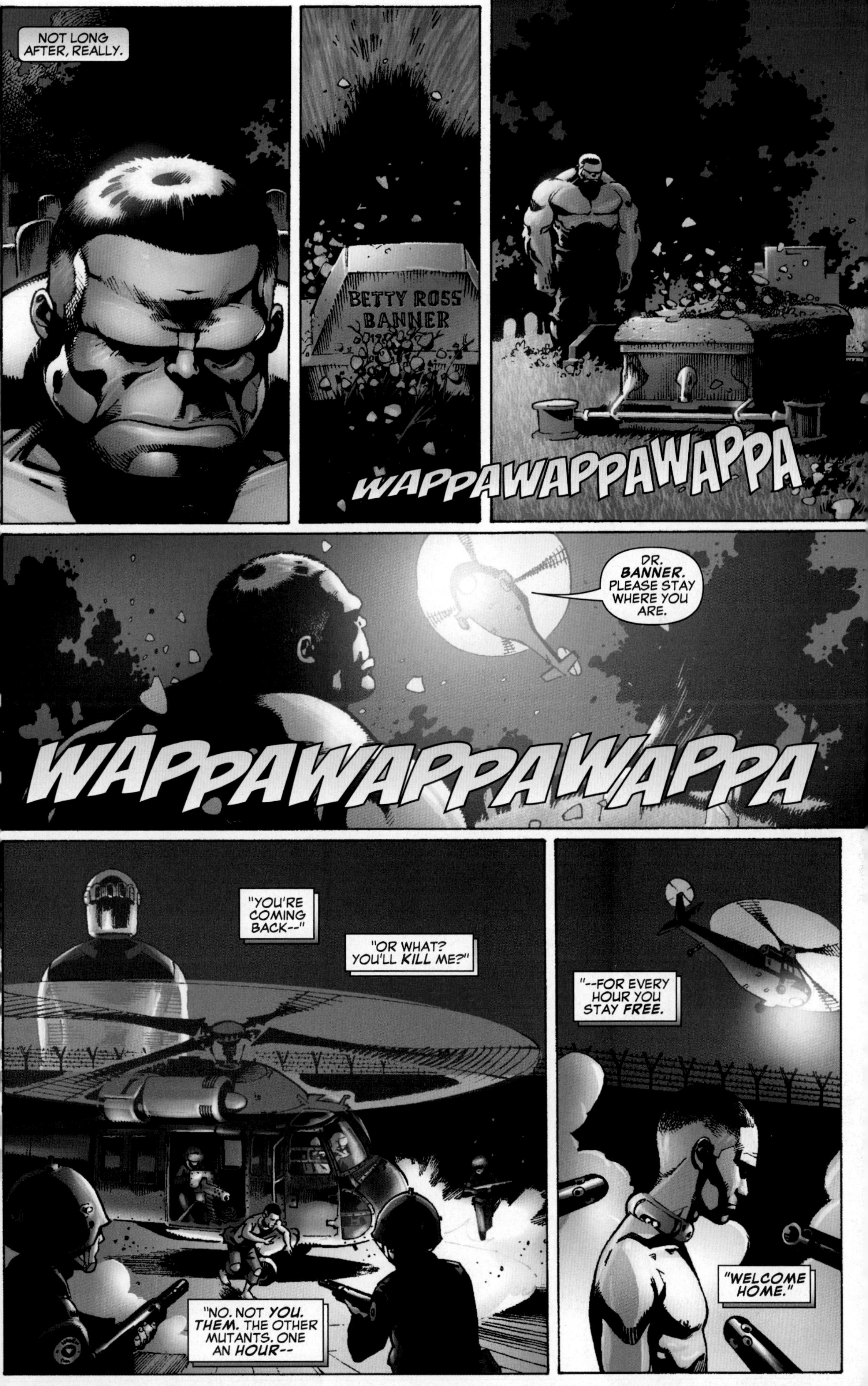
NOT LONG AFTER, REALLY.
BETTY ROSS BANNER
WAPPAWAPPAWAPPA
DR. BANNER. PLEASE STAY WHERE YOU ARE.
WAPPAWAPPAWAPPA
"YOU'RE COMING BACK--"
"OR WHAT? YOU'LL KILL ME?"
"NO. NOT YOU. THEM. THE OTHER MUTANTS. ONE AN HOUR--
"--FOR EVERY HOUR YOU STAY FREE.
"WELCOME HOME."

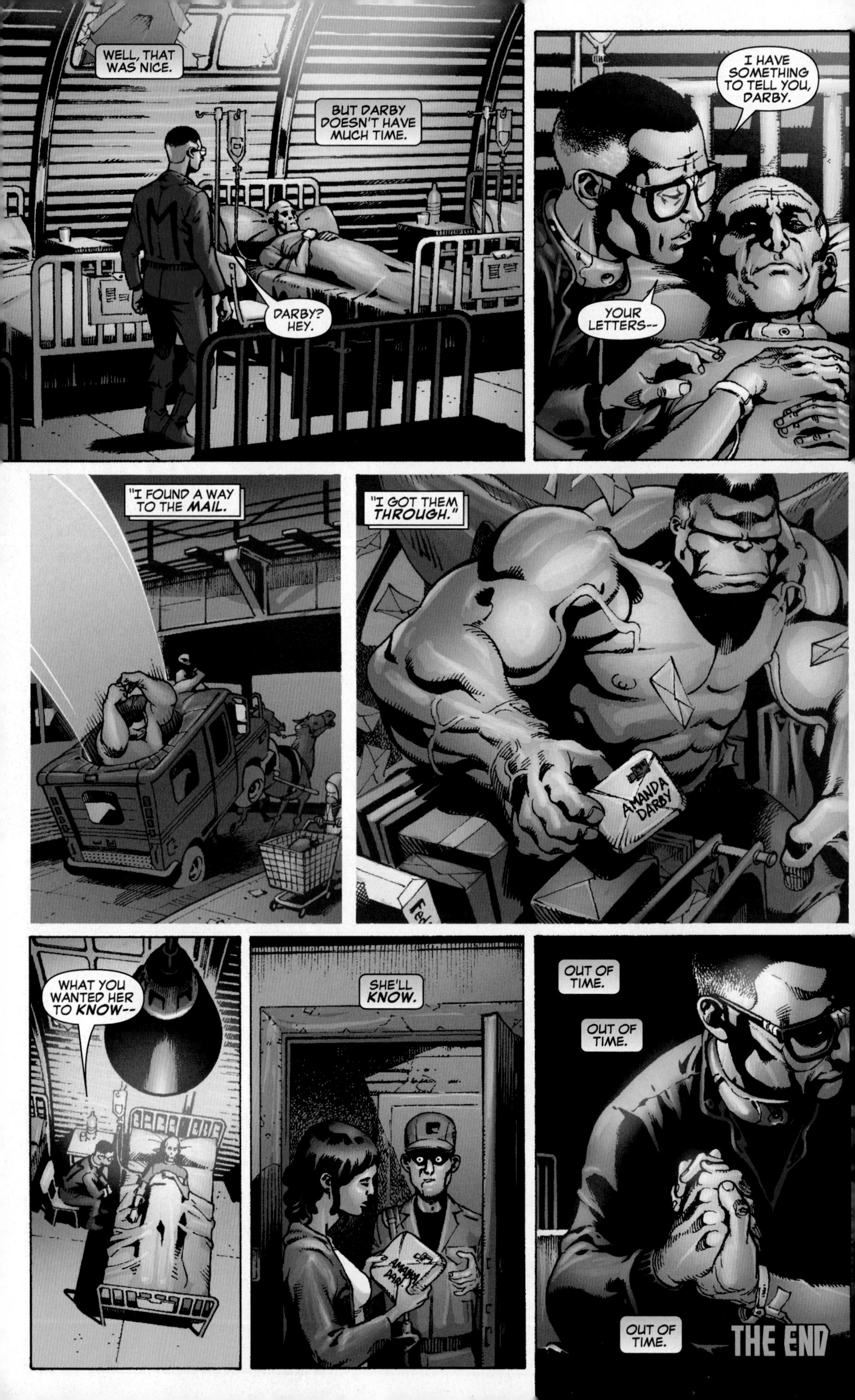
WELL, THAT WAS NICE.
BUT DARBY DOESN'T HAVE MUCH TIME.
DARBY? HEY.
I HAVE SOMETHING TO TELL YOU, DARBY.
YOUR LETTERS--
"I FOUND A WAY TO THE MAIL.
"I GOT THEM THROUGH."
AMANDA DARBY
WHAT YOU WANTED HER TO KNOW--
SHE'LL KNOW.
OUT OF TIME.
OUT OF TIME.
OUT OF TIME.
THE END

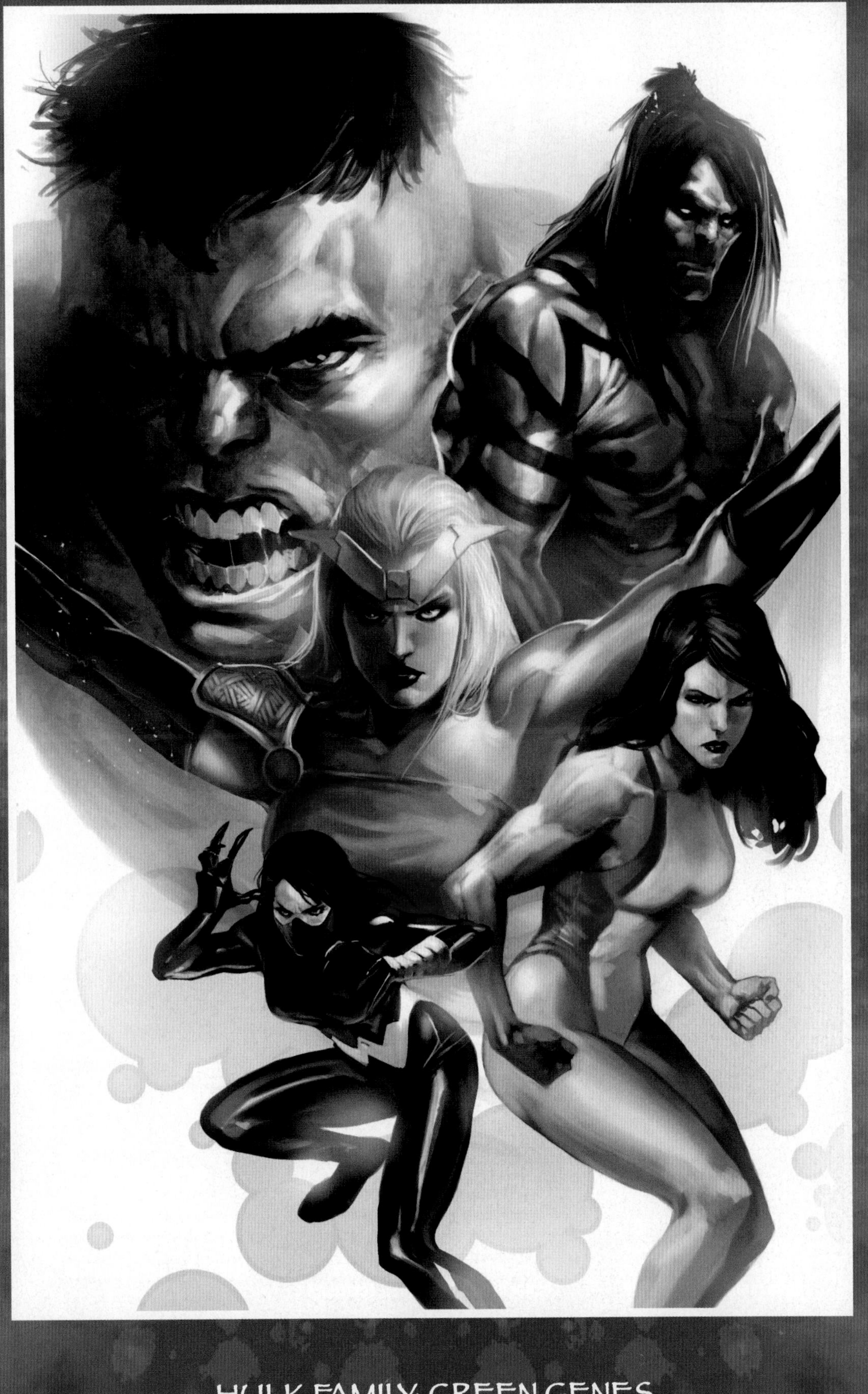

HULK FAMILY: GREEN GENES

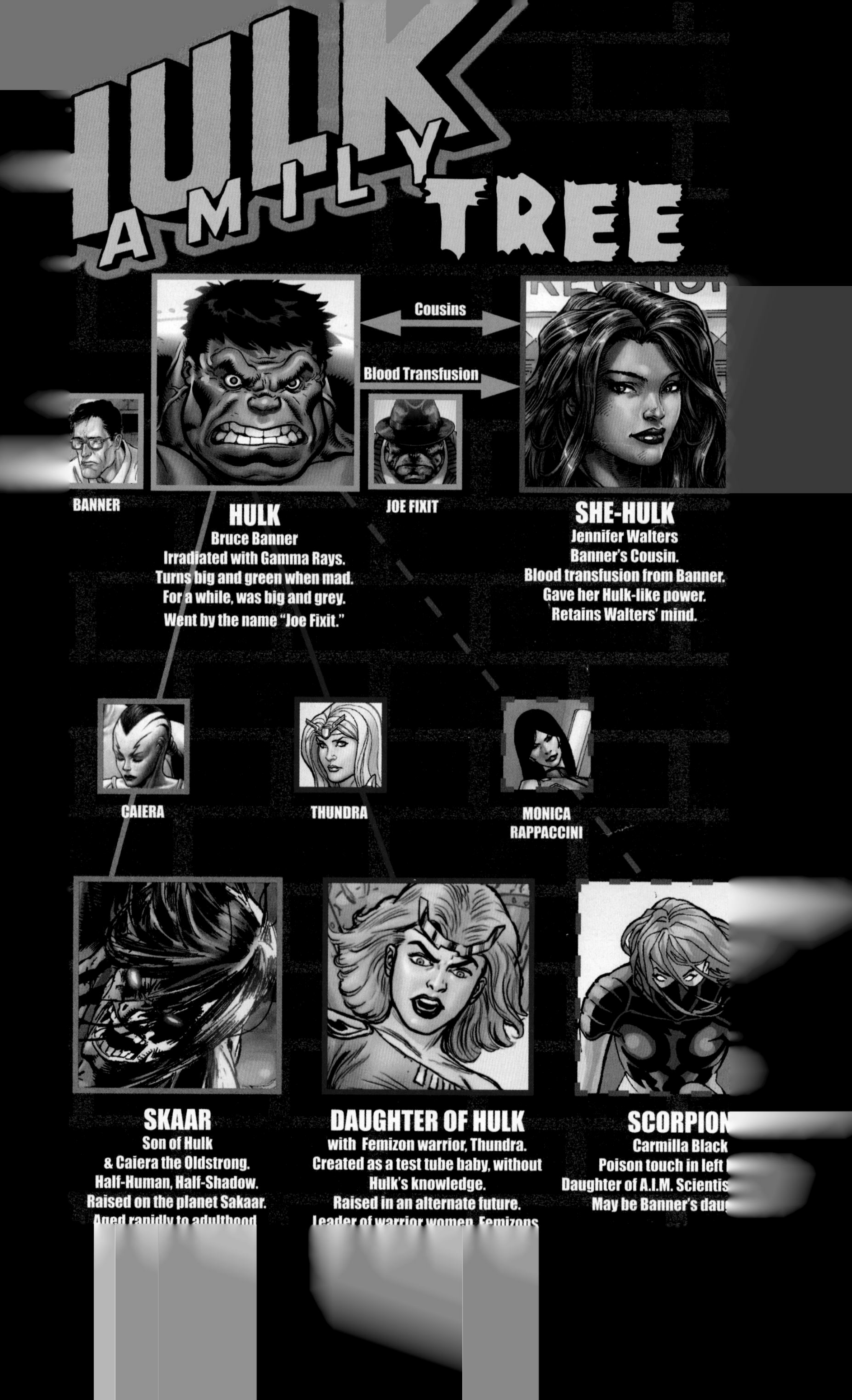
HULK
FAMILY
TREE
Cousins
Blood Transfusion
BANNER
HULK
Bruce Banner
Irradiated with Gamma Rays.
Turns big and green when mad.
For a while, was big and grey.
Went by the name "Joe Fixit."
JOE FIXIT
SHE-HULK
Jennifer Walters
Banner's Cousin.
Blood transfusion from Banner.
Gave her Hulk-like power.
Retains Walters' mind.
CAIERA
THUNDRA
MONICA
RAPPACCINI
SKAAR
Son of Hulk
& Caiera the Oldstrong.
Half-Human, Half-Shadow.
Raised on the planet Sakaar.
Aged rapidly to adulthood
DAUGHTER OF HULK
with Femizon warrior, Thundra.
Created as a test tube baby, without
Hulk's knowledge.
Raised in an alternate future.
Leader of warrior women, Femizons
SCORPION
Carmilla Black
Poison touch in left
Daughter of A.I.M. Scientis
May be Banner's daug

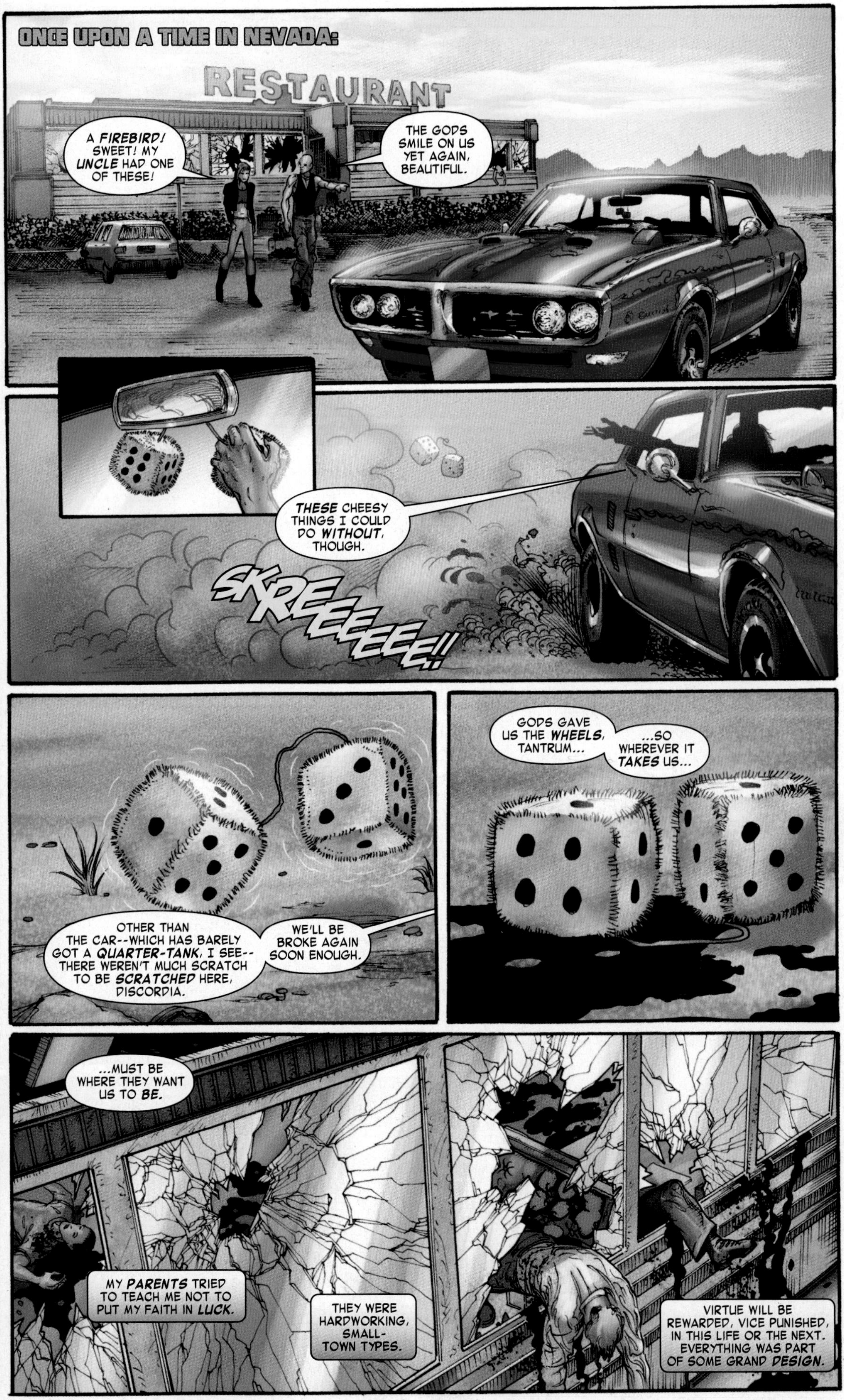
ONCE UPON A TIME IN NEVADA:
RESTAURANT
A FIREBIRD! SWEET! MY UNCLE HAD ONE OF THESE!
THE GODS SMILE ON US YET AGAIN, BEAUTIFUL.
THESE CHEESY THINGS I COULD DO WITHOUT, THOUGH.
SKREEEEEEE!!
OTHER THAN THE CAR--WHICH HAS BARELY GOT A QUARTER-TANK, I SEE--THERE WEREN'T MUCH SCRATCH TO BE SCRATCHED HERE, DISCORDIA.
WE'LL BE BROKE AGAIN SOON ENOUGH.
GODS GAVE US THE WHEELS, TANTRUM...
...SO WHEREVER IT TAKES US...
...MUST BE WHERE THEY WANT US TO BE.
MY PARENTS TRIED TO TEACH ME NOT TO PUT MY FAITH IN LUCK.
THEY WERE HARDWORKING, SMALL-TOWN TYPES.
VIRTUE WILL BE REWARDED, VICE PUNISHED, IN THIS LIFE OR THE NEXT. EVERYTHING WAS PART OF SOME GRAND DESIGN.

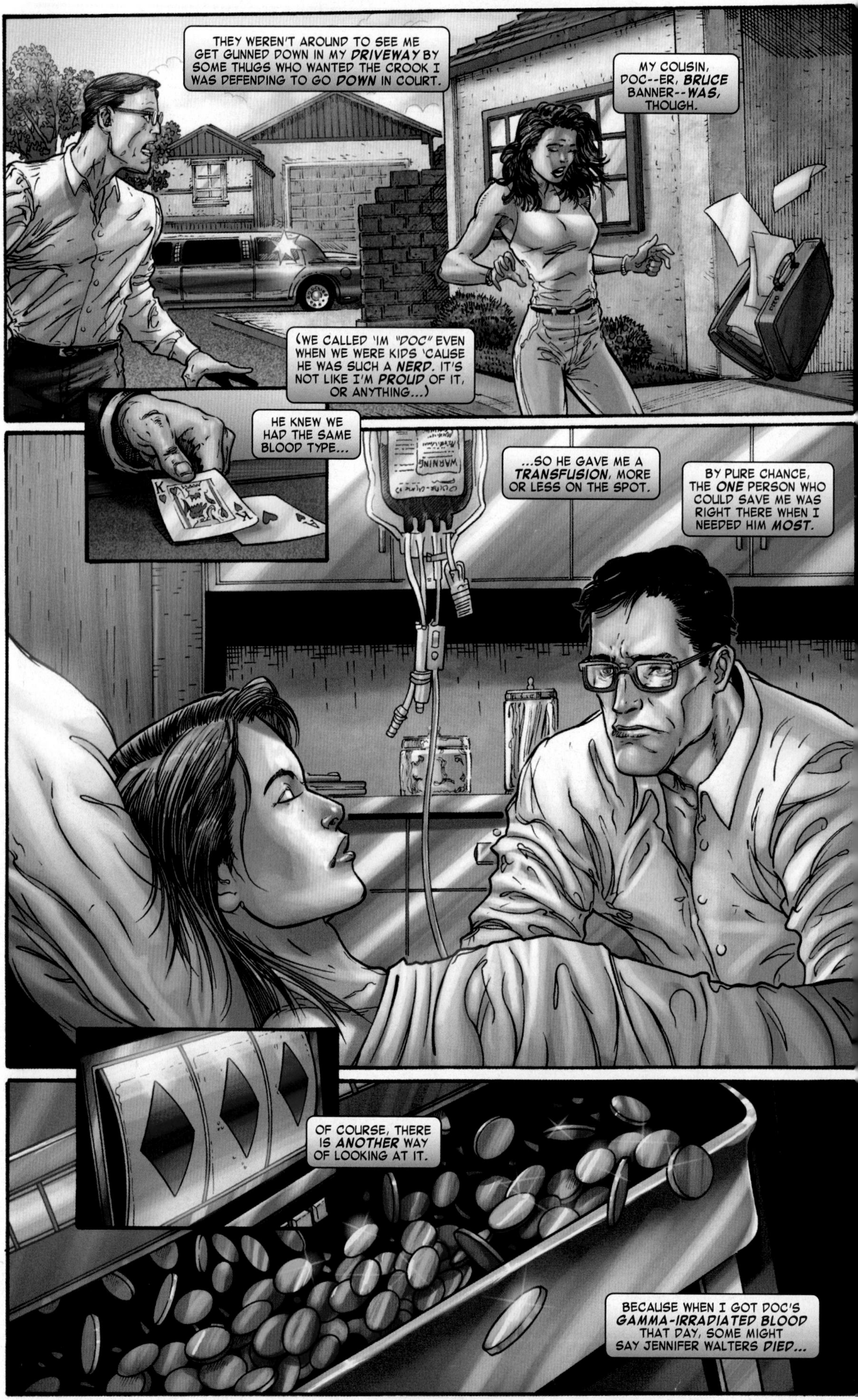
THEY WEREN'T AROUND TO SEE ME GET GUNNED DOWN IN MY DRIVEWAY BY SOME THUGS WHO WANTED THE CROOK I WAS DEFENDING TO GO DOWN IN COURT.
MY COUSIN, DOC--ER, BRUCE BANNER--WAS, THOUGH.
(WE CALLED 'IM "DOC" EVEN WHEN WE WERE KIDS 'CAUSE HE WAS SUCH A NERD. IT'S NOT LIKE I'M PROUD OF IT, OR ANYTHING...)
HE KNEW WE HAD THE SAME BLOOD TYPE...
...SO HE GAVE ME A TRANSFUSION, MORE OR LESS ON THE SPOT.
BY PURE CHANCE, THE ONE PERSON WHO COULD SAVE ME WAS RIGHT THERE WHEN I NEEDED HIM MOST.
WARNING
OF COURSE, THERE IS ANOTHER WAY OF LOOKING AT IT.
BECAUSE WHEN I GOT DOC'S GAMMA-IRRADIATED BLOOD THAT DAY, SOME MIGHT SAY JENNIFER WALTERS DIED...

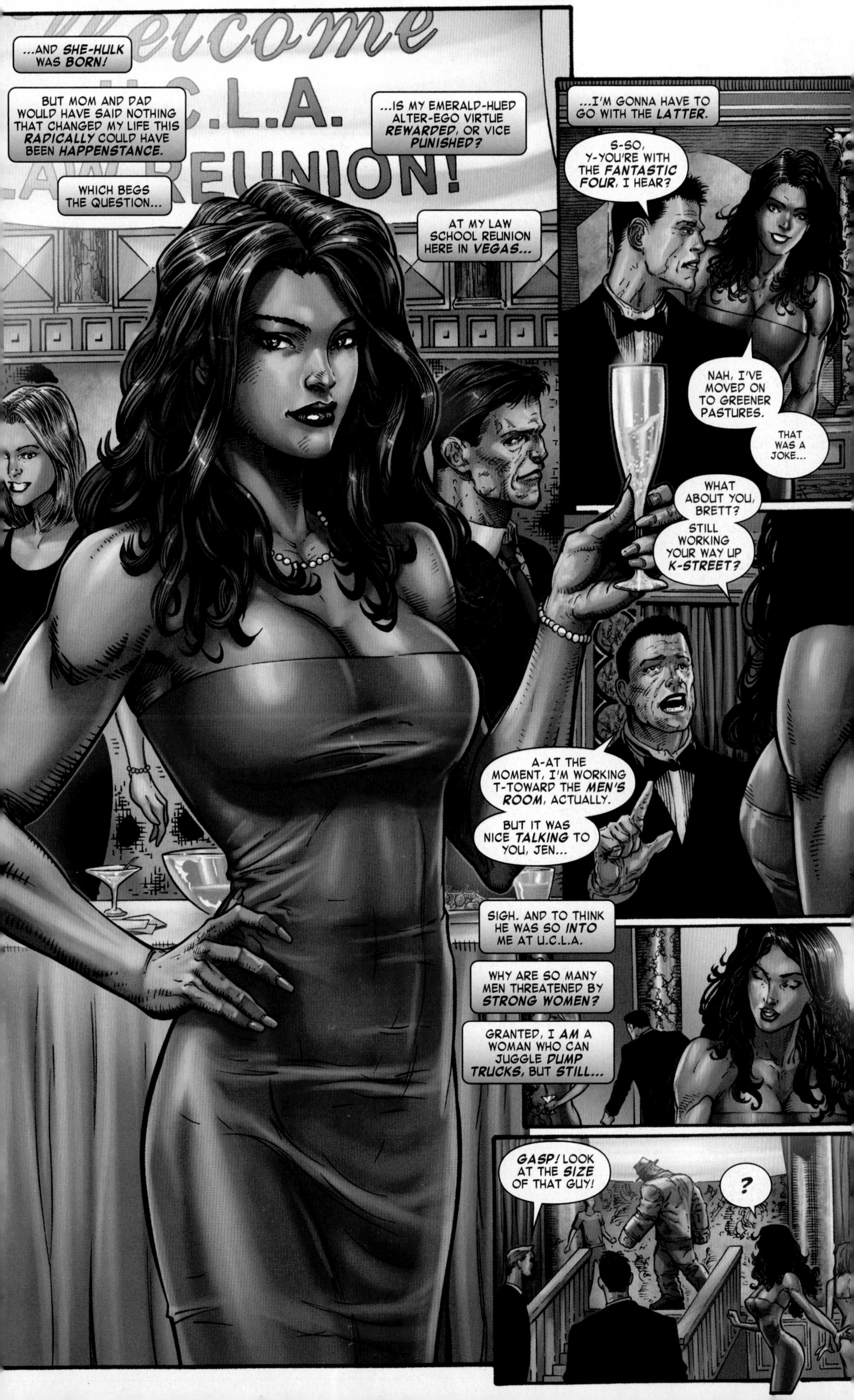
WELCOME U.C.L.A. LAW REUNION!
...AND SHE-HULK WAS BORN!
BUT MOM AND DAD WOULD HAVE SAID NOTHING THAT CHANGED MY LIFE THIS RADICALLY COULD HAVE BEEN HAPPENSTANCE.
WHICH BEGS THE QUESTION...
...IS MY EMERALD-HUED ALTER-EGO VIRTUE REWARDED, OR VICE PUNISHED?
AT MY LAW SCHOOL REUNION HERE IN VEGAS...
...I'M GONNA HAVE TO GO WITH THE LATTER.
S-SO, Y-YOU'RE WITH THE FANTASTIC FOUR, I HEAR?
NAH, I'VE MOVED ON TO GREENER PASTURES.
THAT WAS A JOKE...
WHAT ABOUT YOU, BRETT?
STILL WORKING YOUR WAY UP K-STREET?
A-AT THE MOMENT, I'M WORKING T-TOWARD THE MEN'S ROOM, ACTUALLY.
BUT IT WAS NICE TALKING TO YOU, JEN...
SIGH. AND TO THINK HE WAS SO INTO ME AT U.C.L.A.
WHY ARE SO MANY MEN THREATENED BY STRONG WOMEN?
GRANTED, I AM A WOMAN WHO CAN JUGGLE DUMP TRUCKS, BUT STILL...
GASP! LOOK AT THE SIZE OF THAT GUY!
?

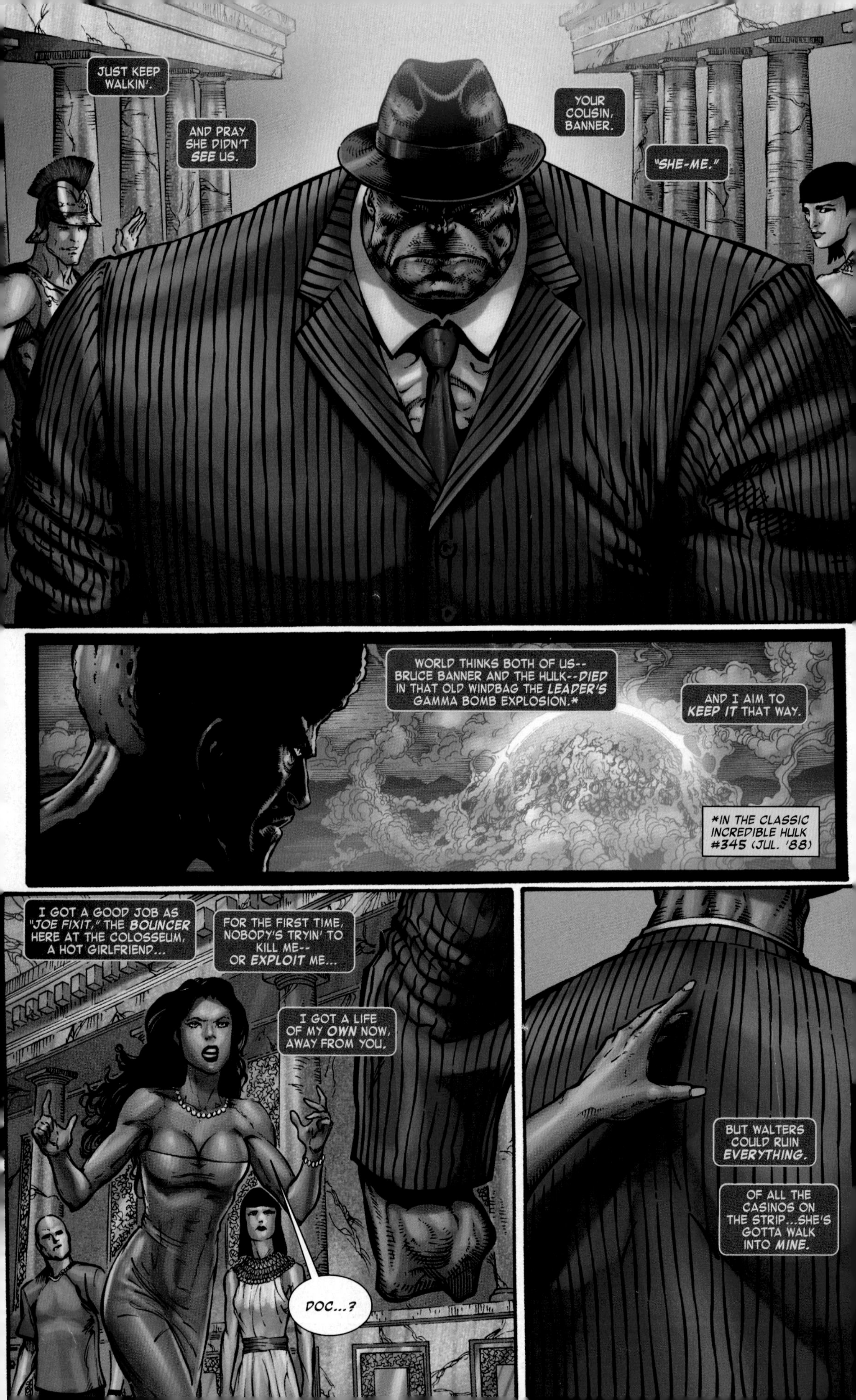

JUST KEEP WALKIN'.
AND PRAY SHE DIDN'T SEE US.
YOUR COUSIN, BANNER.
"SHE-ME."
WORLD THINKS BOTH OF US-- BRUCE BANNER AND THE HULK--DIED IN THAT OLD WINDBAG THE LEADER'S GAMMA BOMB EXPLOSION.*
AND I AIM TO KEEP IT THAT WAY.
*IN THE CLASSIC INCREDIBLE HULK #345 (JUL. '88)
I GOT A GOOD JOB AS "JOE FIXIT," THE BOUNCER HERE AT THE COLOSSEUM, A HOT GIRLFRIEND...
FOR THE FIRST TIME, NOBODY'S TRYIN' TO KILL ME-- OR EXPLOIT ME...
I GOT A LIFE OF MY OWN NOW, AWAY FROM YOU.
DOC...?
BUT WALTERS COULD RUIN EVERYTHING.
OF ALL THE CASINOS ON THE STRIP...SHE'S GOTTA WALK INTO MINE.

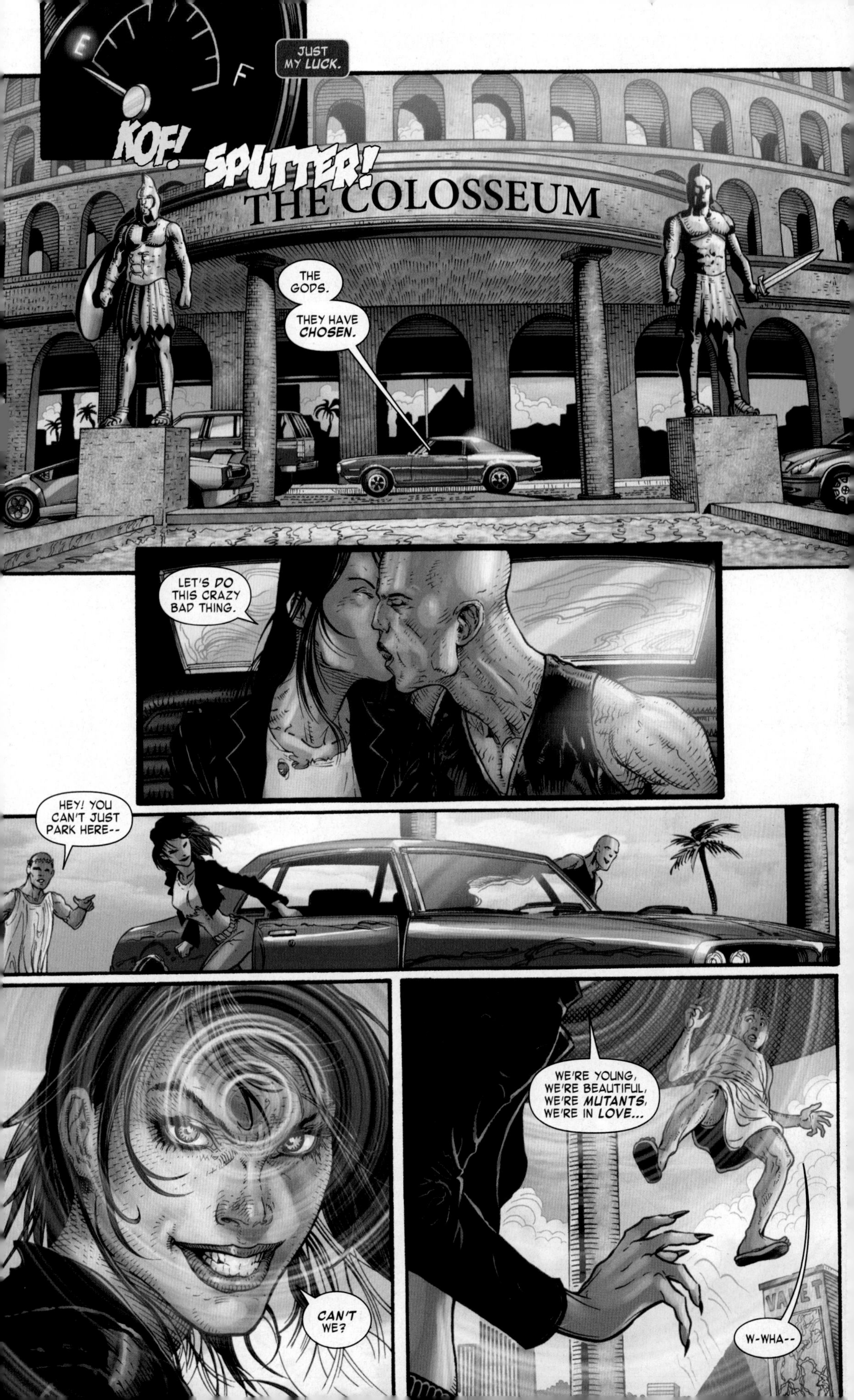
JUST MY LUCK.
KOF!
SPUTTER!
THE COLOSSEUM
THE GODS.
THEY HAVE CHOSEN.
LET'S DO THIS CRAZY BAD THING.
HEY! YOU CAN'T JUST PARK HERE--
CAN'T WE?
WE'RE YOUNG, WE'RE BEAUTIFUL, WE'RE MUTANTS, WE'RE IN LOVE...
W-WHA--
VALET

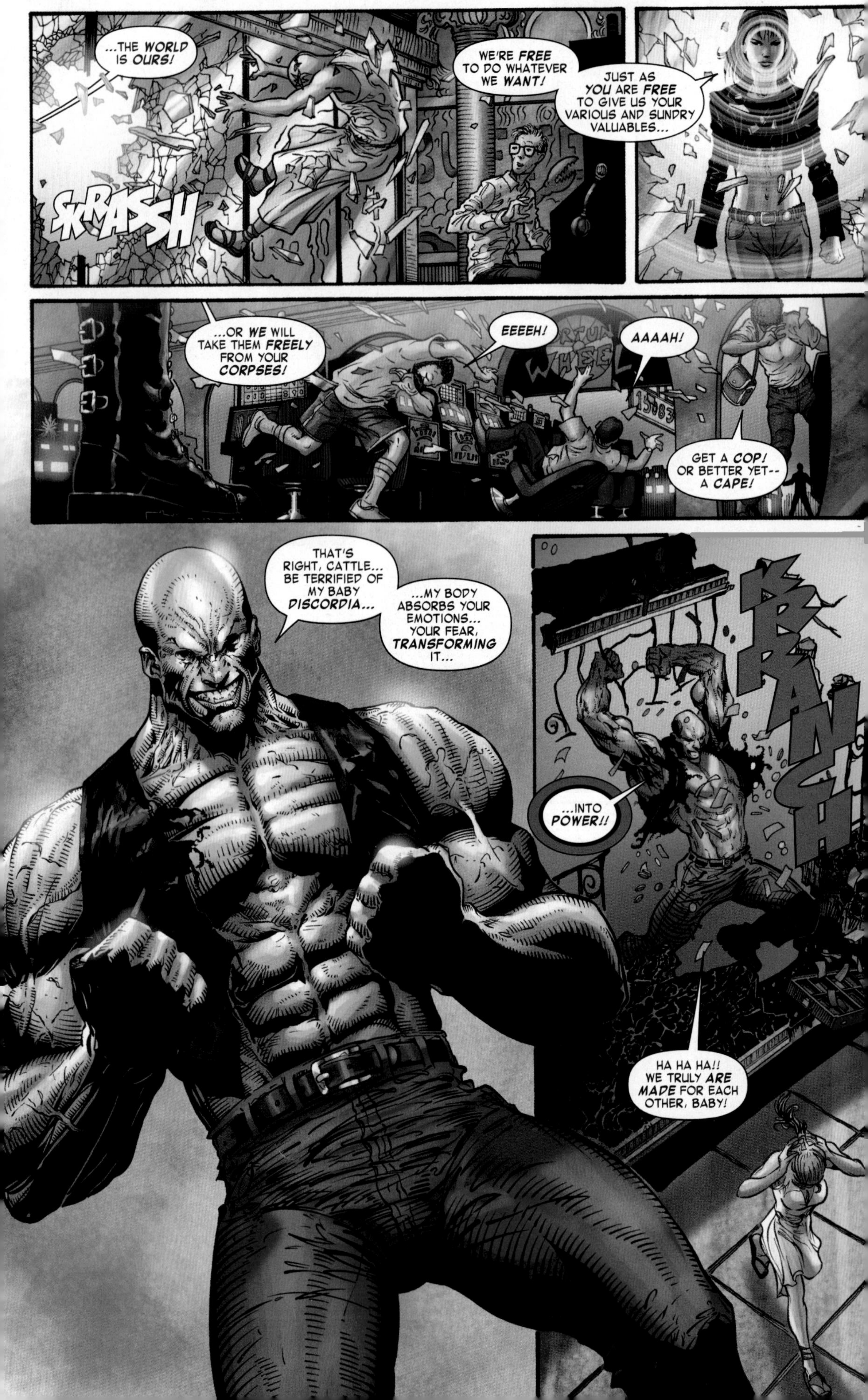

...THE WORLD IS OURS!
SKRASSH
WE'RE FREE TO DO WHATEVER WE WANT!
JUST AS YOU ARE FREE TO GIVE US YOUR VARIOUS AND SUNDRY VALUABLES...
...OR WE WILL TAKE THEM FREELY FROM YOUR CORPSES!
EEEEH!
AAAAH!
GET A COP! OR BETTER YET-- A CAPE!
THAT'S RIGHT, CATTLE... BE TERRIFIED OF MY BABY DISCORDIA...
...MY BODY ABSORBS YOUR EMOTIONS... YOUR FEAR, TRANSFORMING IT...
...INTO POWER!!
KRANCH
HA HA HA!! WE TRULY ARE MADE FOR EACH OTHER, BABY!

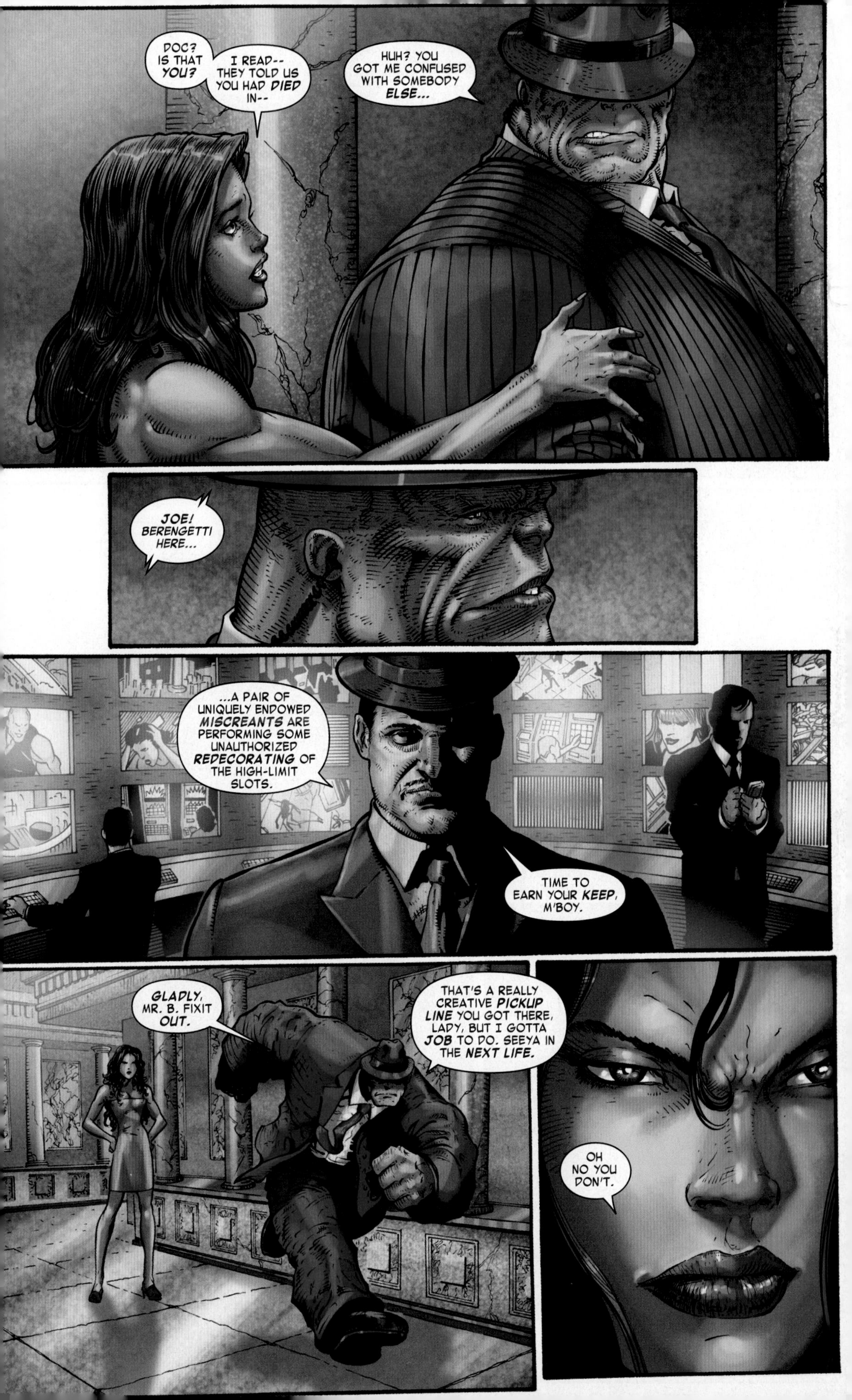
DOC? IS THAT YOU?
I READ-- THEY TOLD US YOU HAD DIED IN--
HUH? YOU GOT ME CONFUSED WITH SOMEBODY ELSE...
JOE! BERENGETTI HERE...
...A PAIR OF UNIQUELY ENDOWED MISCREANTS ARE PERFORMING SOME UNAUTHORIZED REDECORATING OF THE HIGH-LIMIT SLOTS.
TIME TO EARN YOUR KEEP, M'BOY.
GLADLY, MR. B. FIXIT OUT.
THAT'S A REALLY CREATIVE PICKUP LINE YOU GOT THERE, LADY, BUT I GOTTA JOB TO DO. SEEYA IN THE NEXT LIFE.
OH NO YOU DON'T.

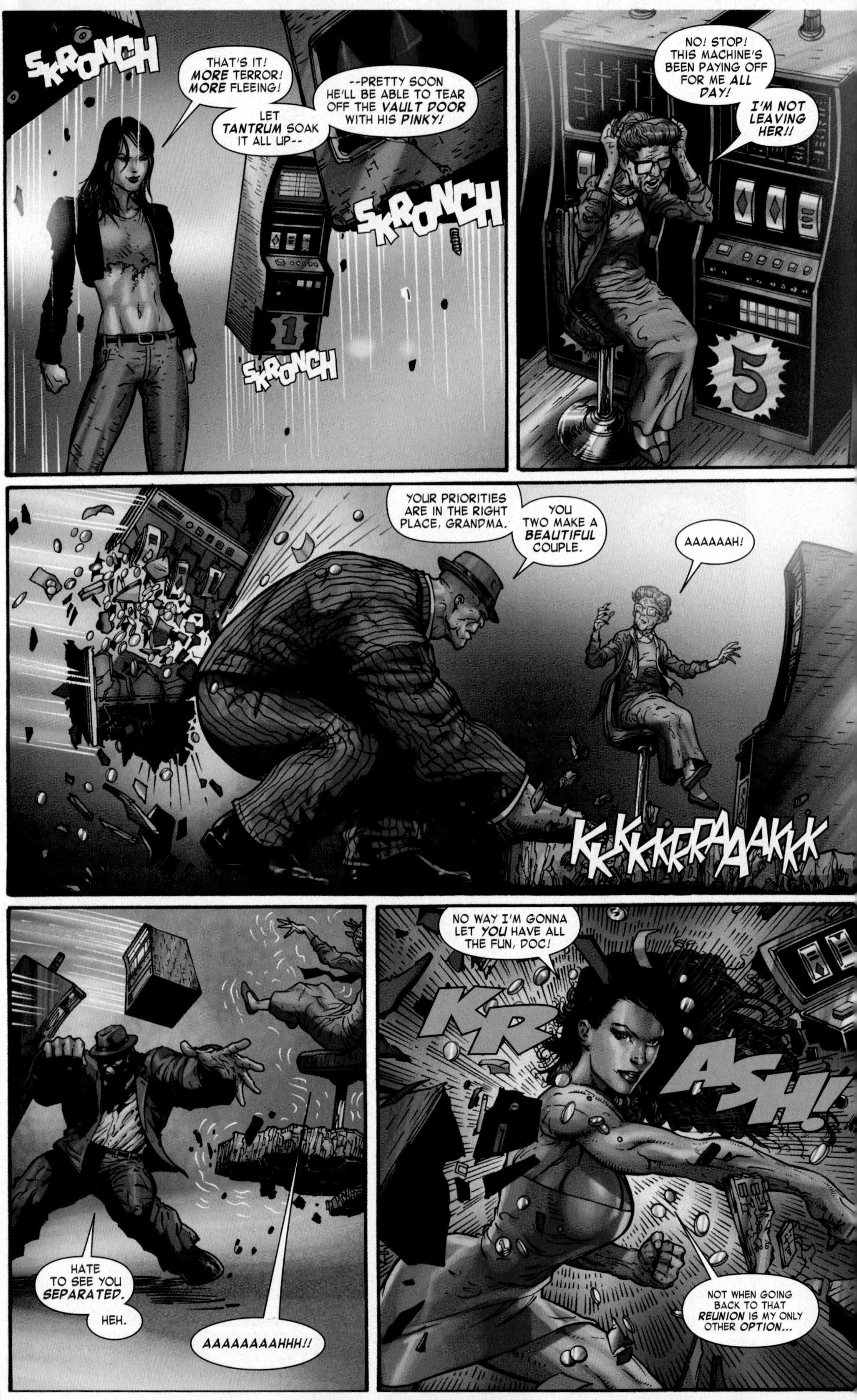
SKRONCH
THAT'S IT! MORE TERROR! MORE FLEEING!
LET TANTRUM SOAK IT ALL UP--
--PRETTY SOON HE'LL BE ABLE TO TEAR OFF THE VAULT DOOR WITH HIS PINKY!
SKRONCH
SKRONCH
NO! STOP! THIS MACHINE'S BEEN PAYING OFF FOR ME ALL DAY!
I'M NOT LEAVING HER!!
YOUR PRIORITIES ARE IN THE RIGHT PLACE, GRANDMA.
YOU TWO MAKE A BEAUTIFUL COUPLE.
AAAAAAH!
KKKKKRRAAAKKK
HATE TO SEE YOU SEPARATED.
HEH.
AAAAAAAAHHH!!
NO WAY I'M GONNA LET YOU HAVE ALL THE FUN, DOC!
KRASH!
NOT WHEN GOING BACK TO THAT REUNION IS MY ONLY OTHER OPTION...

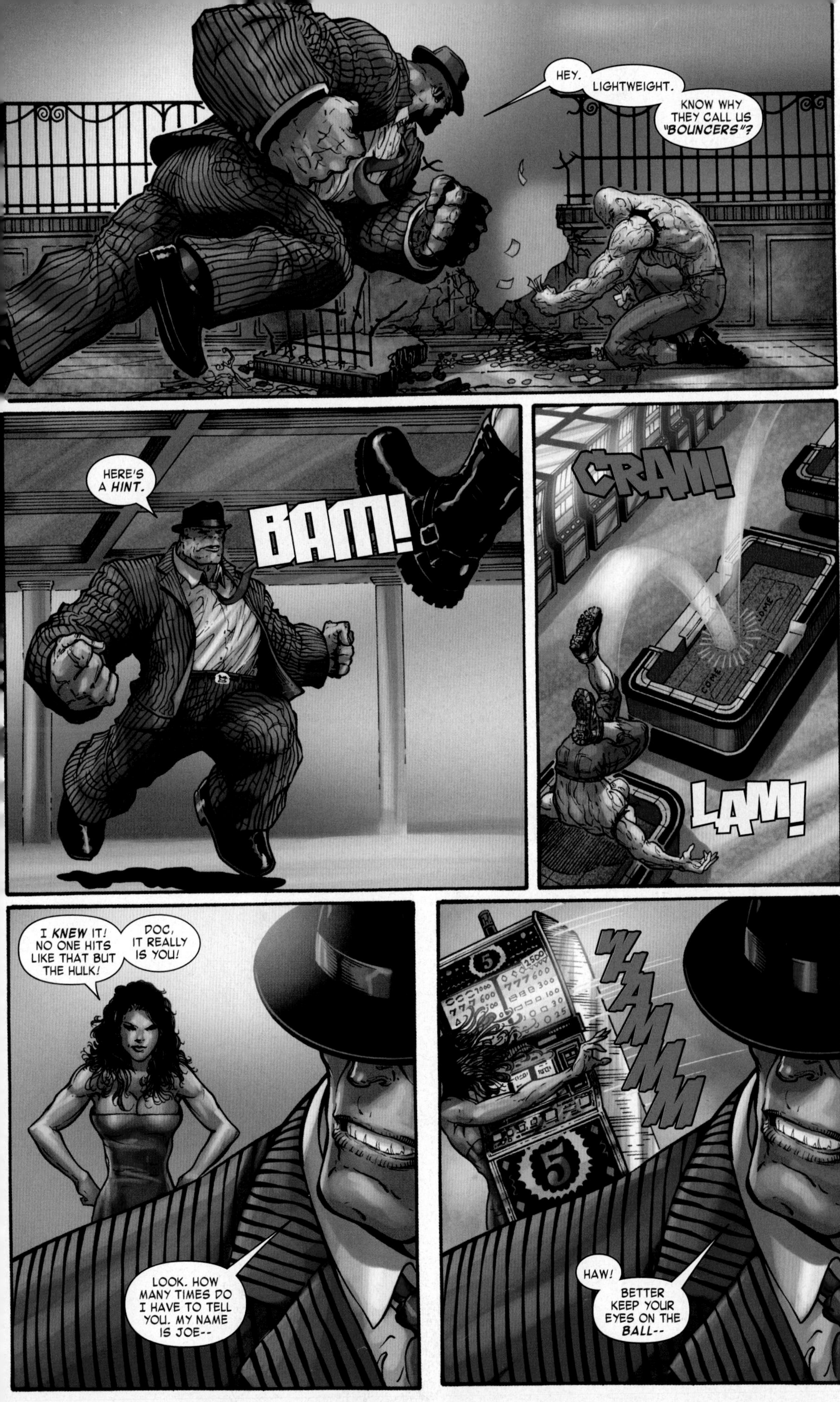
HEY.
LIGHTWEIGHT.
KNOW WHY THEY CALL US "BOUNCERS"?
HERE'S A HINT.
BAM!
CRAM!
LAM!
I KNEW IT! NO ONE HITS LIKE THAT BUT THE HULK!
DOC, IT REALLY IS YOU!
LOOK. HOW MANY TIMES DO I HAVE TO TELL YOU. MY NAME IS JOE--
WHAMMM
HAW!
BETTER KEEP YOUR EYES ON THE BALL--

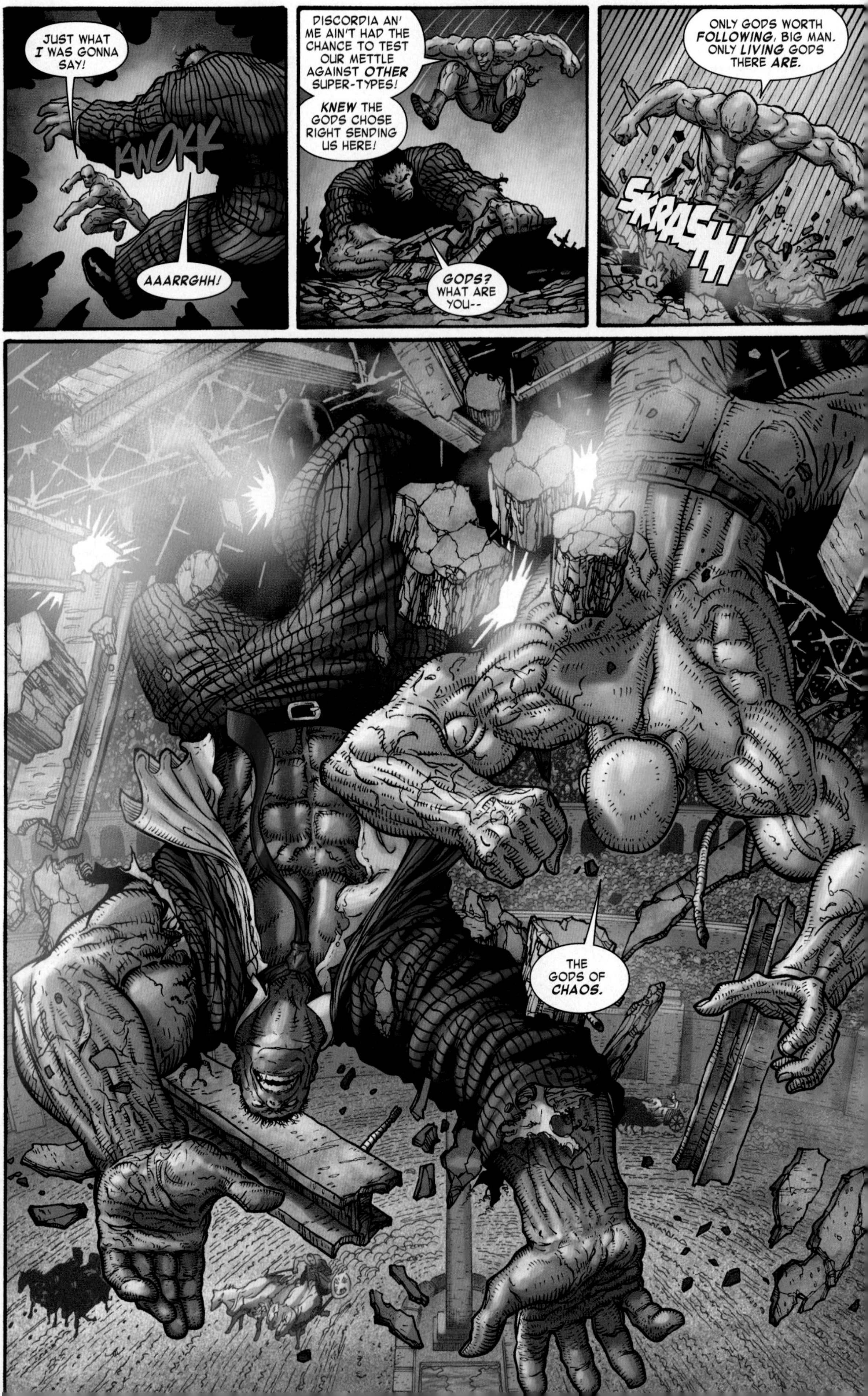
JUST WHAT I WAS GONNA SAY!
KWOKK
AAARRGHH!
DISCORDIA AN' ME AIN'T HAD THE CHANCE TO TEST OUR METTLE AGAINST OTHER SUPER-TYPES!
KNEW THE GODS CHOSE RIGHT SENDING US HERE!
GODS? WHAT ARE YOU--
ONLY GODS WORTH FOLLOWING, BIG MAN. ONLY LIVING GODS THERE ARE.
SKRASHH
THE GODS OF CHAOS.

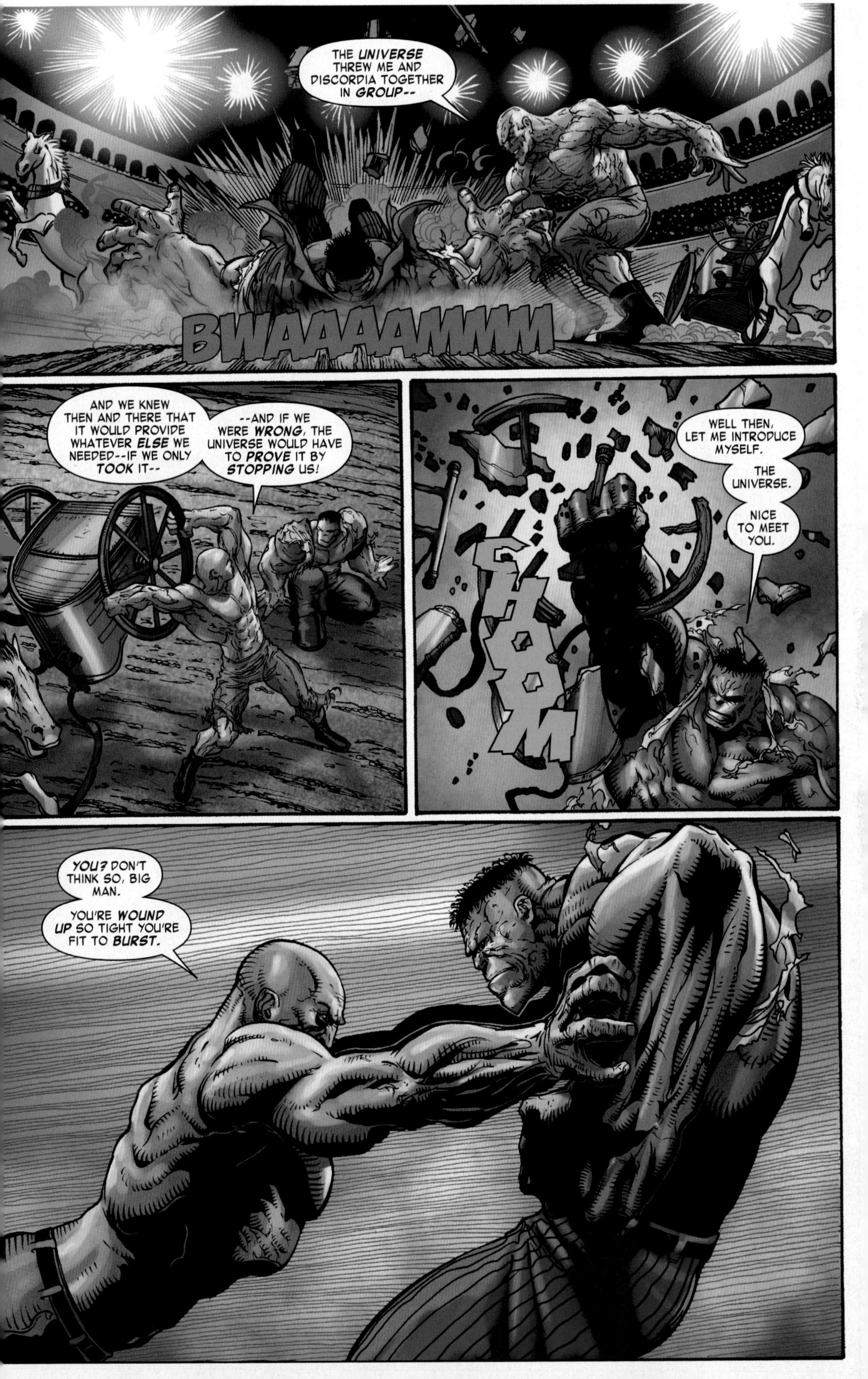
THE UNIVERSE THREW ME AND DISCORDIA TOGETHER IN GROUP--
BWAAAAMMMM
AND WE KNEW THEN AND THERE THAT IT WOULD PROVIDE WHATEVER ELSE WE NEEDED--IF WE ONLY TOOK IT--
--AND IF WE WERE WRONG, THE UNIVERSE WOULD HAVE TO PROVE IT BY STOPPING US!
WELL THEN, LET ME INTRODUCE MYSELF.
THE UNIVERSE.
NICE TO MEET YOU.
SHOOM
YOU? DON'T THINK SO, BIG MAN.
YOU'RE WOUND UP SO TIGHT YOU'RE FIT TO BURST.

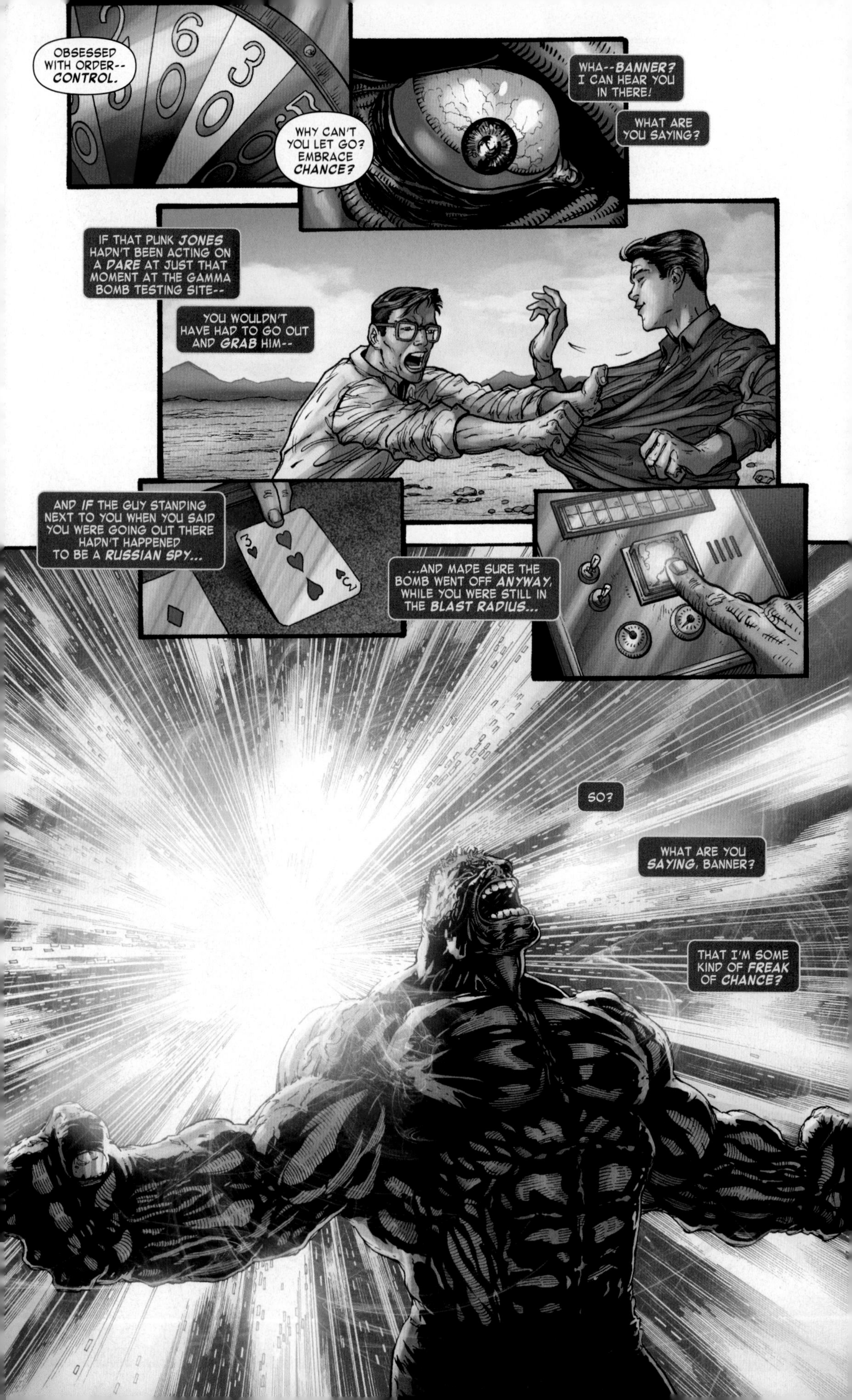
OBSESSED WITH ORDER-- CONTROL.
WHY CAN'T YOU LET GO? EMBRACE CHANCE?
WHA--BANNER? I CAN HEAR YOU IN THERE!
WHAT ARE YOU SAYING?
IF THAT PUNK JONES HADN'T BEEN ACTING ON A DARE AT JUST THAT MOMENT AT THE GAMMA BOMB TESTING SITE--
YOU WOULDN'T HAVE HAD TO GO OUT AND GRAB HIM--
AND IF THE GUY STANDING NEXT TO YOU WHEN YOU SAID YOU WERE GOING OUT THERE HADN'T HAPPENED TO BE A RUSSIAN SPY...
...AND MADE SURE THE BOMB WENT OFF ANYWAY, WHILE YOU WERE STILL IN THE BLAST RADIUS...
SO?
WHAT ARE YOU SAYING, BANNER?
THAT I'M SOME KIND OF FREAK OF CHANCE?

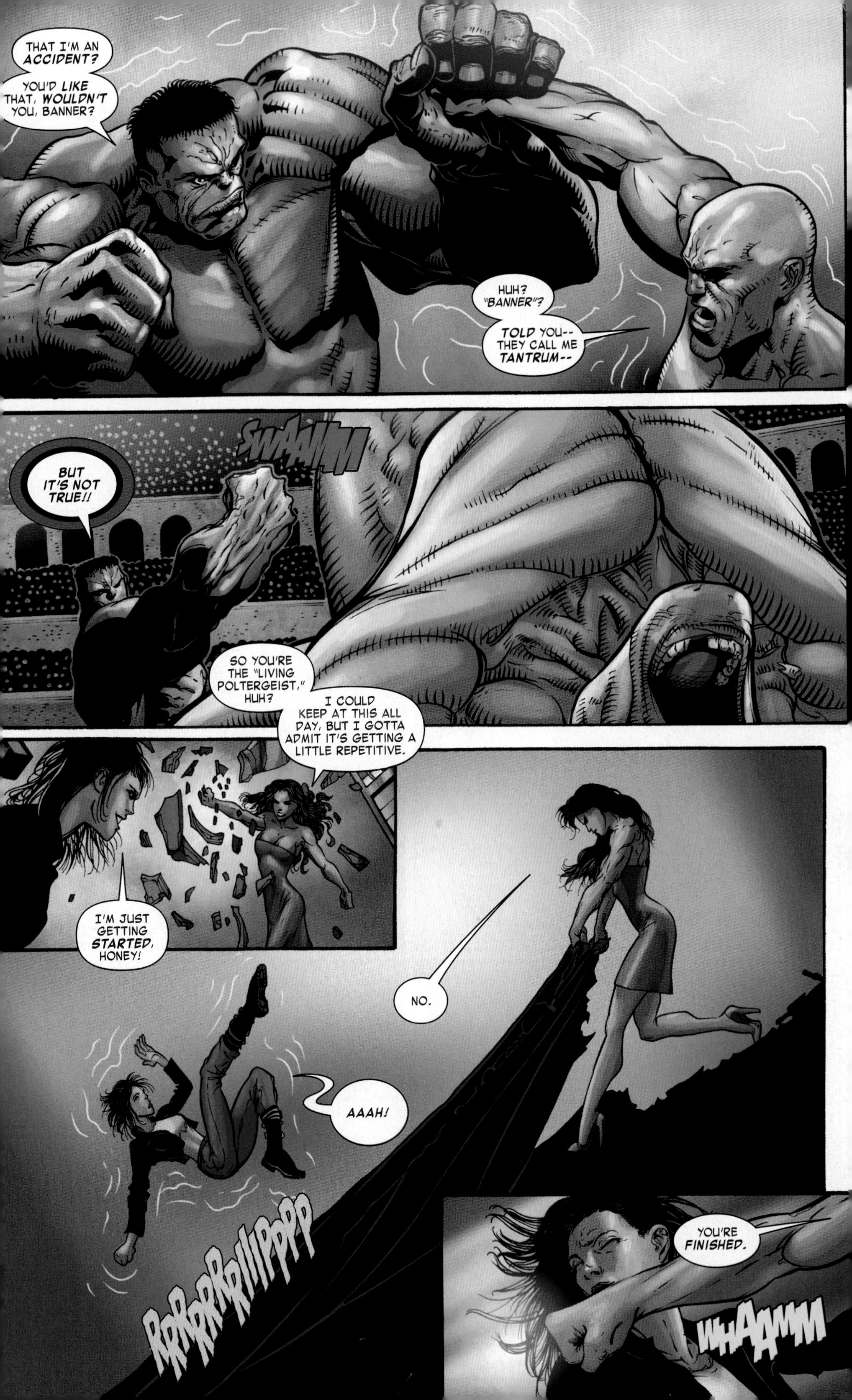
THAT I'M AN ACCIDENT?
YOU'D LIKE THAT, WOULDN'T YOU, BANNER?
HUH? "BANNER"?
TOLD YOU-- THEY CALL ME TANTRUM--
SWAAMM
BUT IT'S NOT TRUE!!
SO YOU'RE THE "LIVING POLTERGEIST," HUH?
I COULD KEEP AT THIS ALL DAY, BUT I GOTTA ADMIT IT'S GETTING A LITTLE REPETITIVE.
I'M JUST GETTING STARTED, HONEY!
NO.
AAAH!
RRRRRRIIPPPP
YOU'RE FINISHED.
WHAAMM

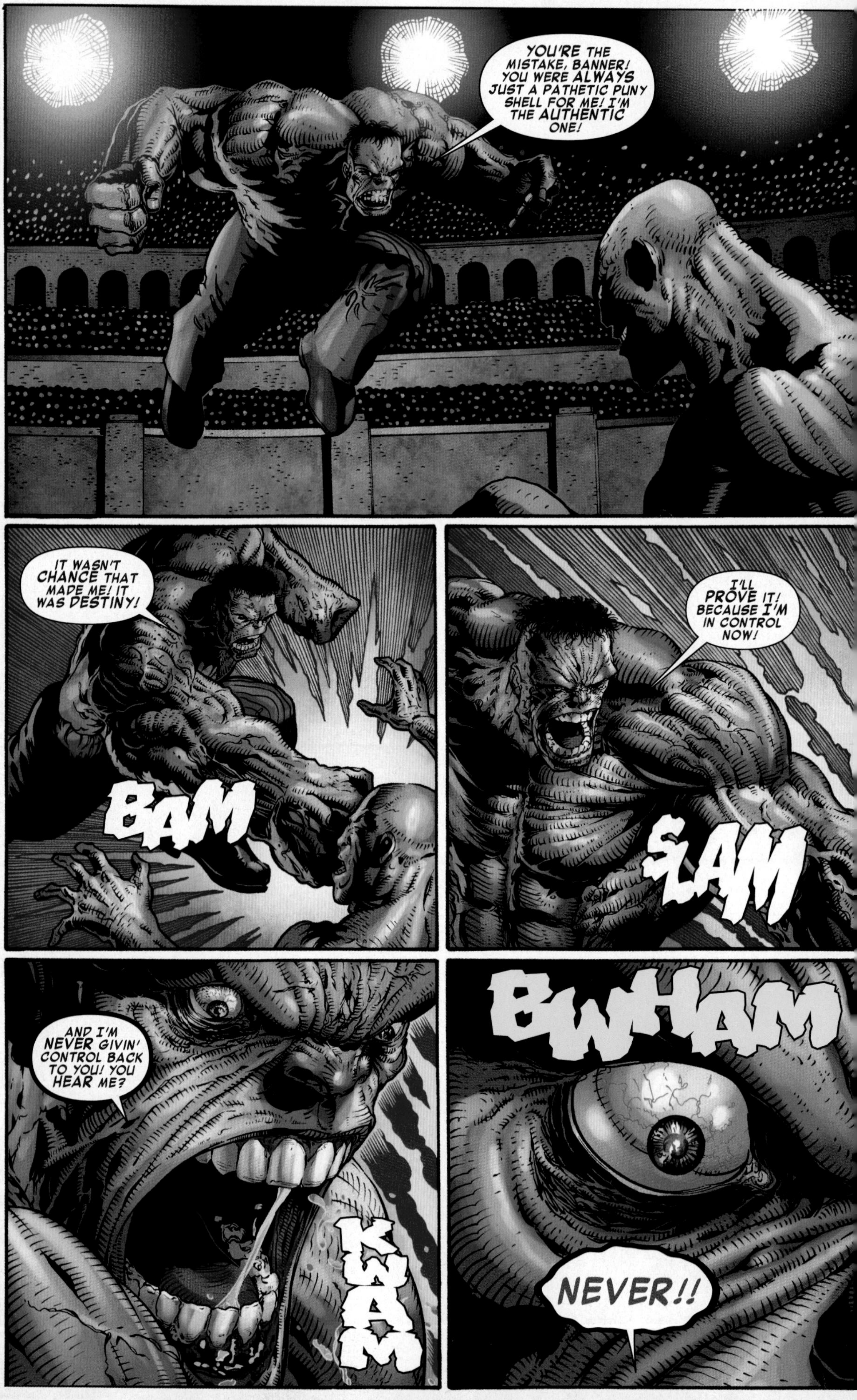
YOU'RE THE MISTAKE, BANNER! YOU WERE ALWAYS JUST A PATHETIC PUNY SHELL FOR ME! I'M THE AUTHENTIC ONE!
IT WASN'T CHANCE THAT MADE ME! IT WAS DESTINY!
BAM
I'LL PROVE IT! BECAUSE I'M IN CONTROL NOW!
SLAM
AND I'M NEVER GIVIN' CONTROL BACK TO YOU! YOU HEAR ME?
KWAM
BWHAM
NEVER!!

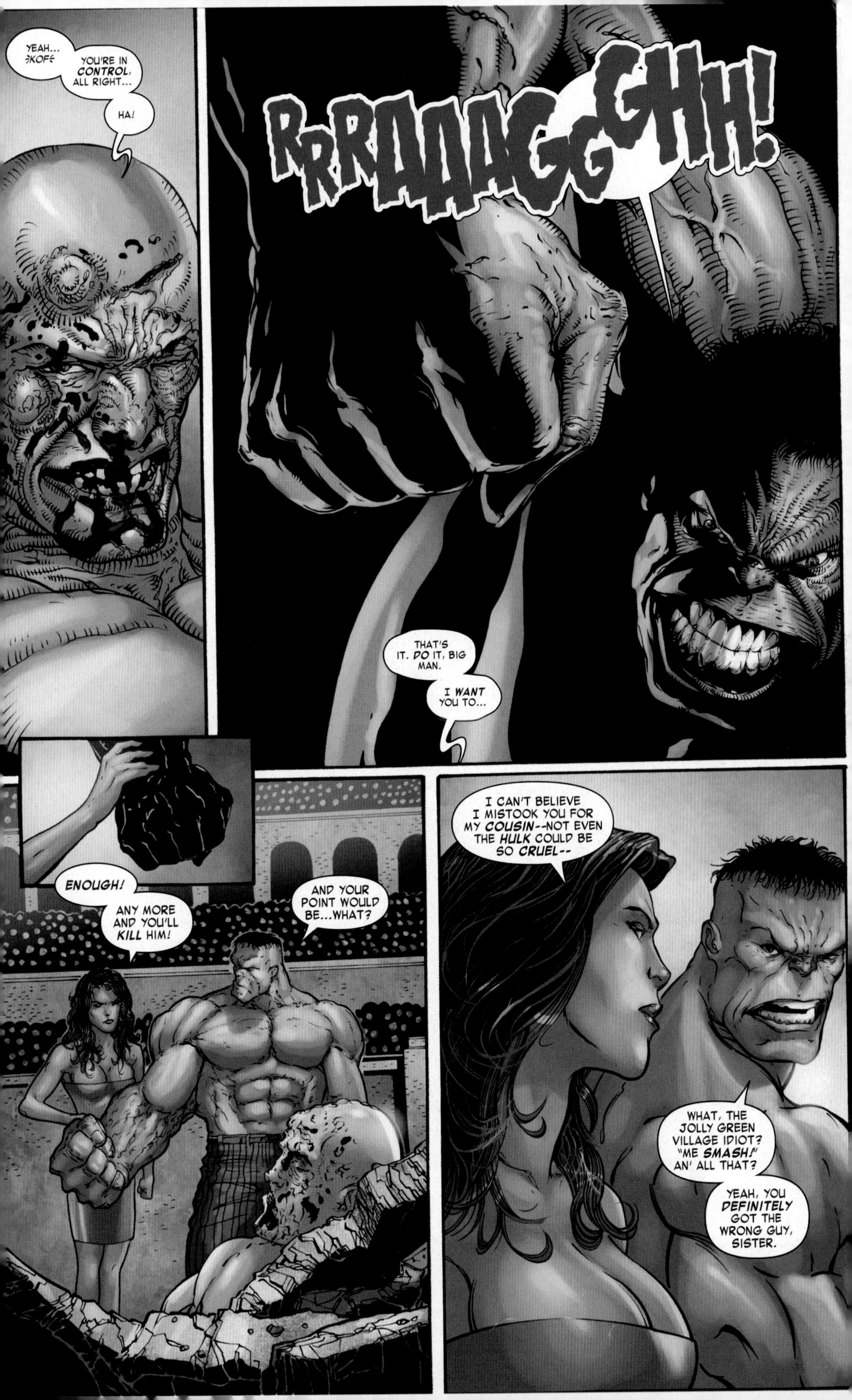
YEAH... ⋟KOF⋞
YOU'RE IN CONTROL, ALL RIGHT...
HA!
RRRAAAGGGHH!
THAT'S IT. DO IT, BIG MAN.
I WANT YOU TO...
ENOUGH!
ANY MORE AND YOU'LL KILL HIM!
AND YOUR POINT WOULD BE...WHAT?
I CAN'T BELIEVE I MISTOOK YOU FOR MY COUSIN--NOT EVEN THE HULK COULD BE SO CRUEL--
WHAT, THE JOLLY GREEN VILLAGE IDIOT? "ME SMASH!" AN' ALL THAT?
YEAH, YOU DEFINITELY GOT THE WRONG GUY, SISTER.

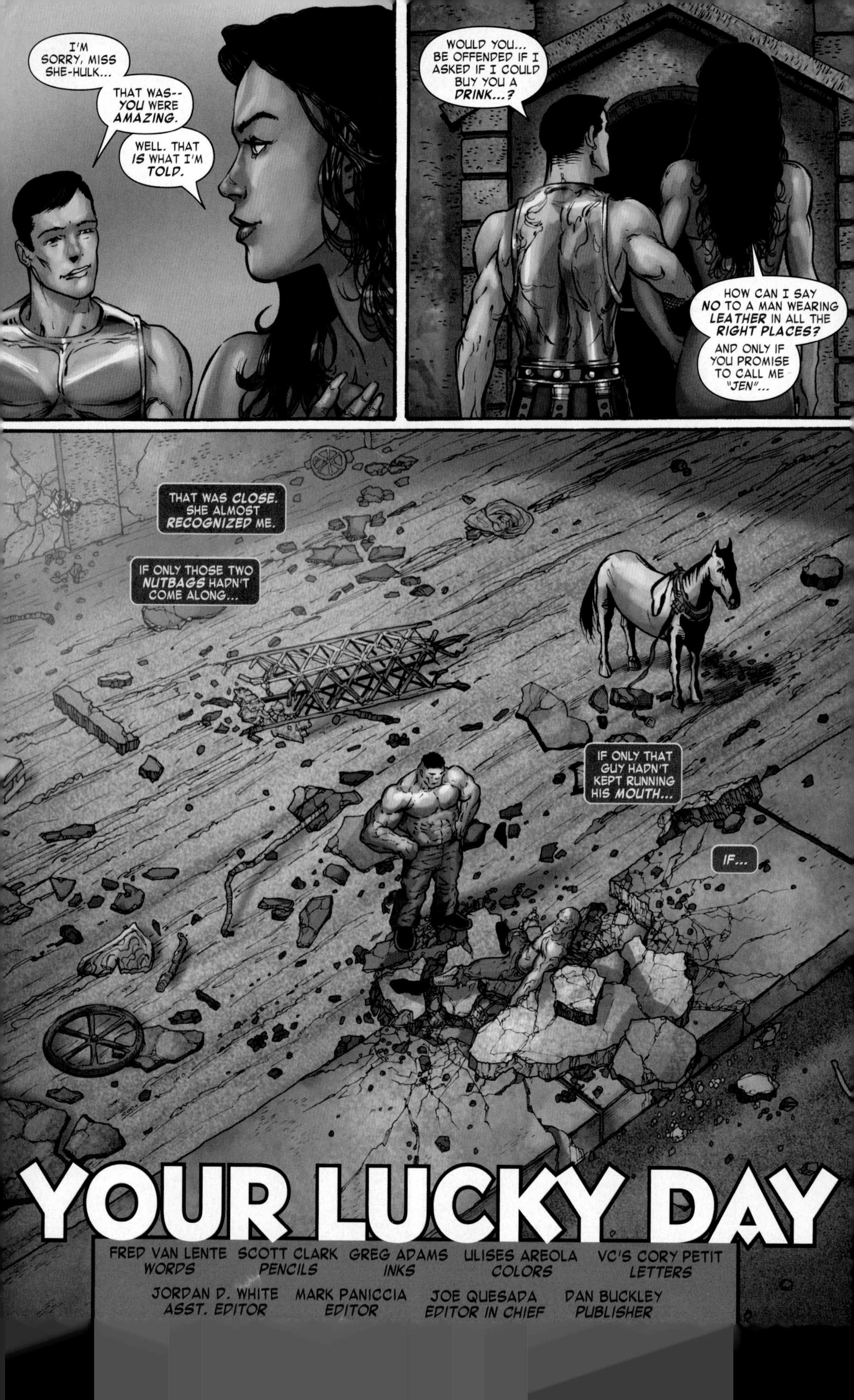

I'M SORRY, MISS SHE-HULK...
THAT WAS-- YOU WERE AMAZING.
WELL. THAT IS WHAT I'M TOLD.
WOULD YOU... BE OFFENDED IF I ASKED IF I COULD BUY YOU A DRINK...?
HOW CAN I SAY NO TO A MAN WEARING LEATHER IN ALL THE RIGHT PLACES?
AND ONLY IF YOU PROMISE TO CALL ME "JEN"...
THAT WAS CLOSE. SHE ALMOST RECOGNIZED ME.
IF ONLY THOSE TWO NUTBAGS HADN'T COME ALONG...
IF ONLY THAT GUY HADN'T KEPT RUNNING HIS MOUTH...
IF...
YOUR LUCKY DAY
FRED VAN LENTE WORDS
SCOTT CLARK PENCILS
GREG ADAMS INKS
ULISES AREOLA COLORS
VC'S CORY PETIT LETTERS
JORDAN D. WHITE ASST. EDITOR
MARK PANICCIA EDITOR
JOE QUESADA EDITOR IN CHIEF
DAN BUCKLEY PUBLISHER

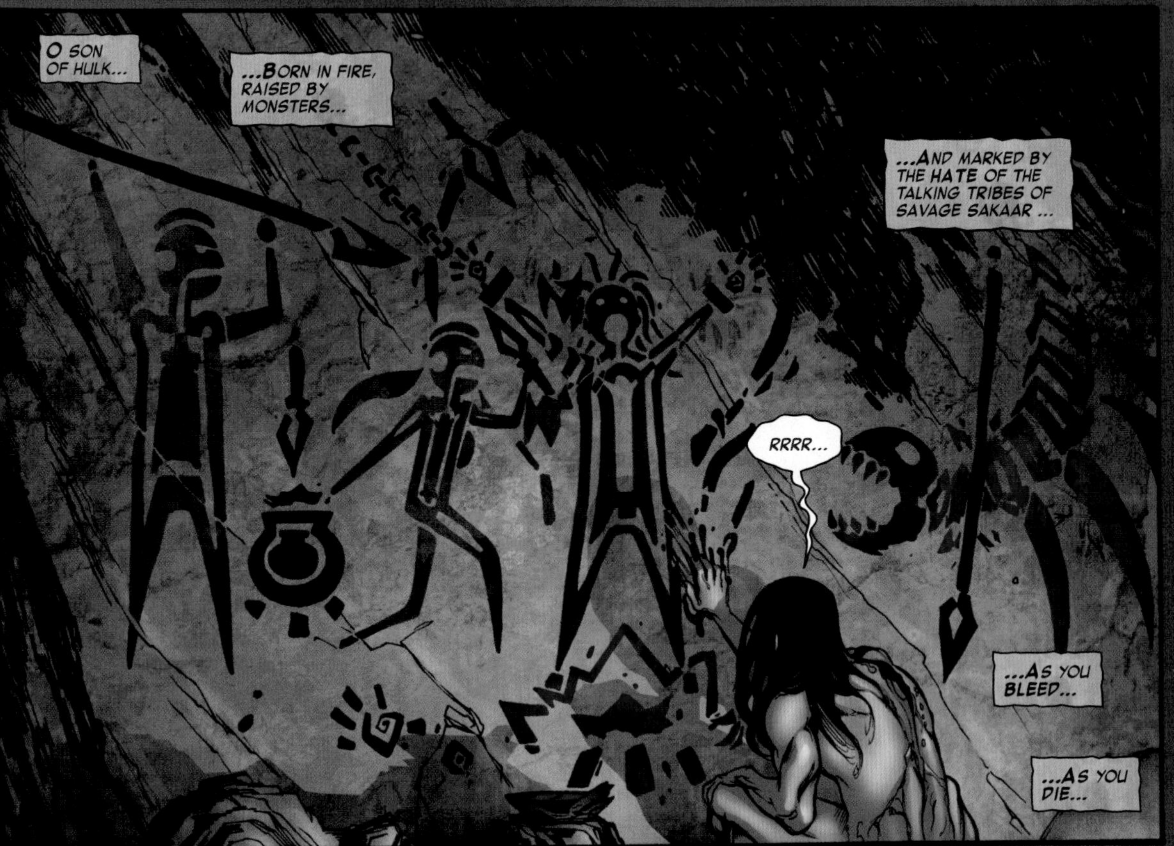
O SON OF HULK...
...BORN IN FIRE, RAISED BY MONSTERS...
...AND MARKED BY THE HATE OF THE TALKING TRIBES OF SAVAGE SAKAAR ...
RRRR...
...AS YOU BLEED...
...AS YOU DIE...

SKAAR: SON OF HULK

SCHOOL FOR SAVAGES

GREG PAK *WORDS* JHEREMY RAAPACK *PENCILS* GREG ADAMS *INKS* CHRIS SOTOMAYOR *COLORS* VC'S JOE CARAMAGNA WITH CORY PETIT *LETTERS*

JORDAN D. WHITE *ASST EDITOR* MARK PANICCIA *EDITOR* JOE QUESADA *EDITOR IN CHIEF* DAN BUCKLEY *PUBLISHER*

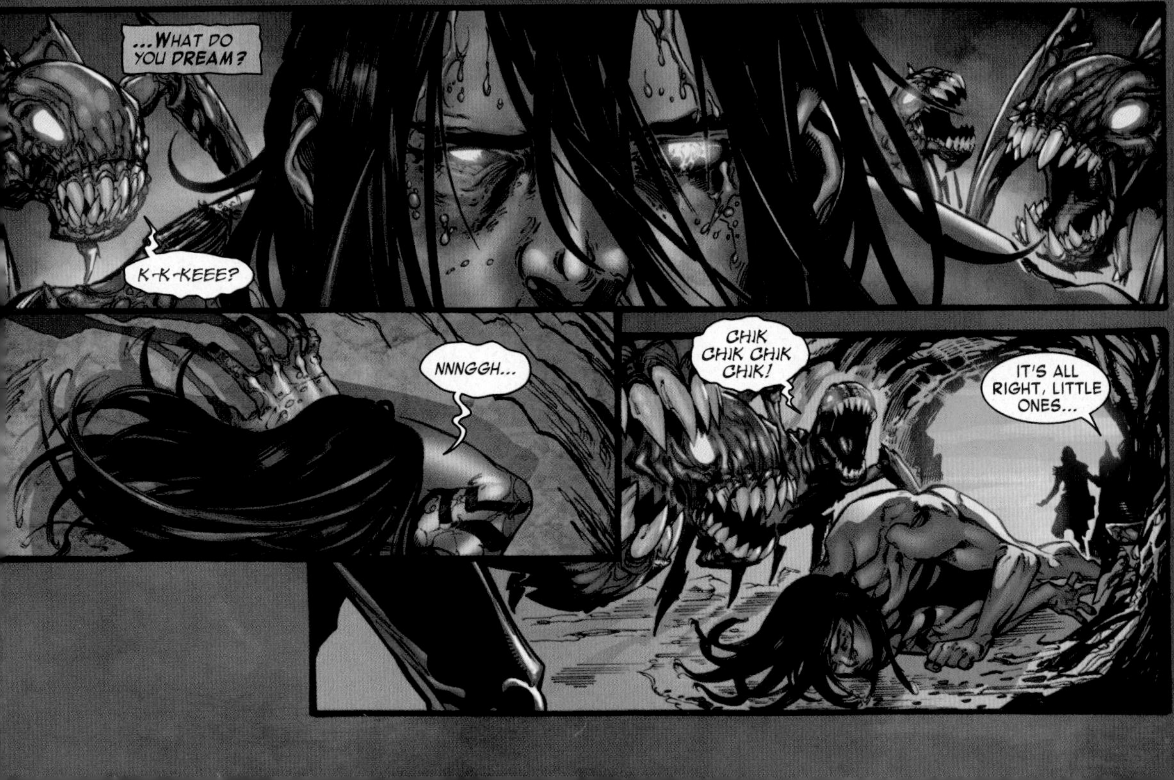
...WHAT DO YOU DREAM?
K-K-KEEE?
NNNGGH...
CHIK CHIK CHIK CHIK!
IT'S ALL RIGHT, LITTLE ONES...

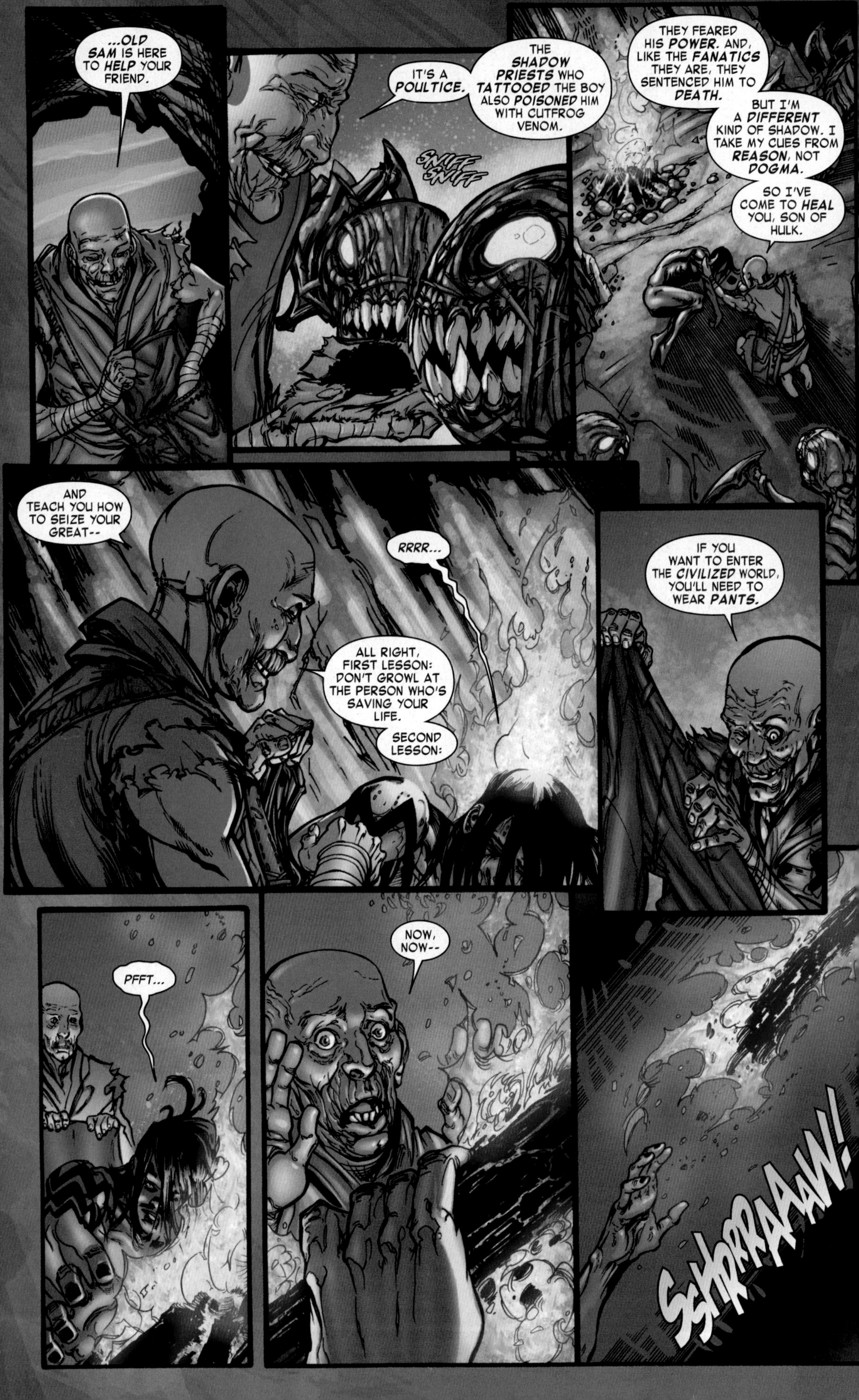

...OLD SAM IS HERE TO HELP YOUR FRIEND.
IT'S A POULTICE.
THE SHADOW PRIESTS WHO TATTOOED THE BOY ALSO POISONED HIM WITH CUTFROG VENOM.
SNIFF SNIFF
THEY FEARED HIS POWER. AND, LIKE THE FANATICS THEY ARE, THEY SENTENCED HIM TO DEATH.
BUT I'M A DIFFERENT KIND OF SHADOW. I TAKE MY CUES FROM REASON, NOT DOGMA.
SO I'VE COME TO HEAL YOU, SON OF HULK.
AND TEACH YOU HOW TO SEIZE YOUR GREAT--
RRRR...
ALL RIGHT, FIRST LESSON: DON'T GROWL AT THE PERSON WHO'S SAVING YOUR LIFE.
SECOND LESSON:
IF YOU WANT TO ENTER THE CIVILIZED WORLD, YOU'LL NEED TO WEAR PANTS.
PFFT...
NOW, NOW--
SSHRRRAAAW!

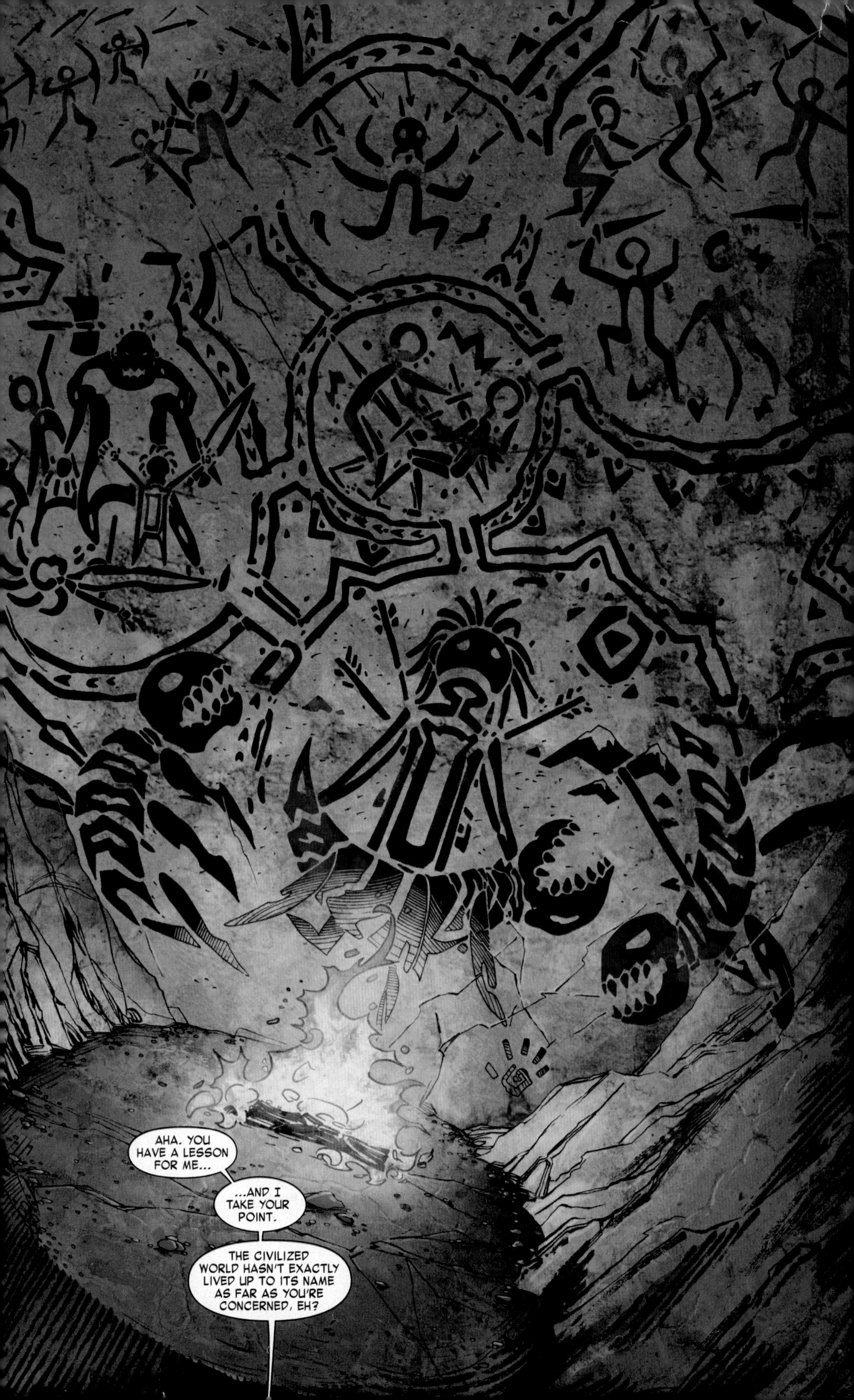
AHA. YOU HAVE A LESSON FOR ME...
...AND I TAKE YOUR POINT.
THE CIVILIZED WORLD HASN'T EXACTLY LIVED UP TO ITS NAME AS FAR AS YOU'RE CONCERNED, EH?

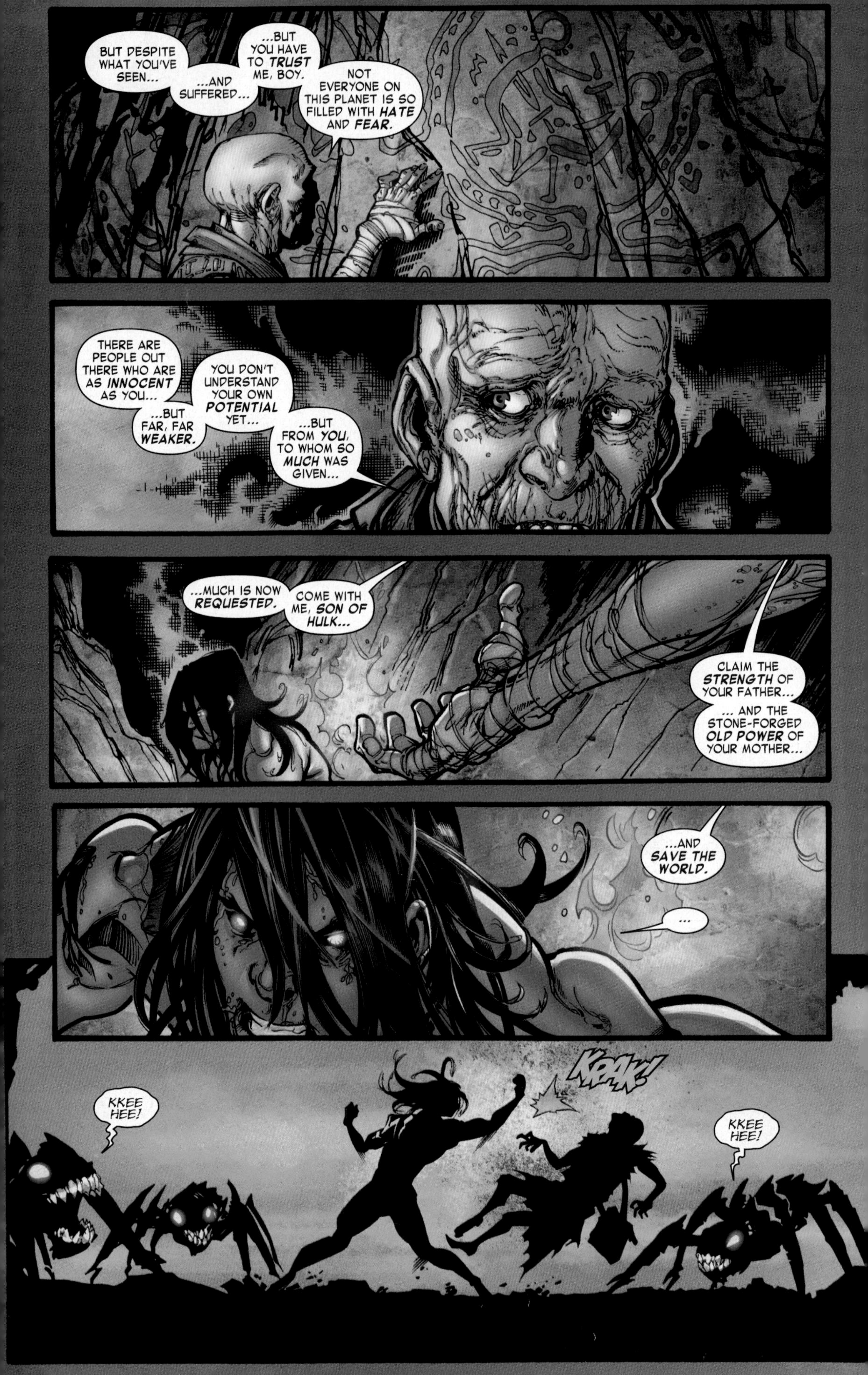
BUT DESPITE WHAT YOU'VE SEEN...
...AND SUFFERED...
...BUT YOU HAVE TO TRUST ME, BOY.
NOT EVERYONE ON THIS PLANET IS SO FILLED WITH HATE AND FEAR.
THERE ARE PEOPLE OUT THERE WHO ARE AS INNOCENT AS YOU...
...BUT FAR, FAR WEAKER.
YOU DON'T UNDERSTAND YOUR OWN POTENTIAL YET...
...BUT FROM YOU, TO WHOM SO MUCH WAS GIVEN...
...MUCH IS NOW REQUESTED.
COME WITH ME, SON OF HULK...
CLAIM THE STRENGTH OF YOUR FATHER...
... AND THE STONE-FORGED OLD POWER OF YOUR MOTHER...
...AND SAVE THE WORLD.
...
KKEE HEE!
KRAK!
KKEE HEE!

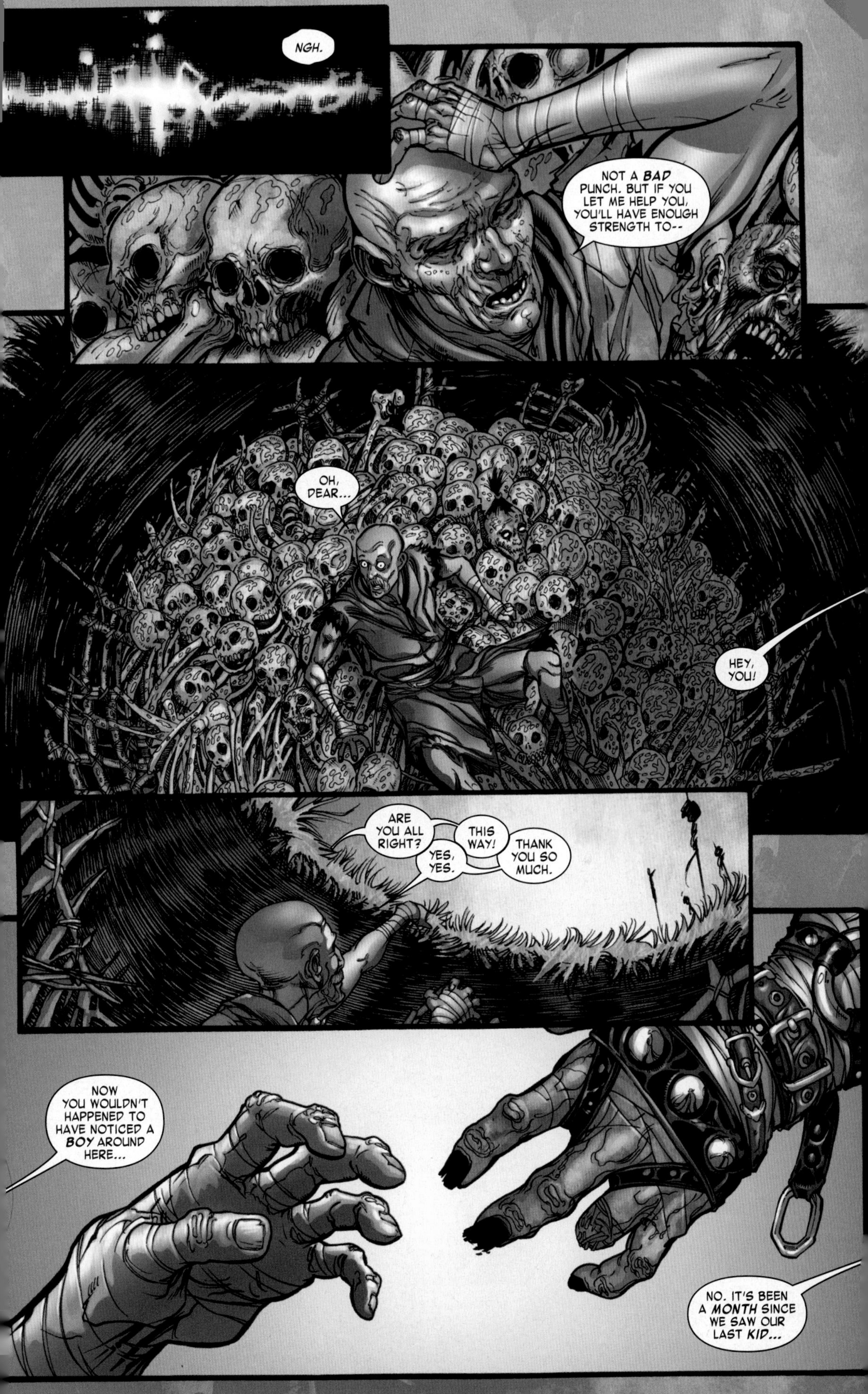
NGH.
NOT A BAD PUNCH. BUT IF YOU LET ME HELP YOU, YOU'LL HAVE ENOUGH STRENGTH TO--
OH, DEAR...
HEY, YOU!
ARE YOU ALL RIGHT?
YES, YES.
THIS WAY!
THANK YOU SO MUCH.
NOW YOU WOULDN'T HAPPENED TO HAVE NOTICED A BOY AROUND HERE...
NO. IT'S BEEN A MONTH SINCE WE SAW OUR LAST KID...

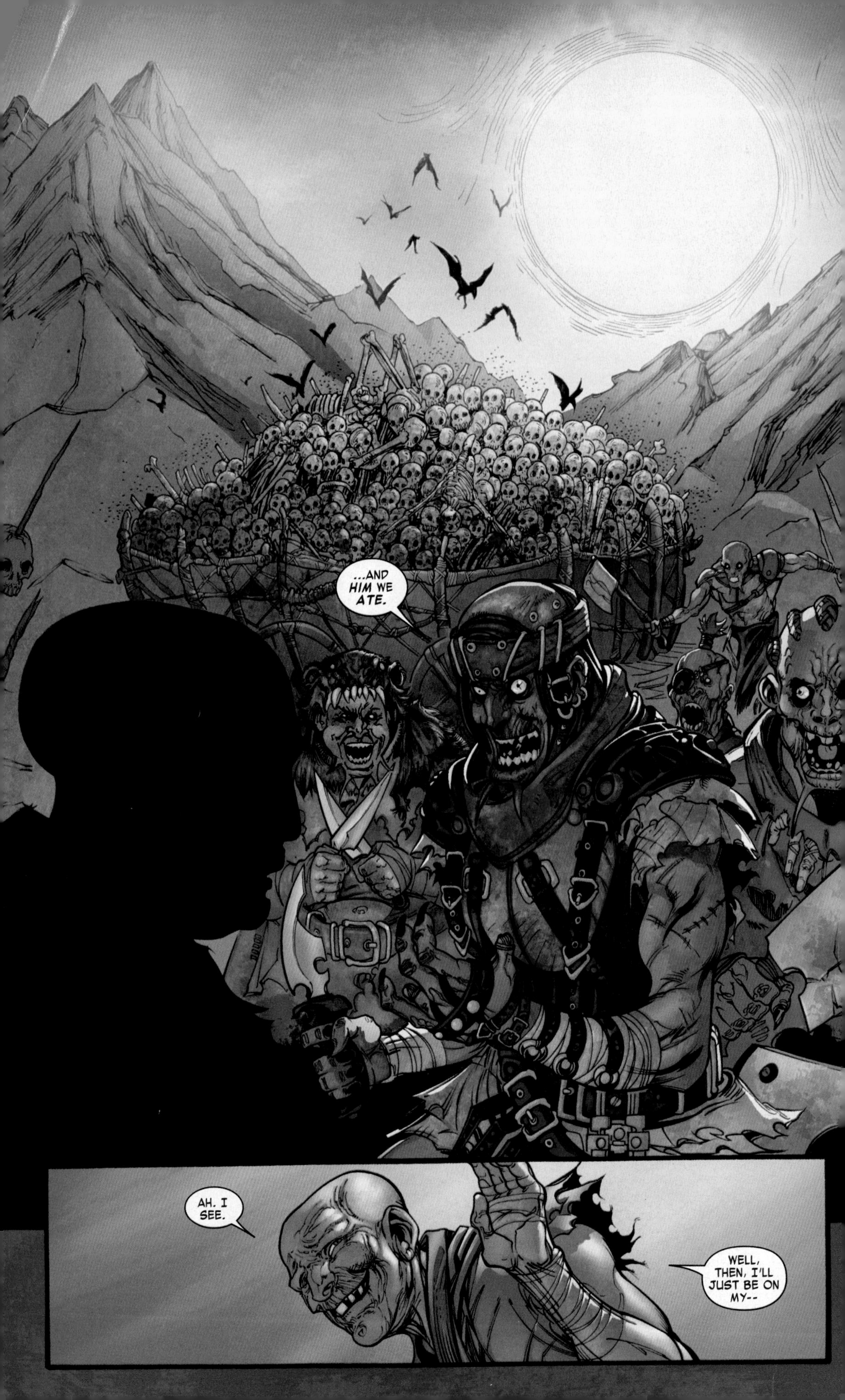
...AND HIM WE ATE.
AH. I SEE.
WELL, THEN, I'LL JUST BE ON MY--

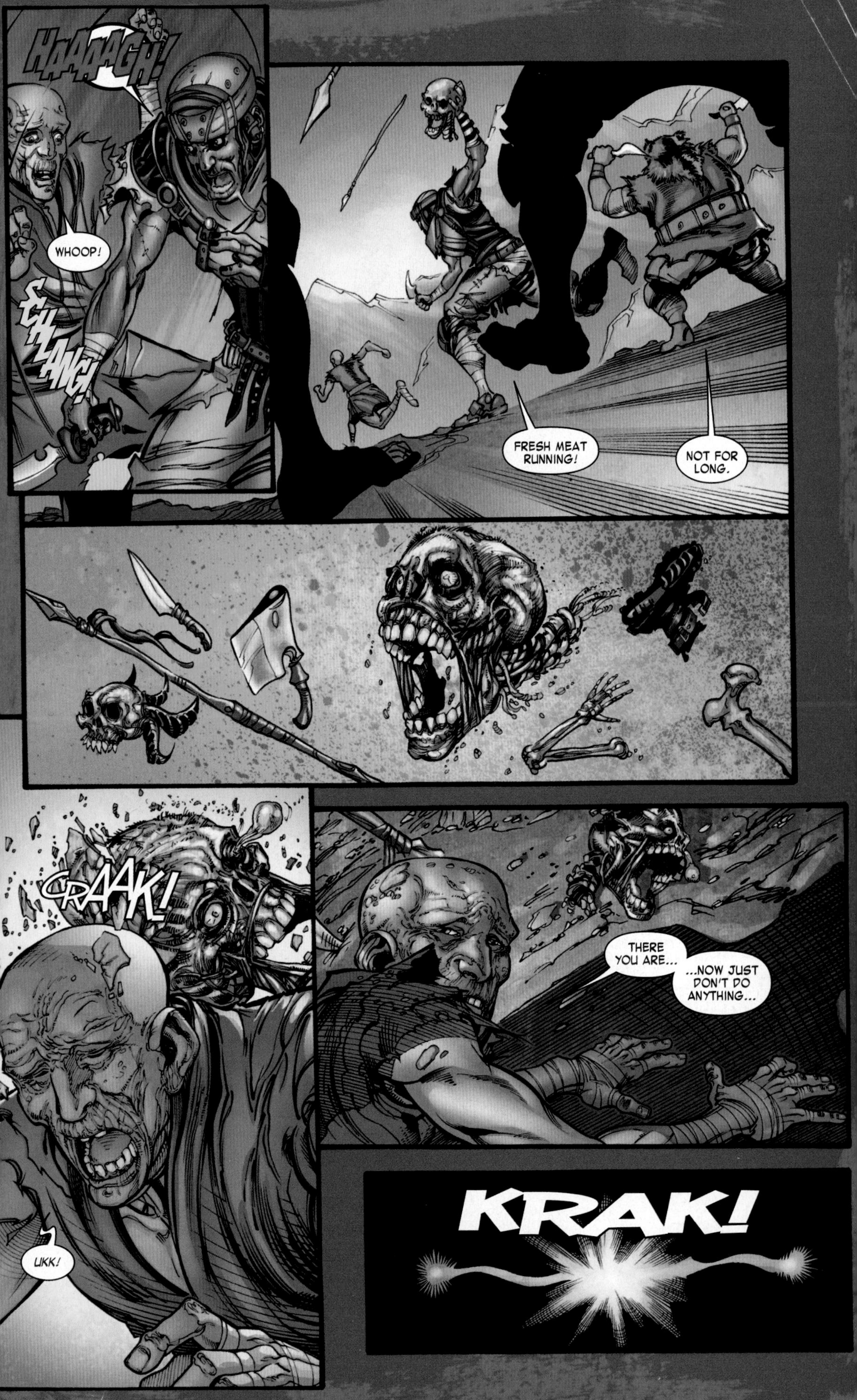
HAAAAGH!
WHOOP!
SCHLANG!
FRESH MEAT RUNNING!
NOT FOR LONG.
CRAAK!
UKK!
THERE YOU ARE...
...NOW JUST DON'T DO ANYTHING...
KRAK!

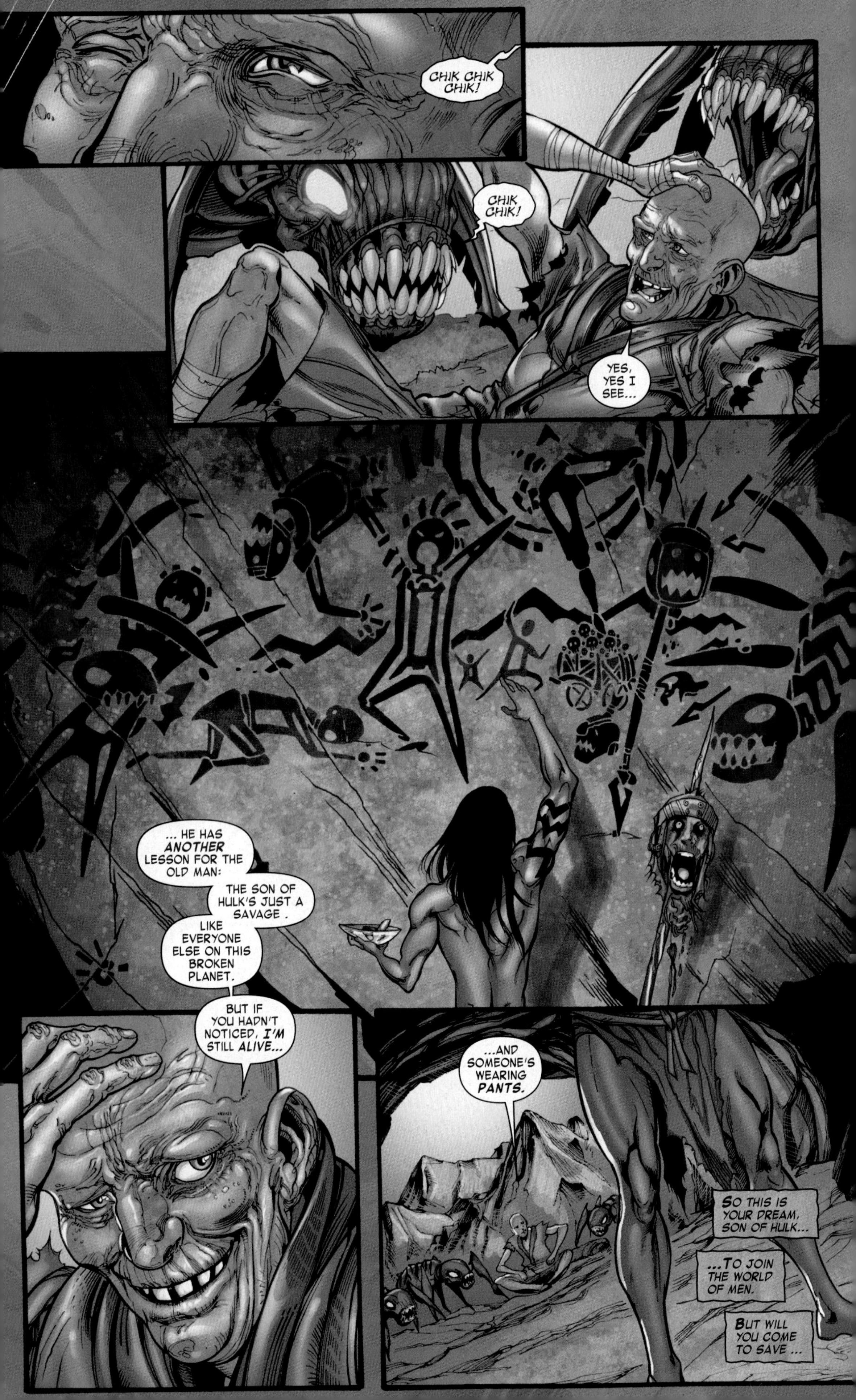
CHIK CHIK CHIK!
CHIK CHIK!
YES, YES I SEE...
... HE HAS ANOTHER LESSON FOR THE OLD MAN:
THE SON OF HULK'S JUST A SAVAGE .
LIKE EVERYONE ELSE ON THIS BROKEN PLANET.
BUT IF YOU HADN'T NOTICED, I'M STILL ALIVE...
...AND SOMEONE'S WEARING PANTS.
SO THIS IS YOUR DREAM, SON OF HULK...
...TO JOIN THE WORLD OF MEN.
BUT WILL YOU COME TO SAVE ...

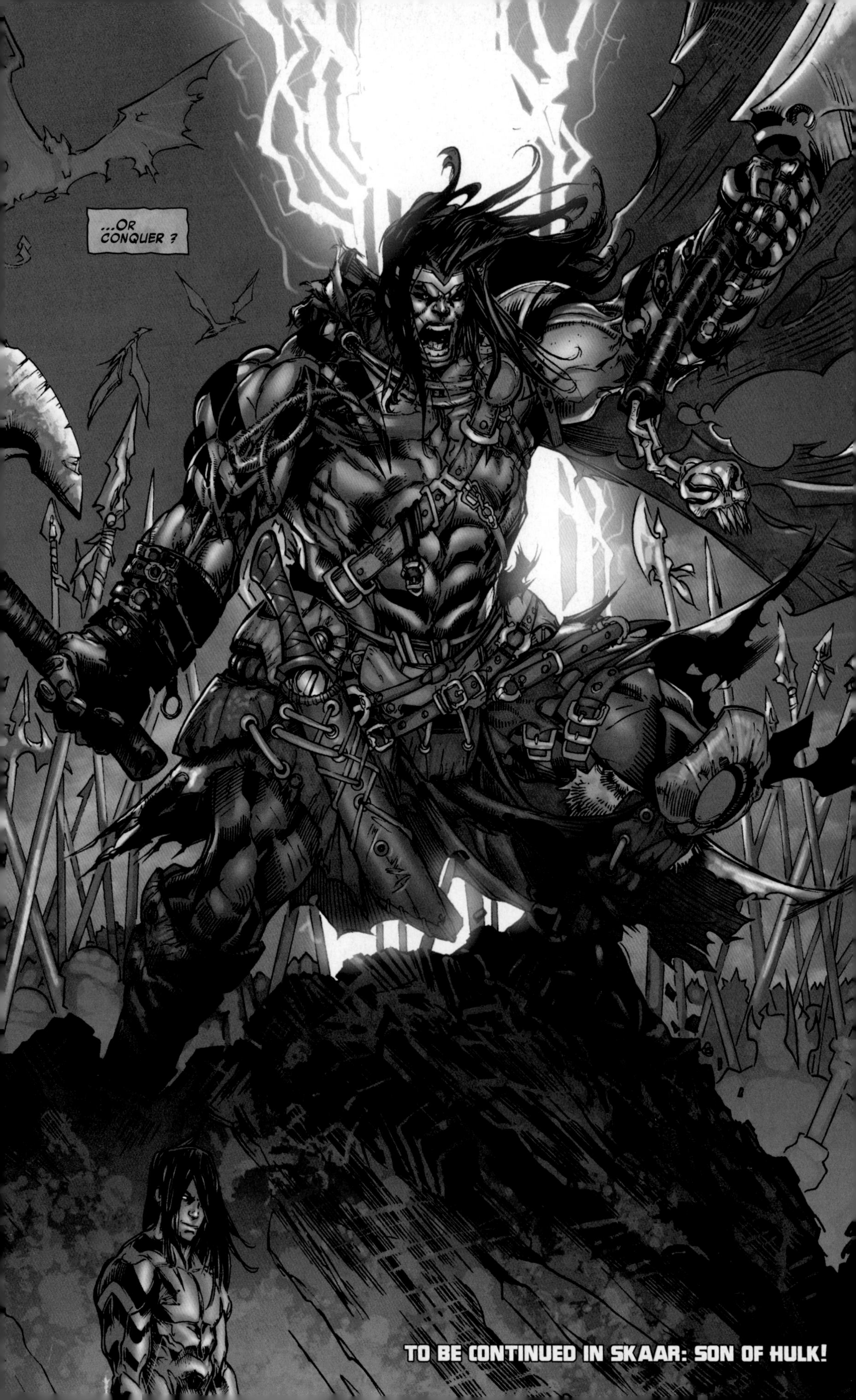
...OR CONQUER ?
TO BE CONTINUED IN SKAAR: SON OF HULK!

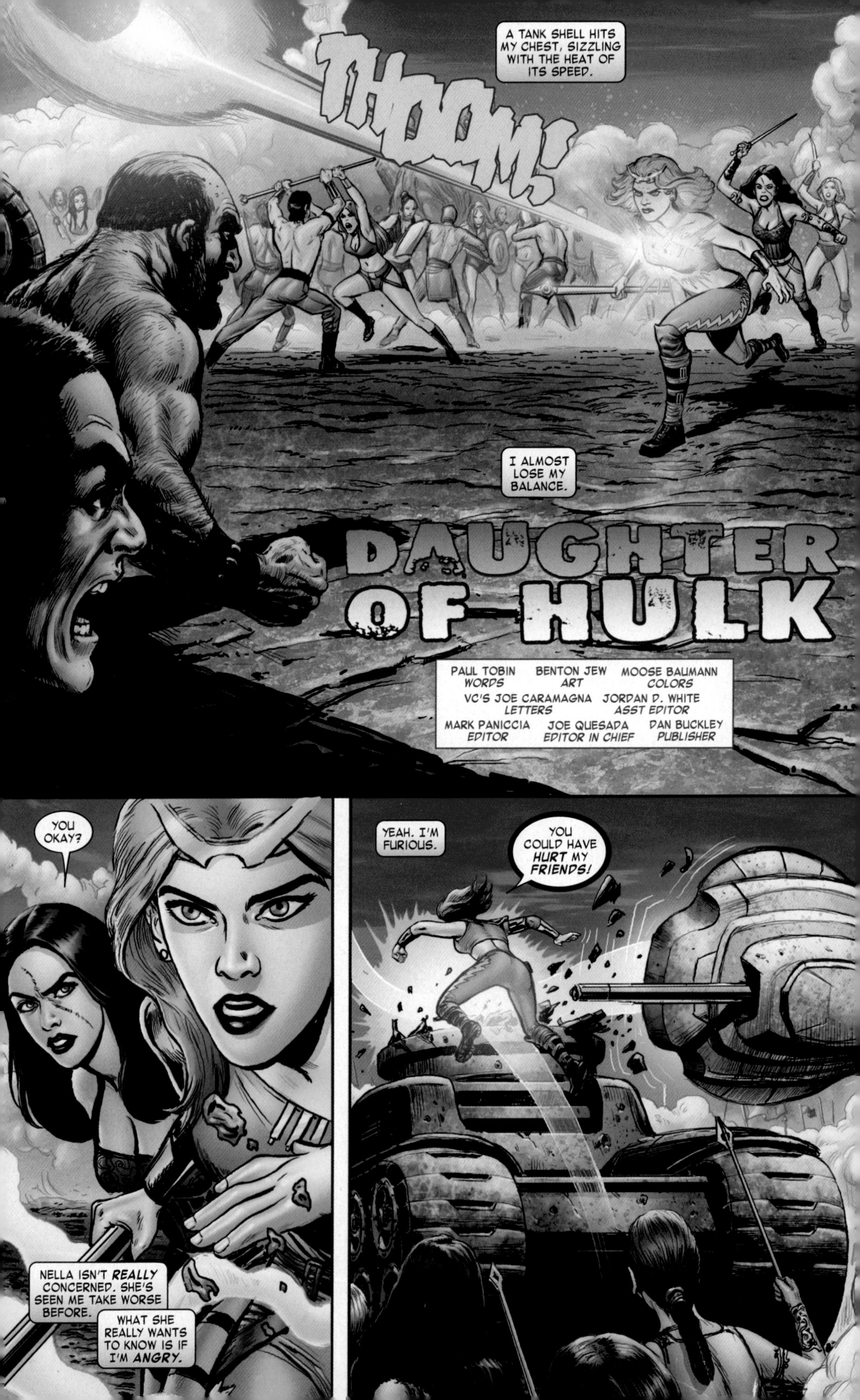
A TANK SHELL HITS MY CHEST, SIZZLING WITH THE HEAT OF ITS SPEED.
THOOM!
I ALMOST LOSE MY BALANCE.
DAUGHTER OF HULK
PAUL TOBIN WORDS
BENTON JEW ART
MOOSE BAUMANN COLORS
VC'S JOE CARAMAGNA LETTERS
JORDAN D. WHITE ASST EDITOR
MARK PANICCIA EDITOR
JOE QUESADA EDITOR IN CHIEF
DAN BUCKLEY PUBLISHER
YOU OKAY?
NELLA ISN'T REALLY CONCERNED. SHE'S SEEN ME TAKE WORSE BEFORE.
WHAT SHE REALLY WANTS TO KNOW IS IF I'M ANGRY.
YEAH. I'M FURIOUS.
YOU COULD HAVE HURT MY FRIENDS!

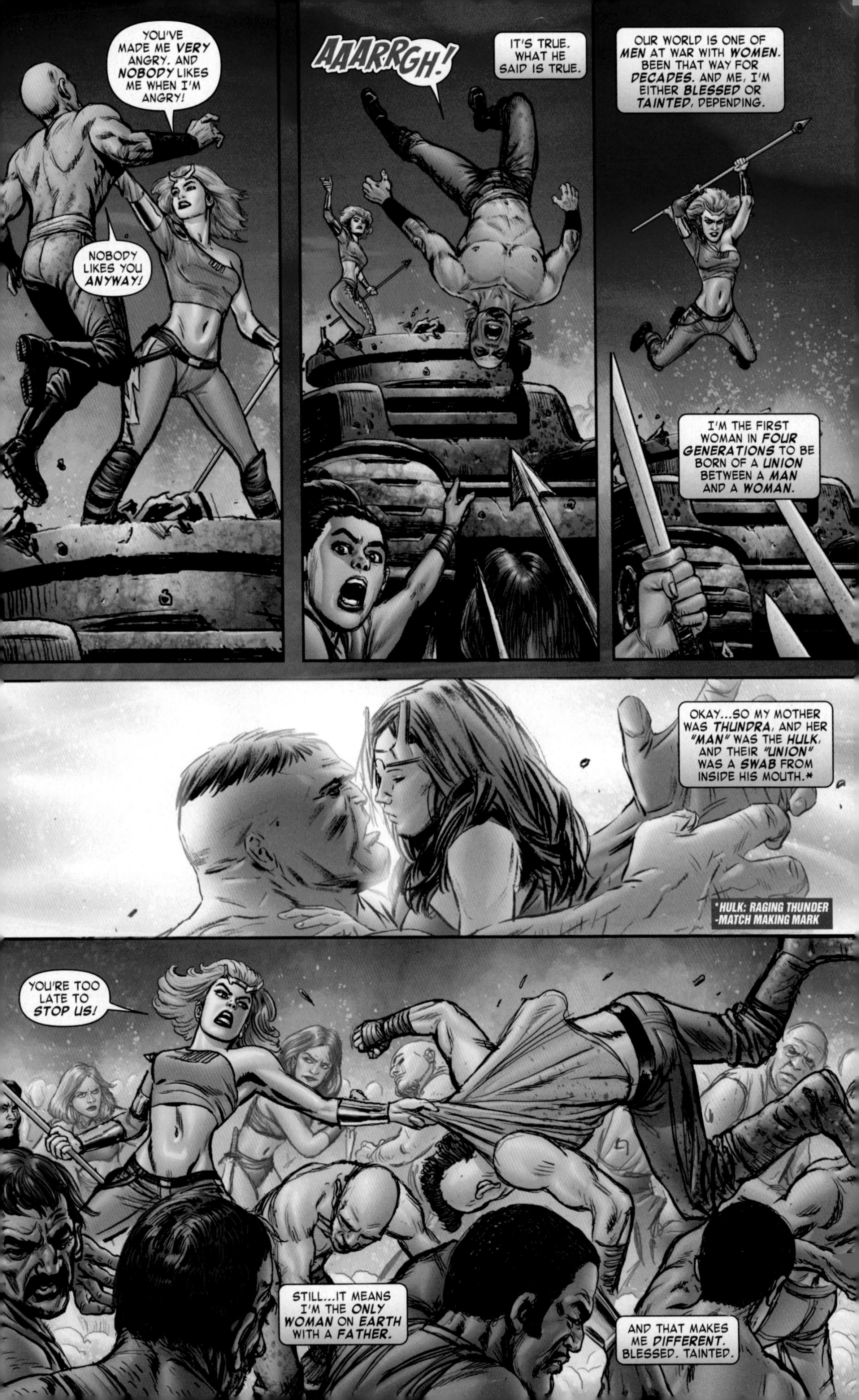
YOU'VE MADE ME VERY ANGRY. AND NOBODY LIKES ME WHEN I'M ANGRY!
NOBODY LIKES YOU ANYWAY!
AAARRGH!
IT'S TRUE. WHAT HE SAID IS TRUE.
OUR WORLD IS ONE OF MEN AT WAR WITH WOMEN. BEEN THAT WAY FOR DECADES. AND ME, I'M EITHER BLESSED OR TAINTED, DEPENDING.
I'M THE FIRST WOMAN IN FOUR GENERATIONS TO BE BORN OF A UNION BETWEEN A MAN AND A WOMAN.
OKAY...SO MY MOTHER WAS THUNDRA, AND HER "MAN" WAS THE HULK, AND THEIR "UNION" WAS A SWAB FROM INSIDE HIS MOUTH.*
*HULK: RAGING THUNDER -MATCH MAKING MARK
YOU'RE TOO LATE TO STOP US!
STILL...IT MEANS I'M THE ONLY WOMAN ON EARTH WITH A FATHER.
AND THAT MAKES ME DIFFERENT. BLESSED. TAINTED.

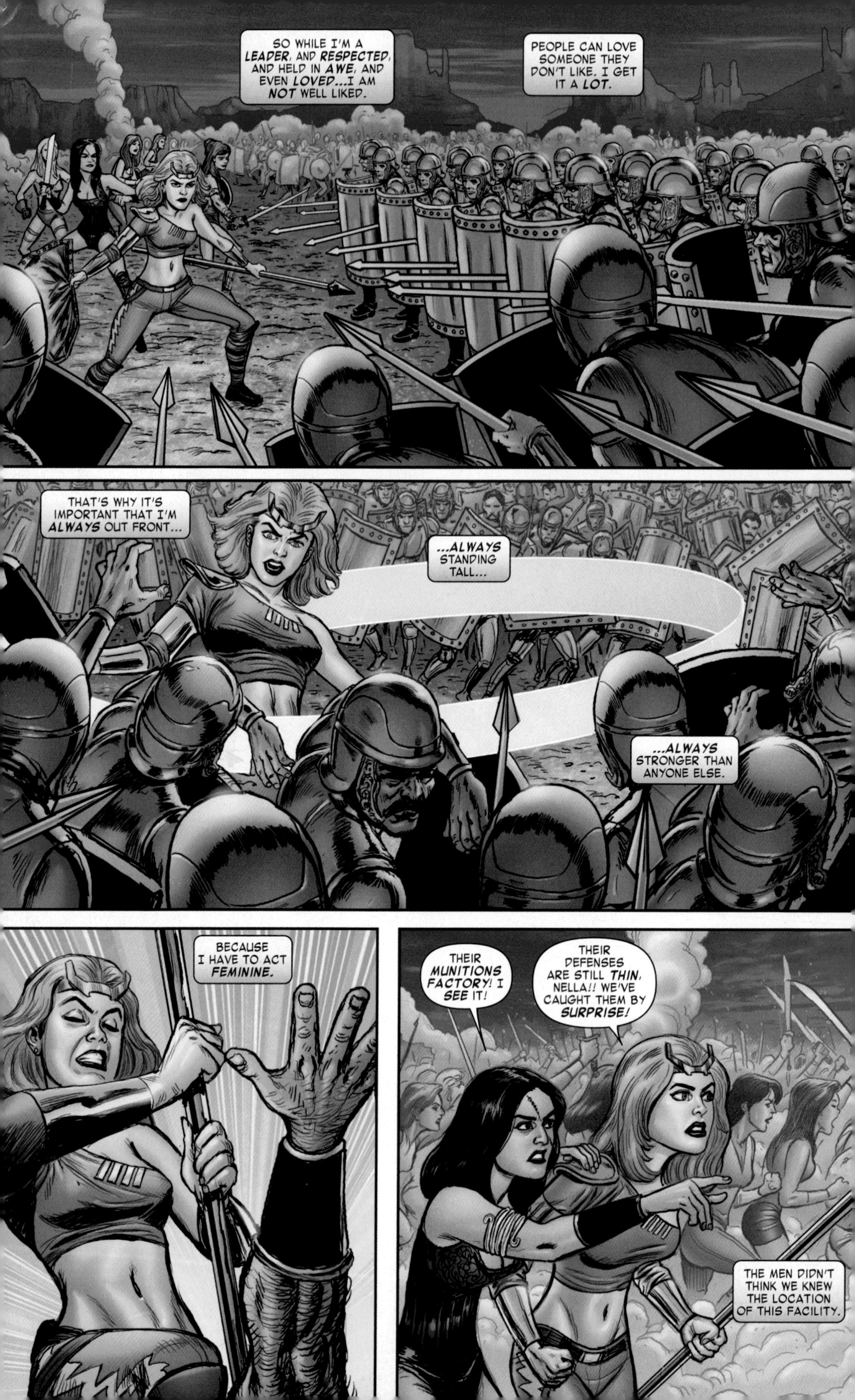

SO WHILE I'M A LEADER, AND RESPECTED, AND HELD IN AWE, AND EVEN LOVED...I AM NOT WELL LIKED.
PEOPLE CAN LOVE SOMEONE THEY DON'T LIKE. I GET IT A LOT.
THAT'S WHY IT'S IMPORTANT THAT I'M ALWAYS OUT FRONT...
...ALWAYS STANDING TALL...
...ALWAYS STRONGER THAN ANYONE ELSE.
BECAUSE I HAVE TO ACT FEMININE.
THEIR MUNITIONS FACTORY! I SEE IT!
THEIR DEFENSES ARE STILL THIN, NELLA!! WE'VE CAUGHT THEM BY SURPRISE!
THE MEN DIDN'T THINK WE KNEW THE LOCATION OF THIS FACILITY.

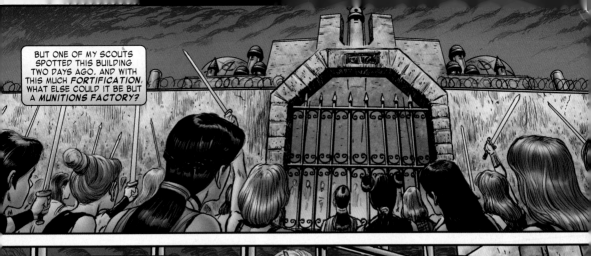

BUT ONE OF MY SCOUTS SPOTTED THIS BUILDING TWO DAYS AGO. AND WITH THIS MUCH *FORTIFICATION*, WHAT ELSE COULD IT BE BUT A *MUNITIONS FACTORY?*

WE CAN DESTROY THE VERY *SOURCE* OF THEIR WEAPONS.

STAY *BACK* UNTIL I *BREACH* THE *WALLS!*

THE FIGHT INSIDE THE WALLS IS *INTENSE,* BUT *SWIFT.* THEY WEREN'T *READY* FOR US. FOR *ME.*

DECADES OF WAR, AND THE MEN *STILL* DON'T THINK WE'LL TAKE THE *OFFENSIVE.*

WELL, THAT'S WHY MEN ARE *FOOLS.*

WE CAN *HOLD* THEM HERE! GO IN AND *DESTROY* THE *FACTORY!*

THERE'S AN *OPEN* DOOR ONLY *TEN FEET AWAY...*

BUT I'M IN THE MOOD FOR A *DISPLAY.*

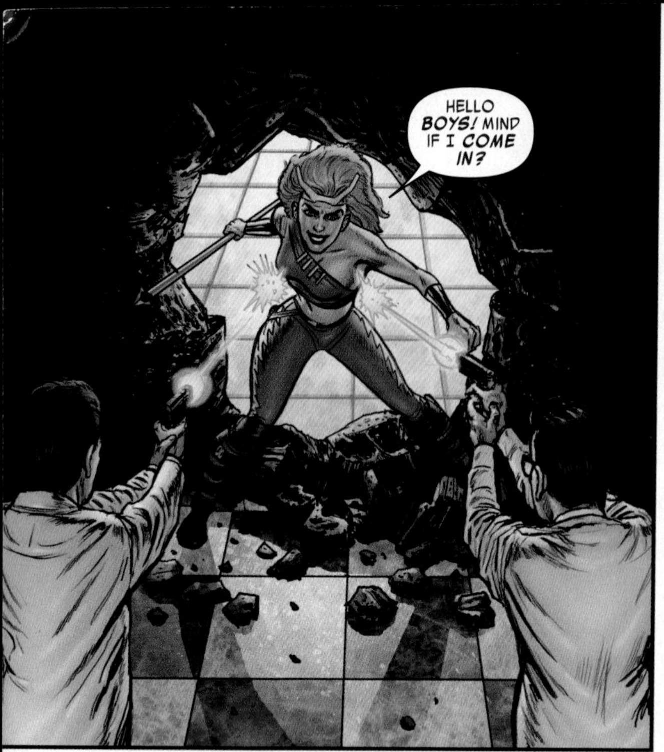
HELLO BOYS! MIND IF I COME IN?

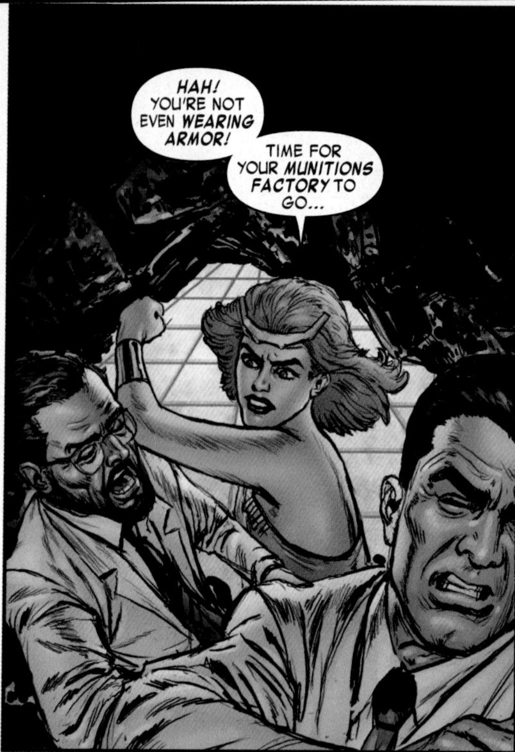
HAH! YOU'RE NOT EVEN WEARING ARMOR!
TIME FOR YOUR MUNITIONS FACTORY TO GO...

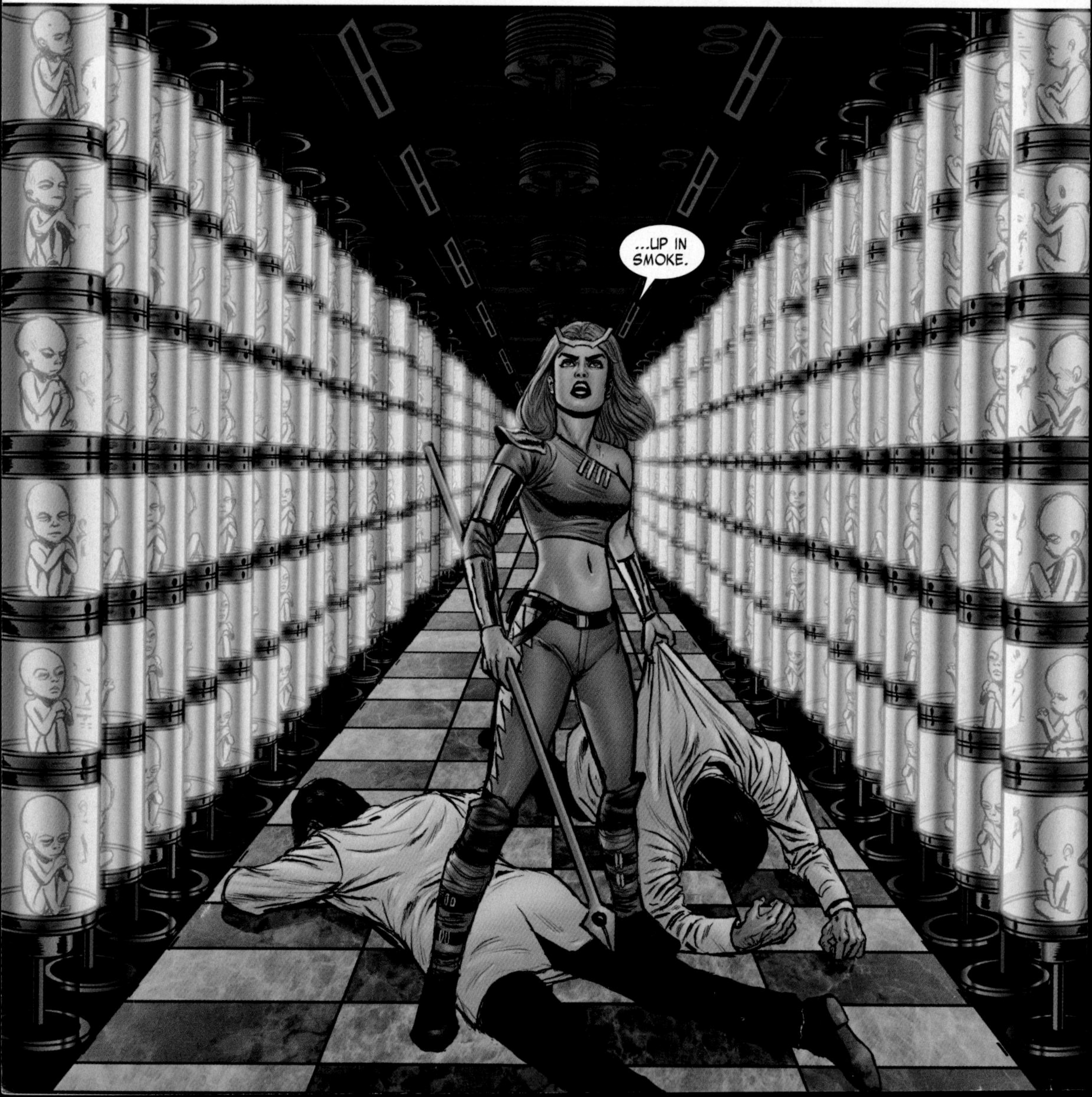
...UP IN SMOKE.

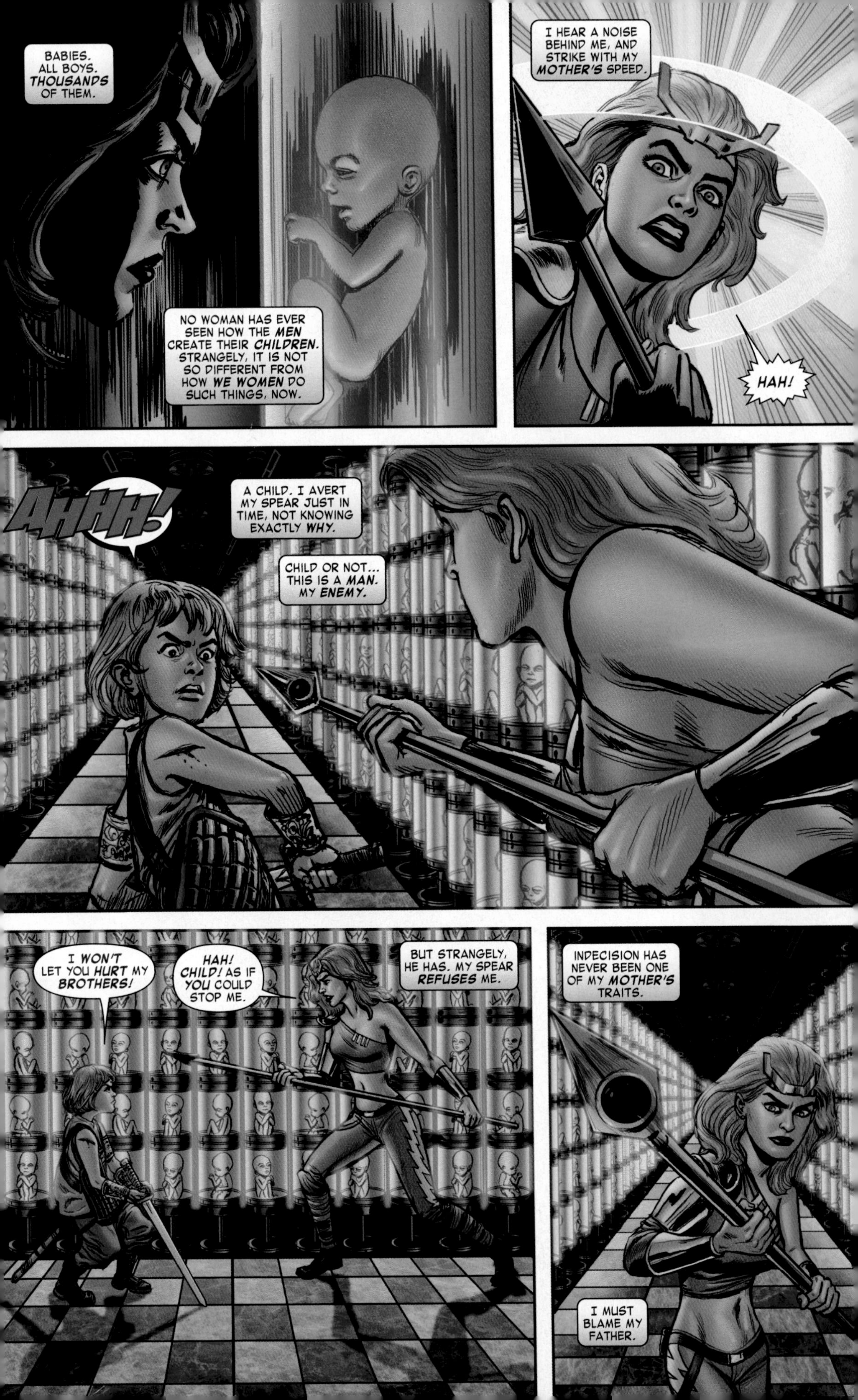
BABIES. ALL BOYS. THOUSANDS OF THEM.
NO WOMAN HAS EVER SEEN HOW THE MEN CREATE THEIR CHILDREN. STRANGELY, IT IS NOT SO DIFFERENT FROM HOW WE WOMEN DO SUCH THINGS, NOW.
I HEAR A NOISE BEHIND ME, AND STRIKE WITH MY MOTHER'S SPEED.
HAH!
AHHH!
A CHILD. I AVERT MY SPEAR JUST IN TIME, NOT KNOWING EXACTLY WHY.
CHILD OR NOT... THIS IS A MAN. MY ENEMY.
I WON'T LET YOU HURT MY BROTHERS!
HAH! CHILD! AS IF YOU COULD STOP ME.
BUT STRANGELY, HE HAS. MY SPEAR REFUSES ME.
INDECISION HAS NEVER BEEN ONE OF MY MOTHER'S TRAITS.
I MUST BLAME MY FATHER.

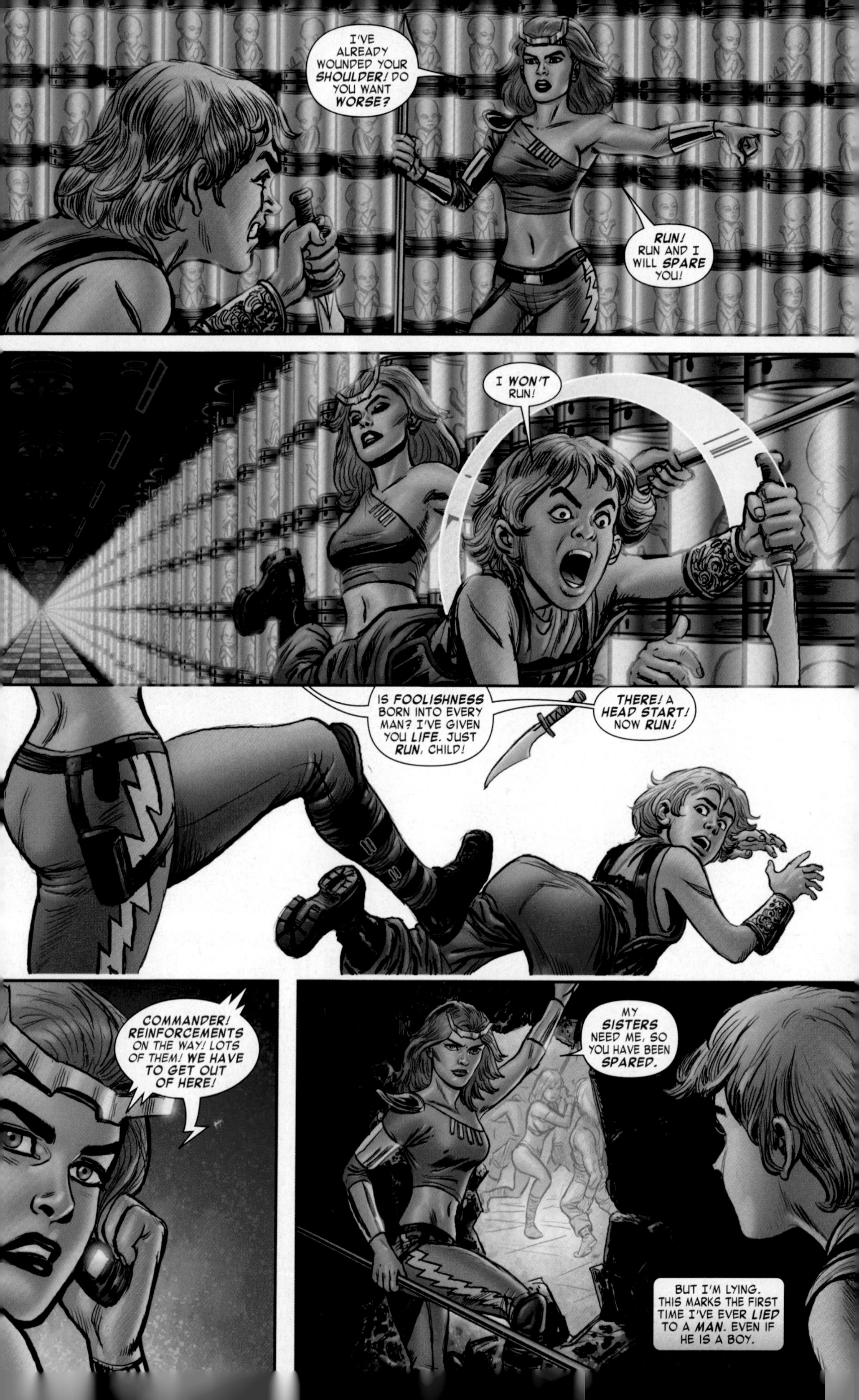
I'VE ALREADY WOUNDED YOUR SHOULDER! DO YOU WANT WORSE?
RUN! RUN AND I WILL SPARE YOU!
I WON'T RUN!
IS FOOLISHNESS BORN INTO EVERY MAN? I'VE GIVEN YOU LIFE. JUST RUN, CHILD!
THERE! A HEAD START! NOW RUN!
COMMANDER! REINFORCEMENTS ON THE WAY! LOTS OF THEM! WE HAVE TO GET OUT OF HERE!
MY SISTERS NEED ME, SO YOU HAVE BEEN SPARED.
BUT I'M LYING. THIS MARKS THE FIRST TIME I'VE EVER LIED TO A MAN. EVEN IF HE IS A BOY.

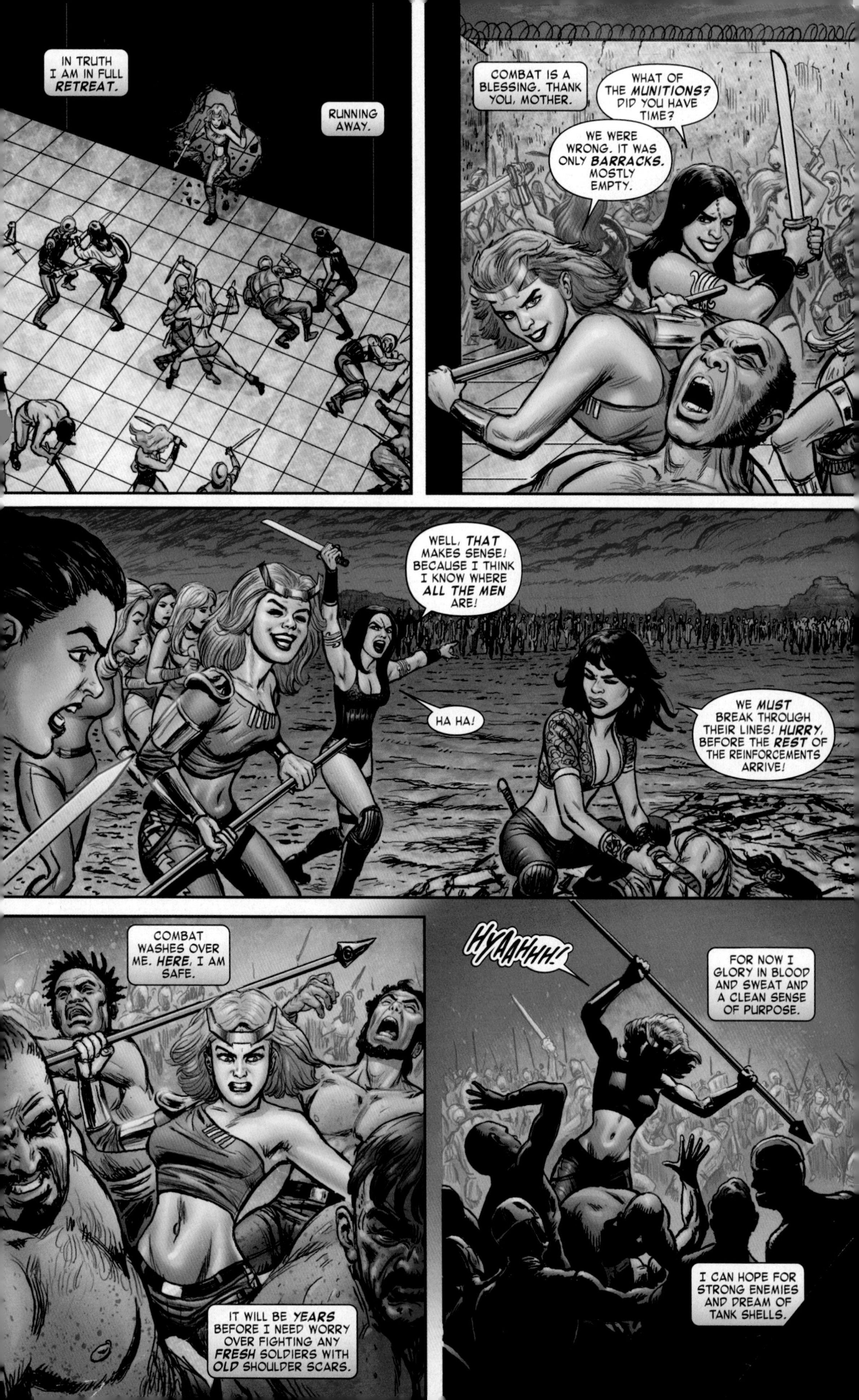
IN TRUTH I AM IN FULL RETREAT.
RUNNING AWAY.
COMBAT IS A BLESSING. THANK YOU, MOTHER.
WHAT OF THE MUNITIONS? DID YOU HAVE TIME?
WE WERE WRONG. IT WAS ONLY BARRACKS. MOSTLY EMPTY.
WELL, THAT MAKES SENSE! BECAUSE I THINK I KNOW WHERE ALL THE MEN ARE!
HA HA!
WE MUST BREAK THROUGH THEIR LINES! HURRY, BEFORE THE REST OF THE REINFORCEMENTS ARRIVE!
COMBAT WASHES OVER ME. HERE, I AM SAFE.
IT WILL BE YEARS BEFORE I NEED WORRY OVER FIGHTING ANY FRESH SOLDIERS WITH OLD SHOULDER SCARS.
HYAAHHH!
FOR NOW I GLORY IN BLOOD AND SWEAT AND A CLEAN SENSE OF PURPOSE.
I CAN HOPE FOR STRONG ENEMIES AND DREAM OF TANK SHELLS.

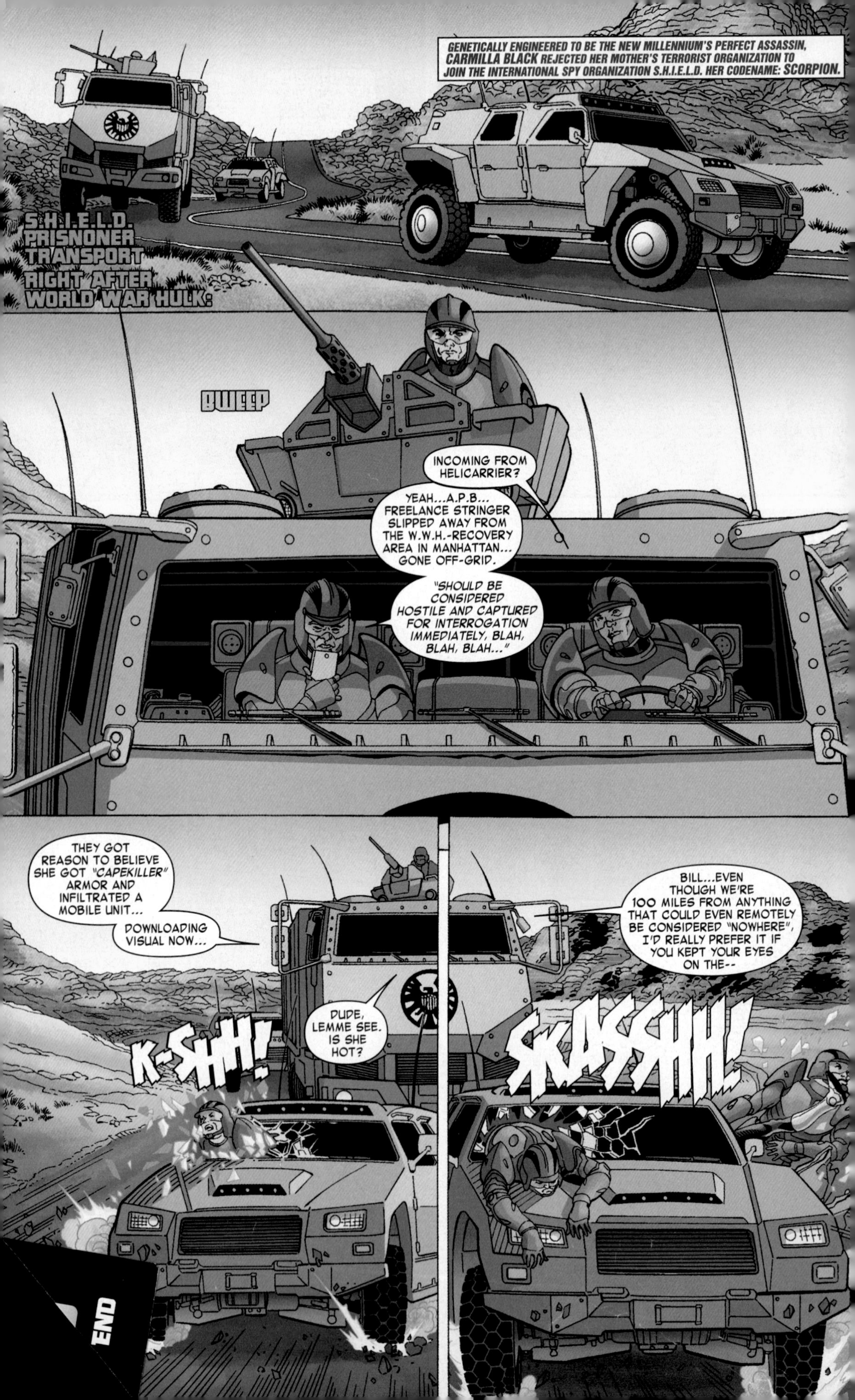
GENETICALLY ENGINEERED TO BE THE NEW MILLENNIUM'S PERFECT ASSASSIN, CARMILLA BLACK REJECTED HER MOTHER'S TERRORIST ORGANIZATION TO JOIN THE INTERNATIONAL SPY ORGANIZATION S.H.I.E.L.D. HER CODENAME: SCORPION.
S.H.I.E.L.D. PRISNONER TRANSPORT RIGHT AFTER WORLD WAR HULK:
BWEEP
INCOMING FROM HELICARRIER?
YEAH...A.P.B... FREELANCE STRINGER SLIPPED AWAY FROM THE W.W.H.-RECOVERY AREA IN MANHATTAN... GONE OFF-GRID.
"SHOULD BE CONSIDERED HOSTILE AND CAPTURED FOR INTERROGATION IMMEDIATELY, BLAH, BLAH, BLAH..."
THEY GOT REASON TO BELIEVE SHE GOT "CAPEKILLER" ARMOR AND INFILTRATED A MOBILE UNIT...
DOWNLOADING VISUAL NOW...
DUDE, LEMME SEE. IS SHE HOT?
K-SHH!
BILL...EVEN THOUGH WE'RE 100 MILES FROM ANYTHING THAT COULD EVEN REMOTELY BE CONSIDERED "NOWHERE", I'D REALLY PREFER IT IF YOU KEPT YOUR EYES ON THE--
SKASSHH!

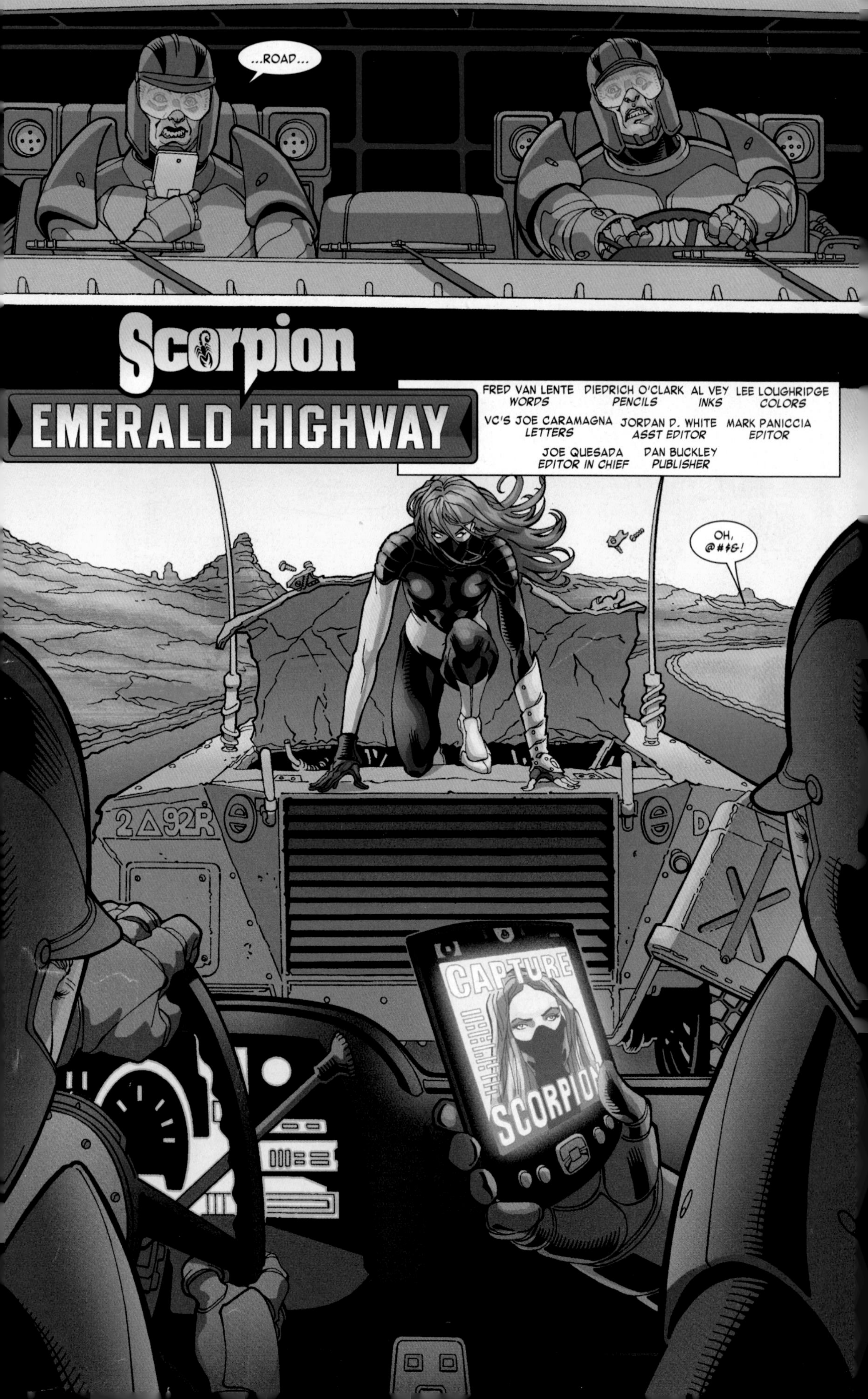
...ROAD...
Scorpion
EMERALD HIGHWAY
FRED VAN LENTE WORDS
DIEDRICH O'CLARK PENCILS
AL VEY INKS
LEE LOUGHRIDGE COLORS
VC'S JOE CARAMAGNA LETTERS
JORDAN D. WHITE ASST EDITOR
MARK PANICCIA EDITOR
JOE QUESADA EDITOR IN CHIEF
DAN BUCKLEY PUBLISHER
OH, @#$&!
2△92R
CAPTURE
SCORPION

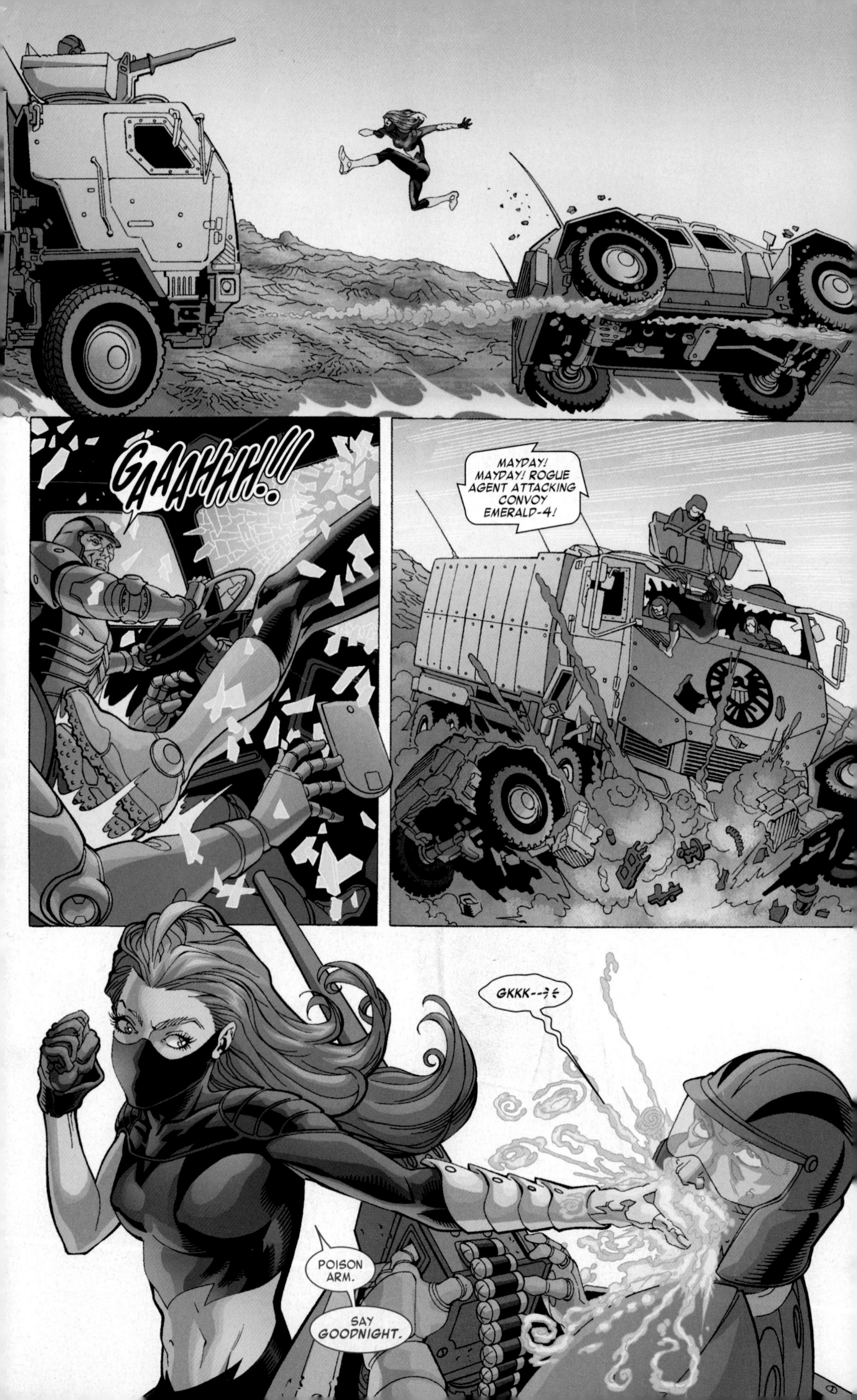
GAAAHHH!!
MAYDAY! MAYDAY! ROGUE AGENT ATTACKING CONVOY EMERALD-4!
GKKK--
POISON ARM.
SAY GOODNIGHT.

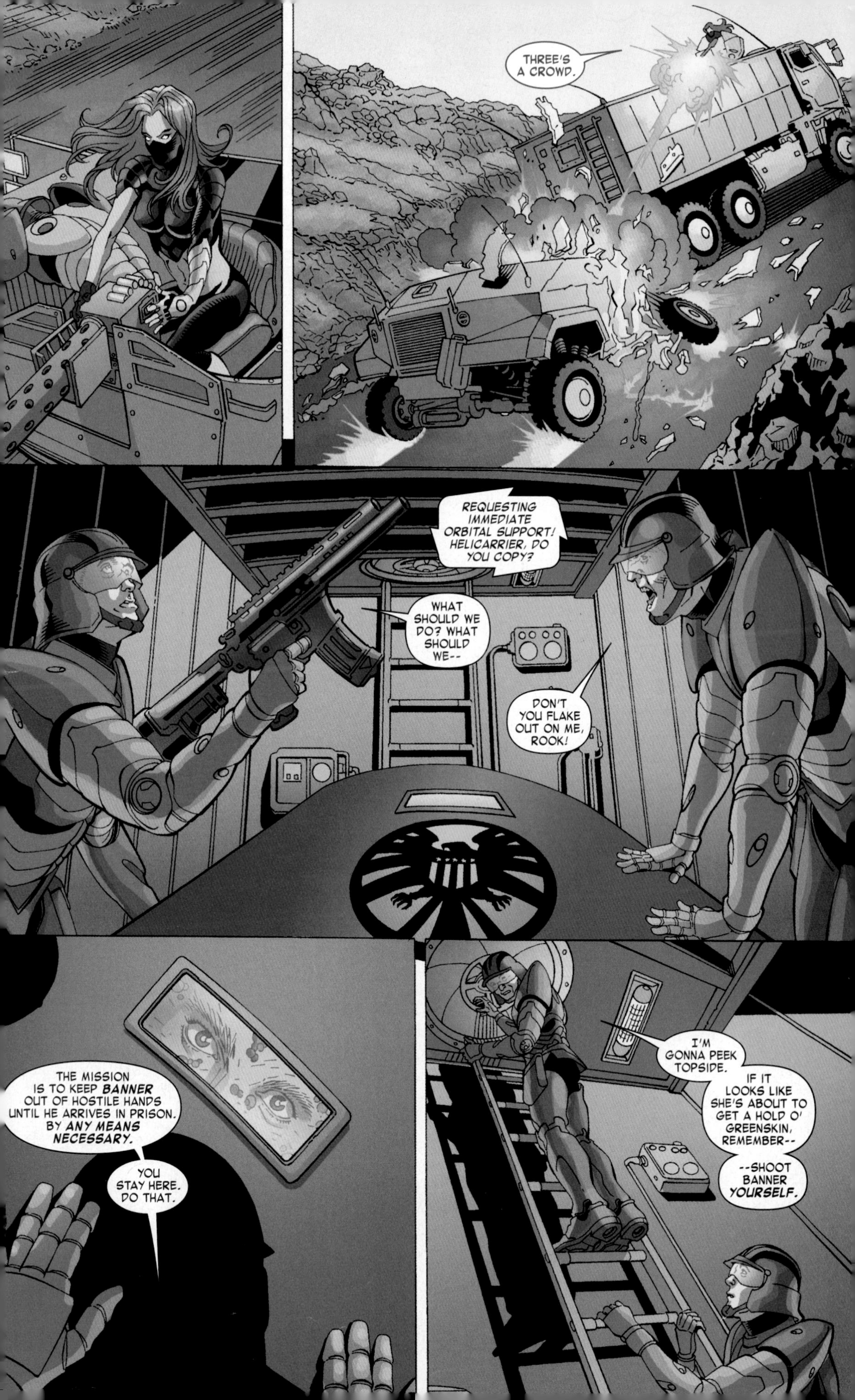
THREE'S A CROWD.
REQUESTING IMMEDIATE ORBITAL SUPPORT! HELICARRIER, DO YOU COPY?
WHAT SHOULD WE DO? WHAT SHOULD WE--
DON'T YOU FLAKE OUT ON ME, ROOK!
THE MISSION IS TO KEEP BANNER OUT OF HOSTILE HANDS UNTIL HE ARRIVES IN PRISON. BY ANY MEANS NECESSARY.
YOU STAY HERE. DO THAT.
I'M GONNA PEEK TOPSIDE.
IF IT LOOKS LIKE SHE'S ABOUT TO GET A HOLD O' GREENSKIN, REMEMBER--
--SHOOT BANNER YOURSELF.

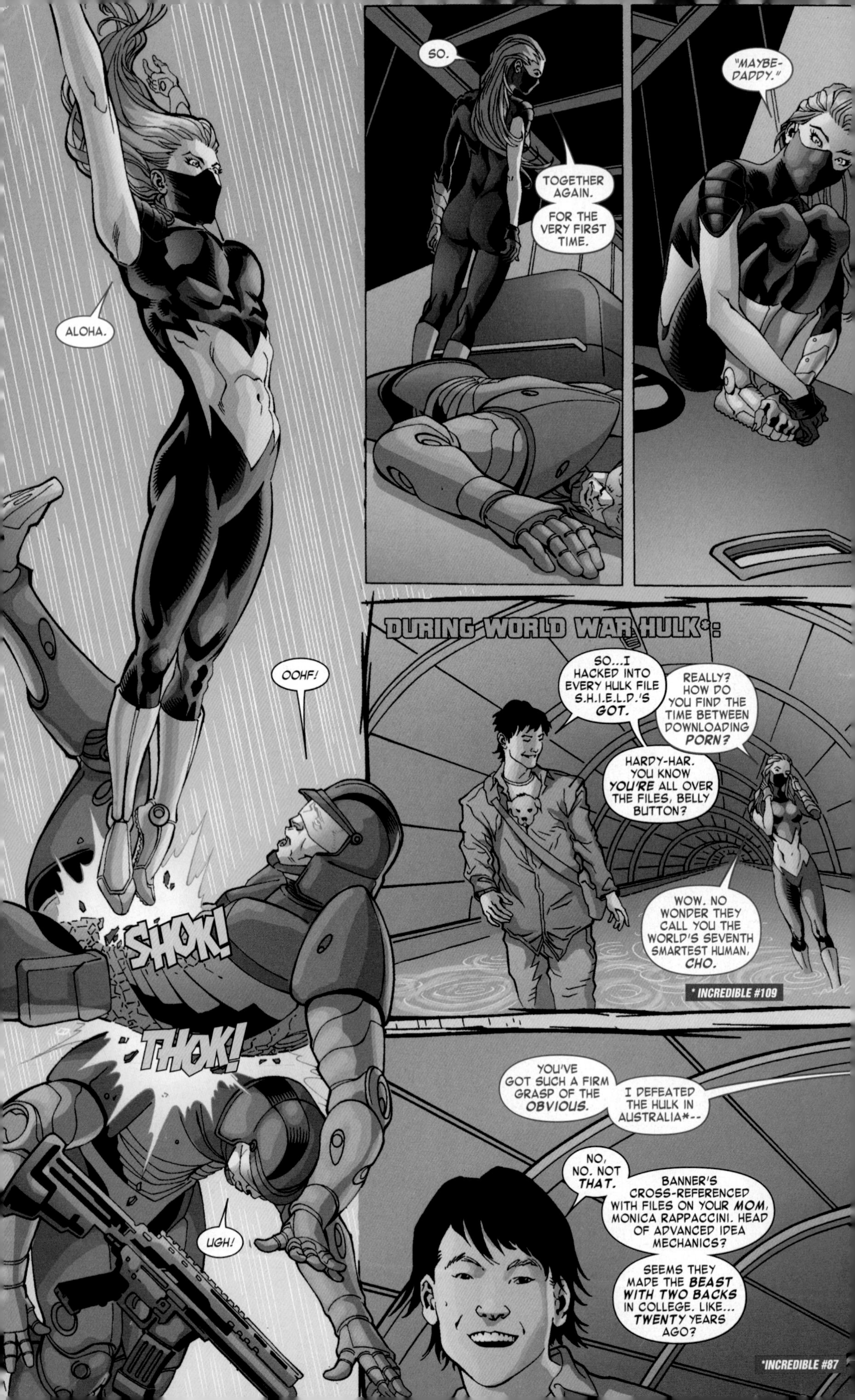
ALOHA.
OOHF!
SHOK!
THOK!
UGH!
SO.
TOGETHER AGAIN.
FOR THE VERY FIRST TIME.
"MAYBE-DADDY."
DURING WORLD WAR HULK*:
SO...I HACKED INTO EVERY HULK FILE S.H.I.E.L.D.'S GOT.
REALLY? HOW DO YOU FIND THE TIME BETWEEN DOWNLOADING PORN?
HARDY-HAR. YOU KNOW YOU'RE ALL OVER THE FILES, BELLY BUTTON?
WOW. NO WONDER THEY CALL YOU THE WORLD'S SEVENTH SMARTEST HUMAN, CHO.
* INCREDIBLE #109
YOU'VE GOT SUCH A FIRM GRASP OF THE OBVIOUS.
I DEFEATED THE HULK IN AUSTRALIA*--
NO, NO. NOT THAT.
BANNER'S CROSS-REFERENCED WITH FILES ON YOUR MOM, MONICA RAPPACCINI. HEAD OF ADVANCED IDEA MECHANICS?
SEEMS THEY MADE THE BEAST WITH TWO BACKS IN COLLEGE. LIKE... TWENTY YEARS AGO?
*INCREDIBLE #87

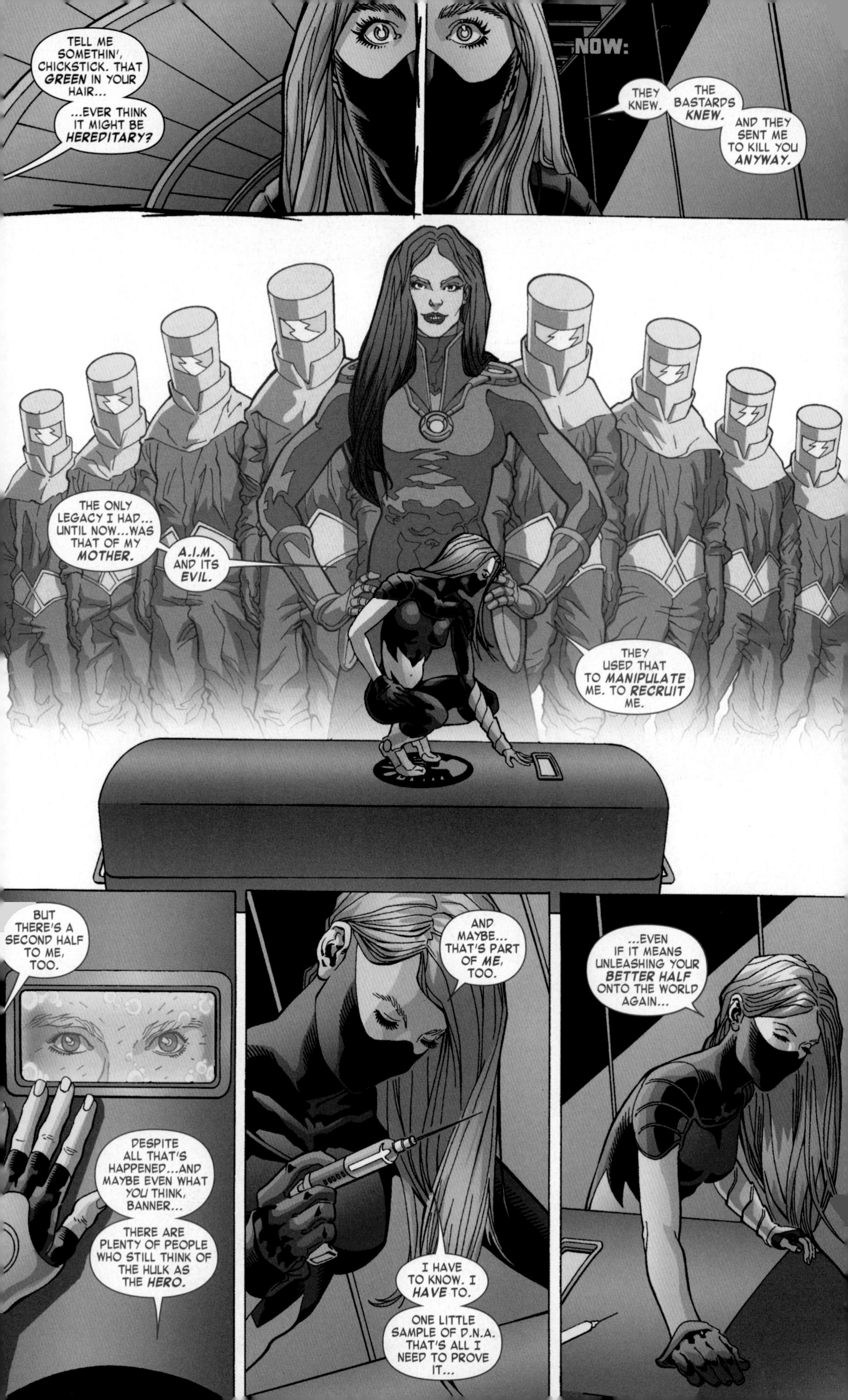
TELL ME SOMETHIN', CHICKSTICK. THAT GREEN IN YOUR HAIR...
...EVER THINK IT MIGHT BE HEREDITARY?
NOW:
THEY KNEW.
THE BASTARDS KNEW.
AND THEY SENT ME TO KILL YOU ANYWAY.
THE ONLY LEGACY I HAD... UNTIL NOW...WAS THAT OF MY MOTHER.
A.I.M. AND ITS EVIL.
THEY USED THAT TO MANIPULATE ME. TO RECRUIT ME.
BUT THERE'S A SECOND HALF TO ME, TOO.
DESPITE ALL THAT'S HAPPENED...AND MAYBE EVEN WHAT YOU THINK, BANNER...
THERE ARE PLENTY OF PEOPLE WHO STILL THINK OF THE HULK AS THE HERO.
AND MAYBE... THAT'S PART OF ME, TOO.
I HAVE TO KNOW. I HAVE TO.
ONE LITTLE SAMPLE OF D.N.A. THAT'S ALL I NEED TO PROVE IT...
...EVEN IF IT MEANS UNLEASHING YOUR BETTER HALF ONTO THE WORLD AGAIN...

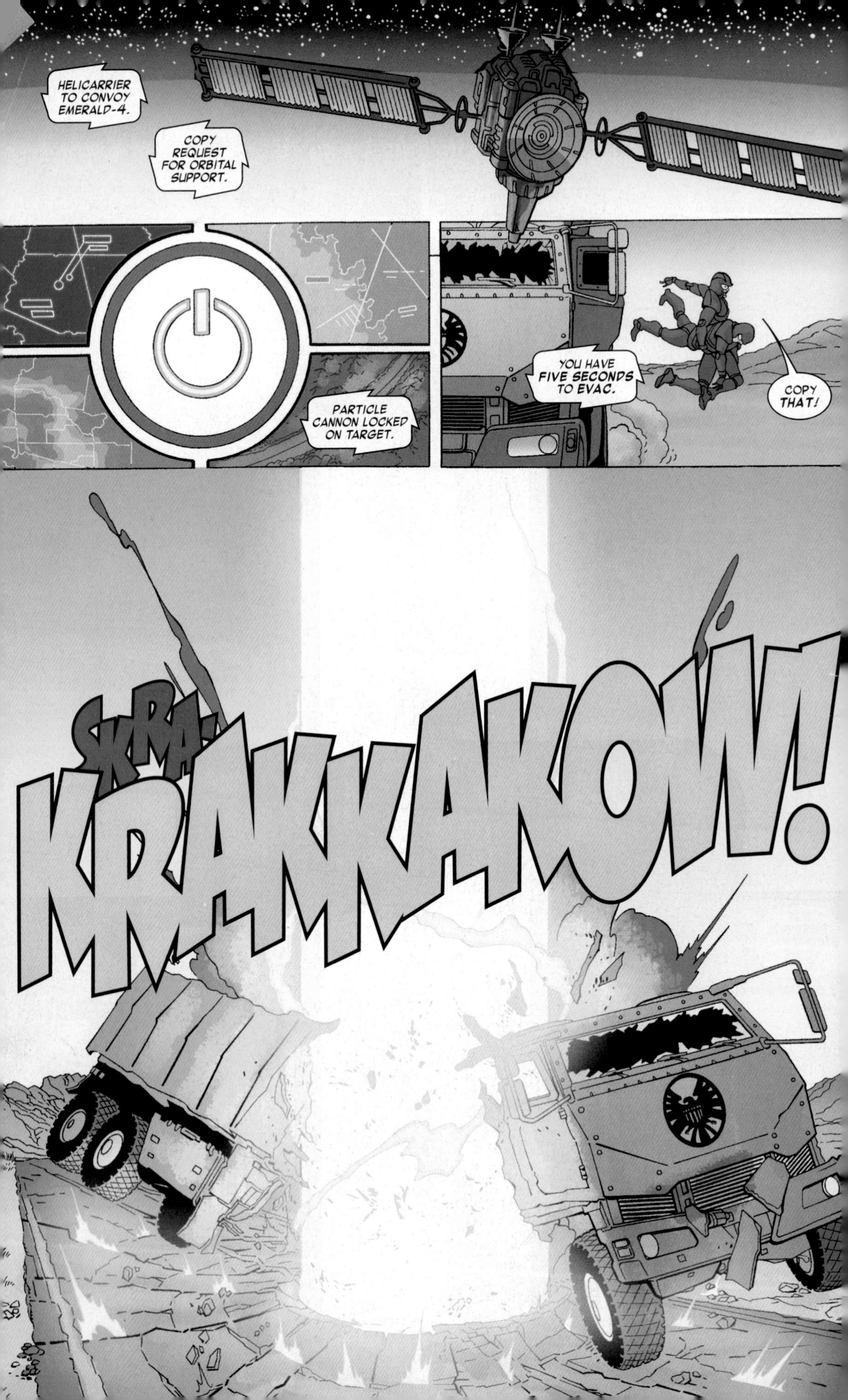
HELICARRIER TO CONVOY EMERALD-4.
COPY REQUEST FOR ORBITAL SUPPORT.
PARTICLE CANNON LOCKED ON TARGET.
YOU HAVE FIVE SECONDS TO EVAC.
COPY THAT!
SKRA-KRAKKAKOW!

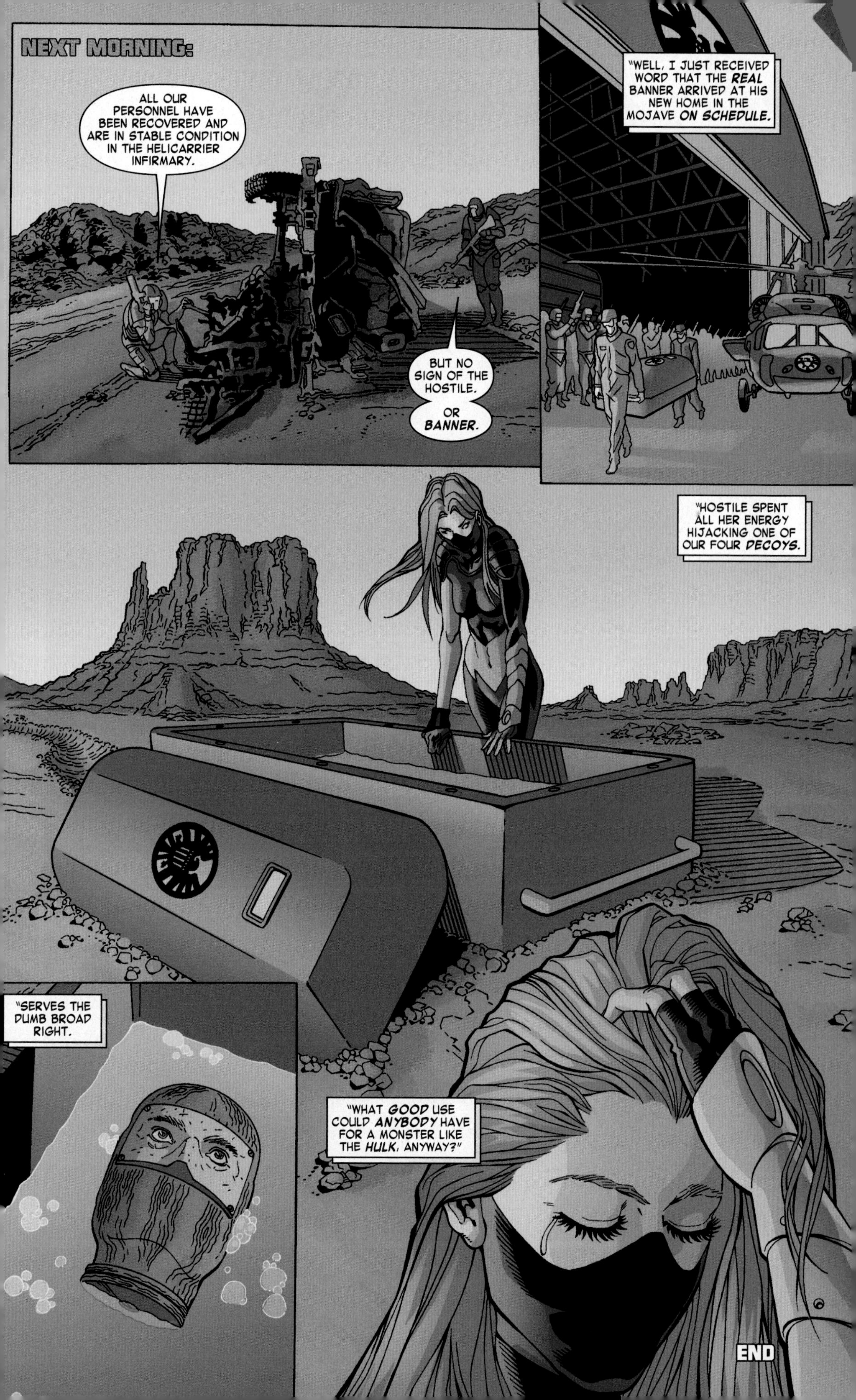
NEXT MORNING:
ALL OUR PERSONNEL HAVE BEEN RECOVERED AND ARE IN STABLE CONDITION IN THE HELICARRIER INFIRMARY.
BUT NO SIGN OF THE HOSTILE.
OR BANNER.
"WELL, I JUST RECEIVED WORD THAT THE REAL BANNER ARRIVED AT HIS NEW HOME IN THE MOJAVE ON SCHEDULE.
"HOSTILE SPENT ALL HER ENERGY HIJACKING ONE OF OUR FOUR DECOYS.
"SERVES THE DUMB BROAD RIGHT.
"WHAT GOOD USE COULD ANYBODY HAVE FOR A MONSTER LIKE THE HULK, ANYWAY?"
END

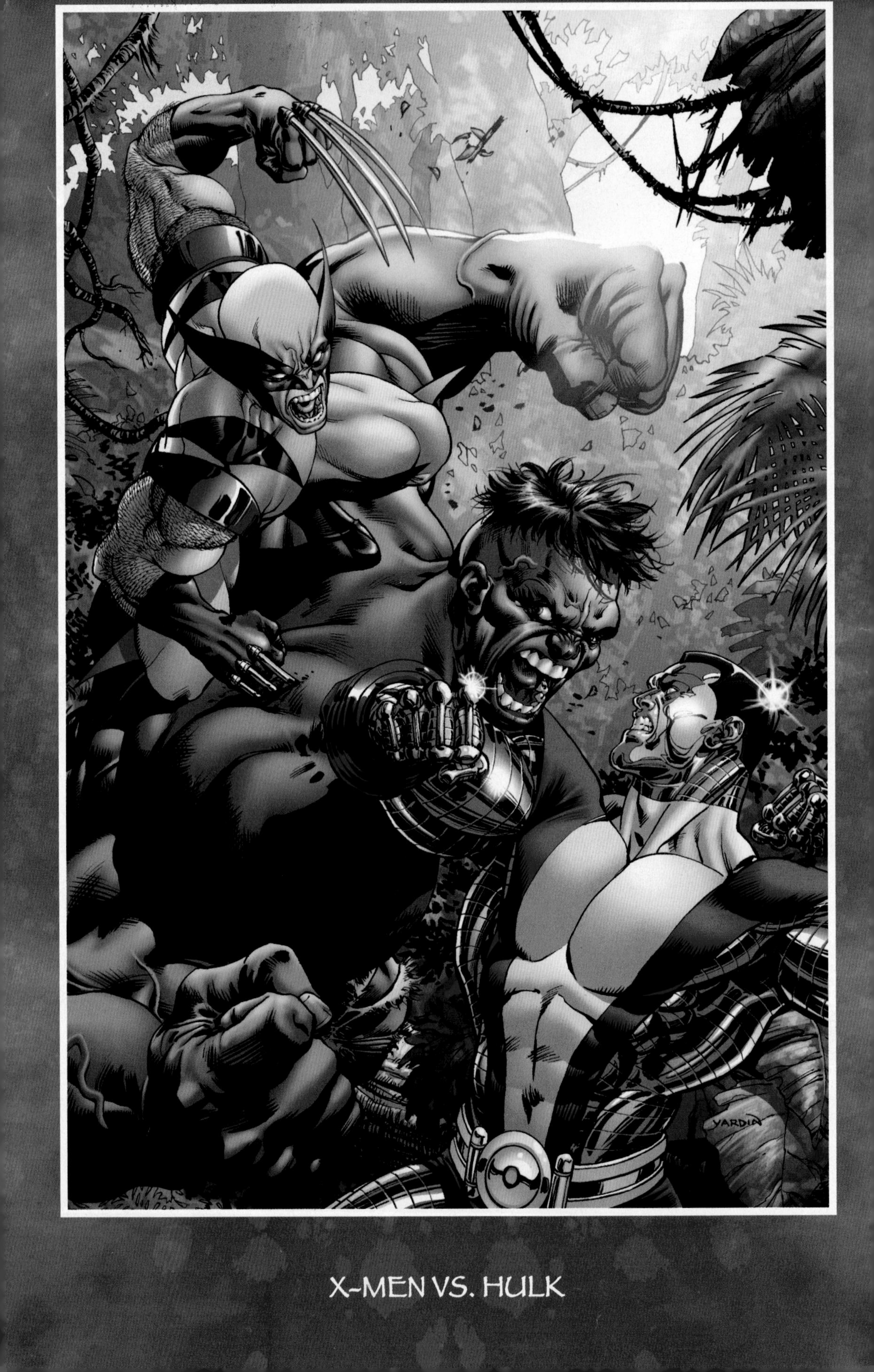
YARDIN

X-MEN VS. HULK

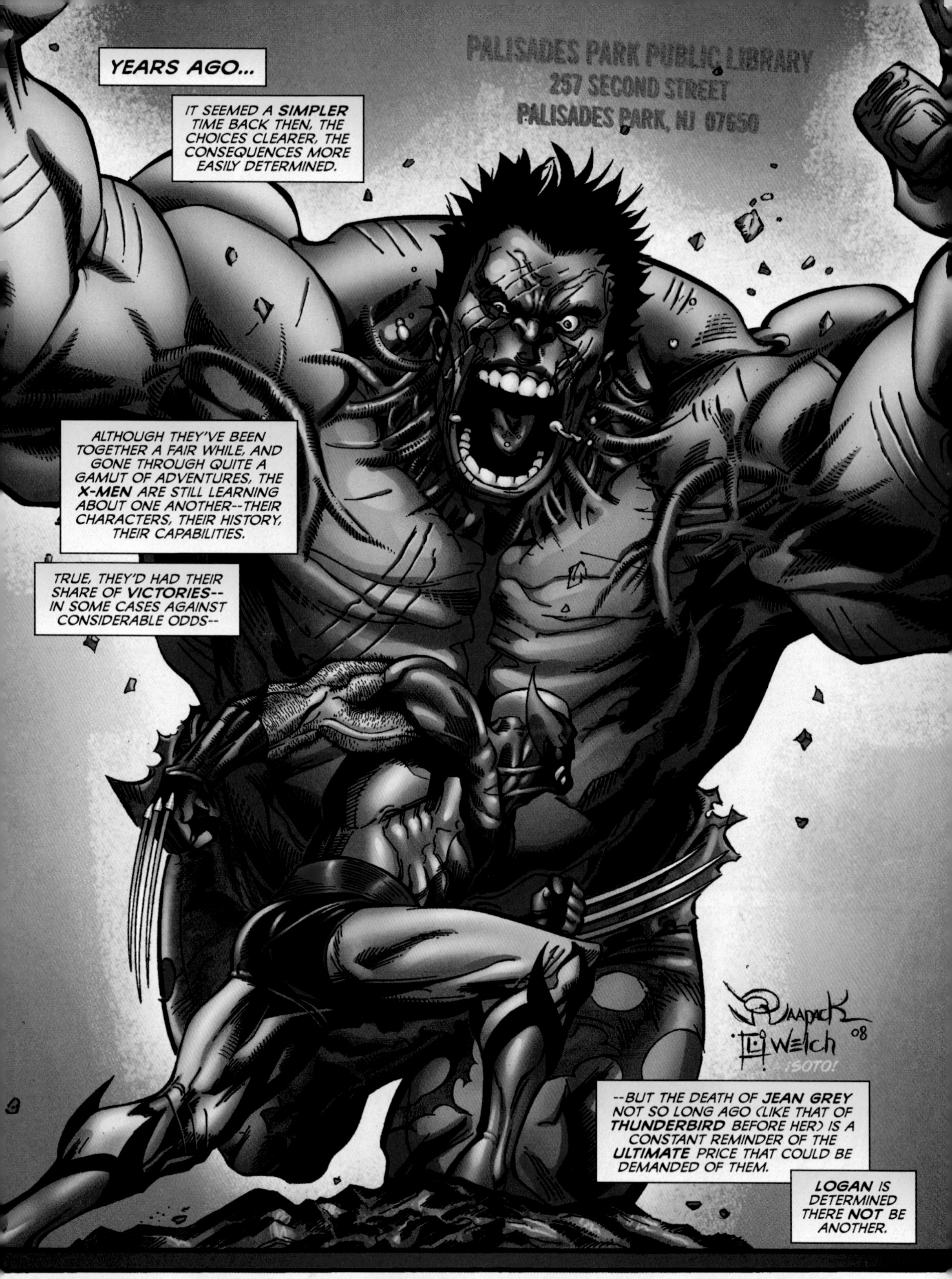
YEARS AGO...
IT SEEMED A SIMPLER TIME BACK THEN, THE CHOICES CLEARER, THE CONSEQUENCES MORE EASILY DETERMINED.
ALTHOUGH THEY'VE BEEN TOGETHER A FAIR WHILE, AND GONE THROUGH QUITE A GAMUT OF ADVENTURES, THE X-MEN ARE STILL LEARNING ABOUT ONE ANOTHER--THEIR CHARACTERS, THEIR HISTORY, THEIR CAPABILITIES.
TRUE, THEY'D HAD THEIR SHARE OF VICTORIES--IN SOME CASES AGAINST CONSIDERABLE ODDS--
--BUT THE DEATH OF JEAN GREY NOT SO LONG AGO (LIKE THAT OF THUNDERBIRD BEFORE HER) IS A CONSTANT REMINDER OF THE ULTIMATE PRICE THAT COULD BE DEMANDED OF THEM.
LOGAN IS DETERMINED THERE NOT BE ANOTHER.

THE MAKING OF A MAN...

By CHRIS CLAREMONT & JHEREMY RAAPACK
LARRY WELCH, INKER
CHRIS SOTOMAYOR, COLORIST
ED DUKESHIRE, LETTERER
DAVID YARDIN & WIL QUINTANA, COVER
CHARLIE BECKERMAN, ASST. EDITOR
MARK PANICCIA, EDITOR
JOE QUESADA, EDITOR IN CHIEF
DAN BUCKLEY, PUBLISHER

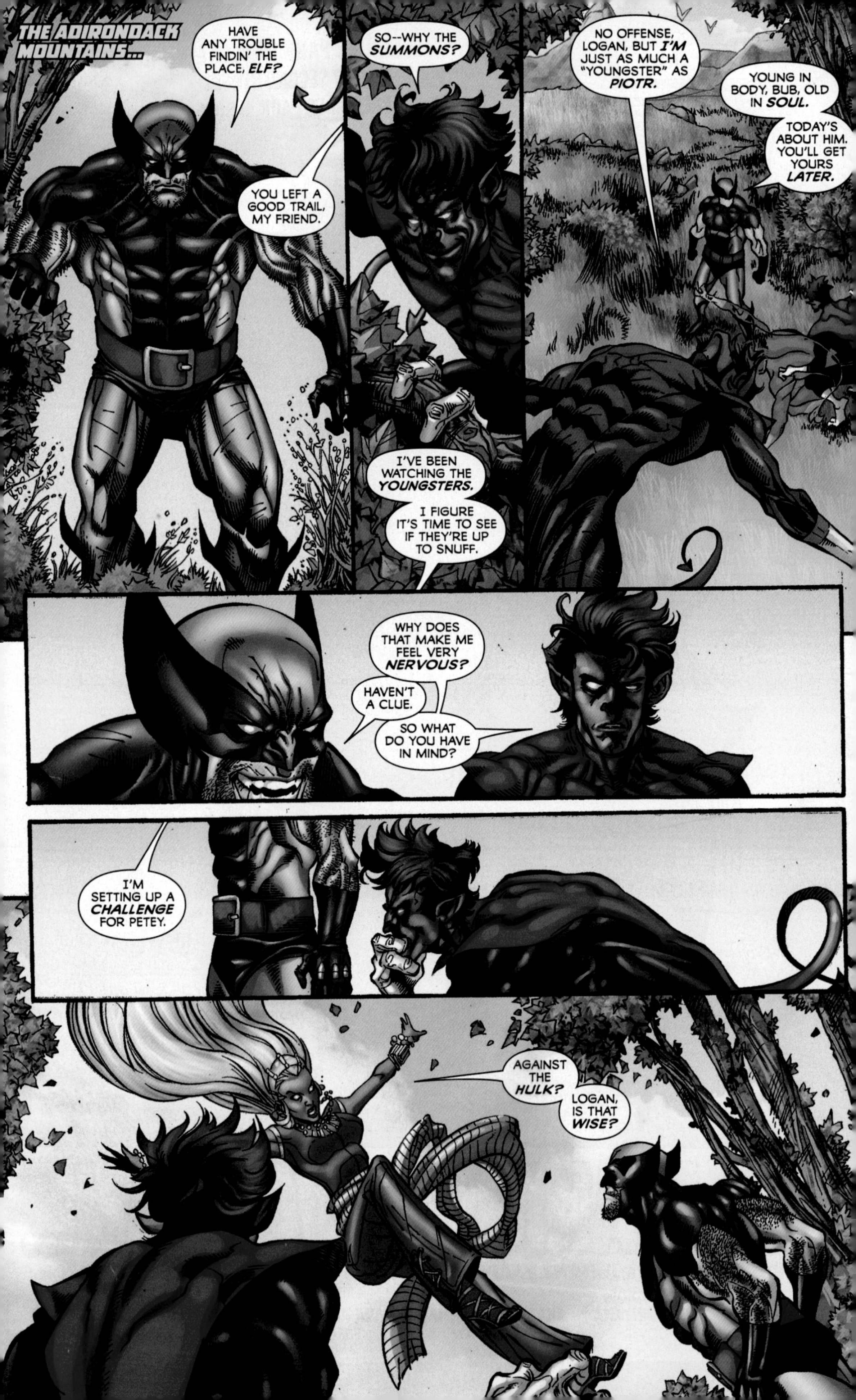
THE ADIRONDACK MOUNTAINS...
HAVE ANY TROUBLE FINDIN' THE PLACE, ELF?
YOU LEFT A GOOD TRAIL, MY FRIEND.
SO--WHY THE SUMMONS?
I'VE BEEN WATCHING THE YOUNGSTERS.
I FIGURE IT'S TIME TO SEE IF THEY'RE UP TO SNUFF.
NO OFFENSE, LOGAN, BUT I'M JUST AS MUCH A "YOUNGSTER" AS PIOTR.
YOUNG IN BODY, BUB, OLD IN SOUL.
TODAY'S ABOUT HIM. YOU'LL GET YOURS LATER.
WHY DOES THAT MAKE ME FEEL VERY NERVOUS?
HAVEN'T A CLUE.
SO WHAT DO YOU HAVE IN MIND?
I'M SETTING UP A CHALLENGE FOR PETEY.
AGAINST THE HULK?
LOGAN, IS THAT WISE?

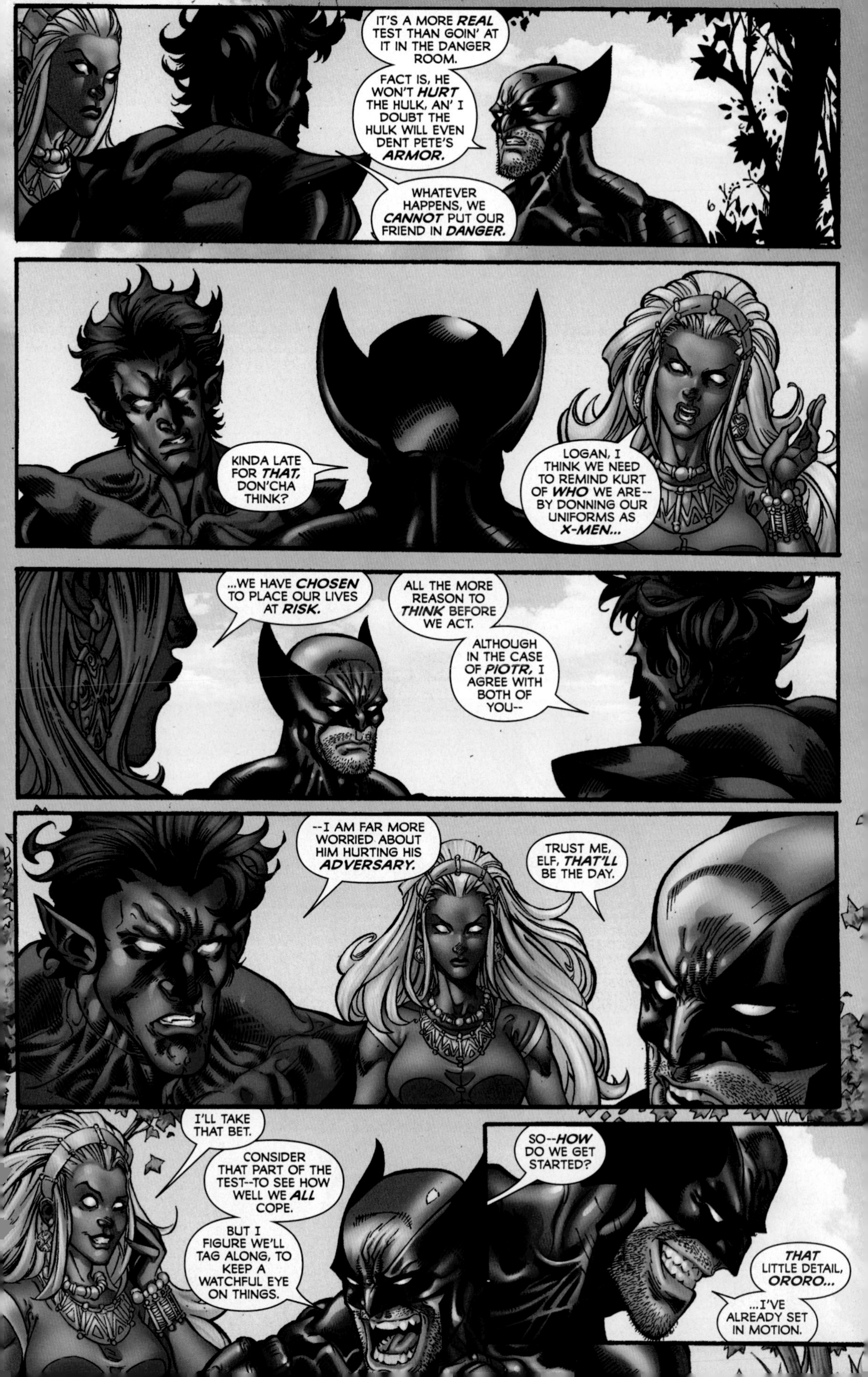
IT'S A MORE REAL TEST THAN GOIN' AT IT IN THE DANGER ROOM.
FACT IS, HE WON'T HURT THE HULK, AN' I DOUBT THE HULK WILL EVEN DENT PETE'S ARMOR.
WHATEVER HAPPENS, WE CANNOT PUT OUR FRIEND IN DANGER.
KINDA LATE FOR THAT, DON'CHA THINK?
LOGAN, I THINK WE NEED TO REMIND KURT OF WHO WE ARE--BY DONNING OUR UNIFORMS AS X-MEN...
...WE HAVE CHOSEN TO PLACE OUR LIVES AT RISK.
ALL THE MORE REASON TO THINK BEFORE WE ACT.
ALTHOUGH IN THE CASE OF PIOTR, I AGREE WITH BOTH OF YOU--
--I AM FAR MORE WORRIED ABOUT HIM HURTING HIS ADVERSARY.
TRUST ME, ELF, THAT'LL BE THE DAY.
I'LL TAKE THAT BET.
CONSIDER THAT PART OF THE TEST--TO SEE HOW WELL WE ALL COPE.
BUT I FIGURE WE'LL TAG ALONG, TO KEEP A WATCHFUL EYE ON THINGS.
SO--HOW DO WE GET STARTED?
THAT LITTLE DETAIL, ORORO...
...I'VE ALREADY SET IN MOTION.

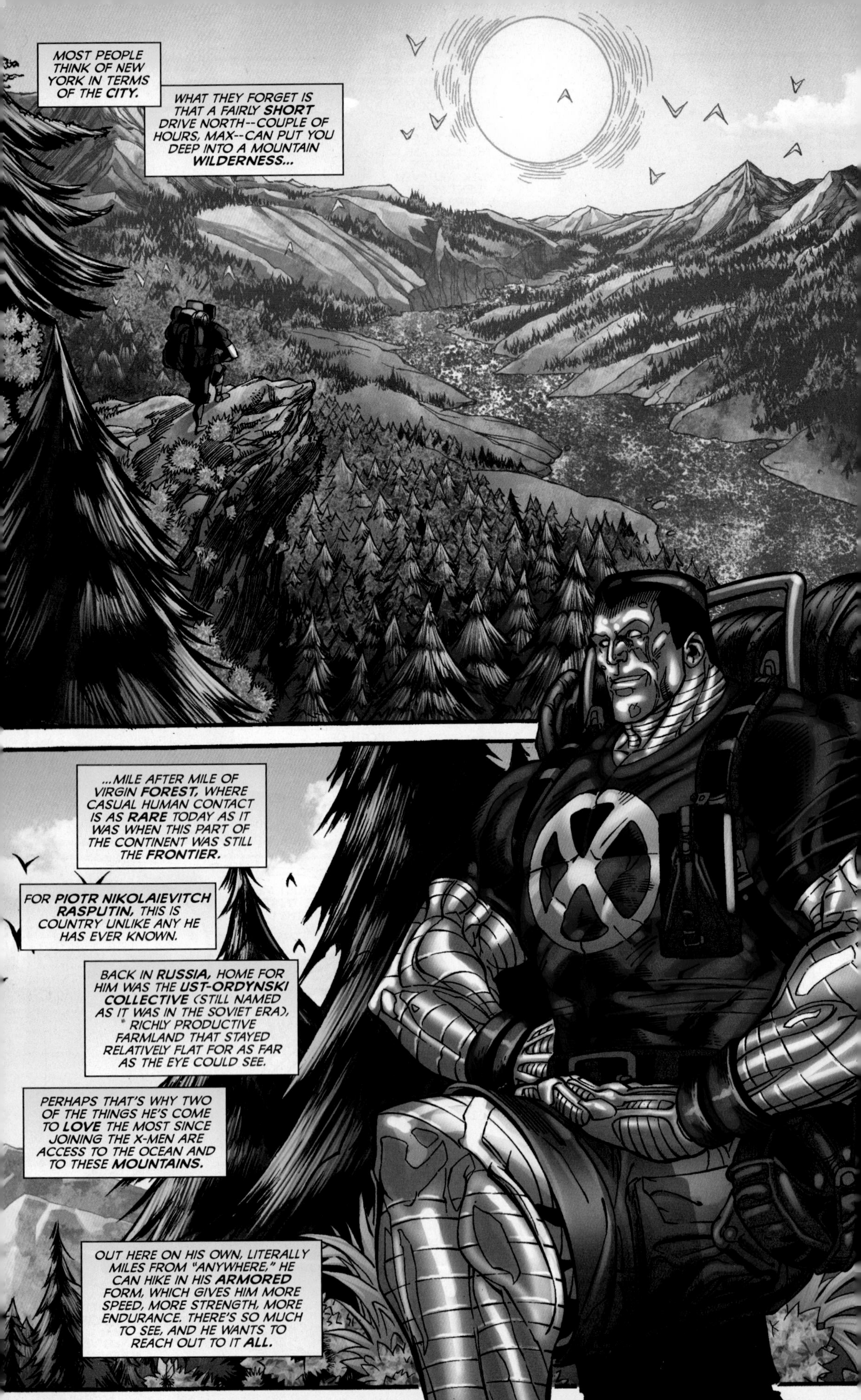
MOST PEOPLE THINK OF NEW YORK IN TERMS OF THE CITY.
WHAT THEY FORGET IS THAT A FAIRLY SHORT DRIVE NORTH--COUPLE OF HOURS, MAX--CAN PUT YOU DEEP INTO A MOUNTAIN WILDERNESS...
...MILE AFTER MILE OF VIRGIN FOREST, WHERE CASUAL HUMAN CONTACT IS AS RARE TODAY AS IT WAS WHEN THIS PART OF THE CONTINENT WAS STILL THE FRONTIER.
FOR PIOTR NIKOLAIEVITCH RASPUTIN, THIS IS COUNTRY UNLIKE ANY HE HAS EVER KNOWN.
BACK IN RUSSIA, HOME FOR HIM WAS THE UST-ORDYNSKI COLLECTIVE (STILL NAMED AS IT WAS IN THE SOVIET ERA), RICHLY PRODUCTIVE FARMLAND THAT STAYED RELATIVELY FLAT FOR AS FAR AS THE EYE COULD SEE.
PERHAPS THAT'S WHY TWO OF THE THINGS HE'S COME TO LOVE THE MOST SINCE JOINING THE X-MEN ARE ACCESS TO THE OCEAN AND TO THESE MOUNTAINS.
OUT HERE ON HIS OWN, LITERALLY MILES FROM "ANYWHERE," HE CAN HIKE IN HIS ARMORED FORM, WHICH GIVES HIM MORE SPEED, MORE STRENGTH, MORE ENDURANCE. THERE'S SO MUCH TO SEE, AND HE WANTS TO REACH OUT TO IT ALL.

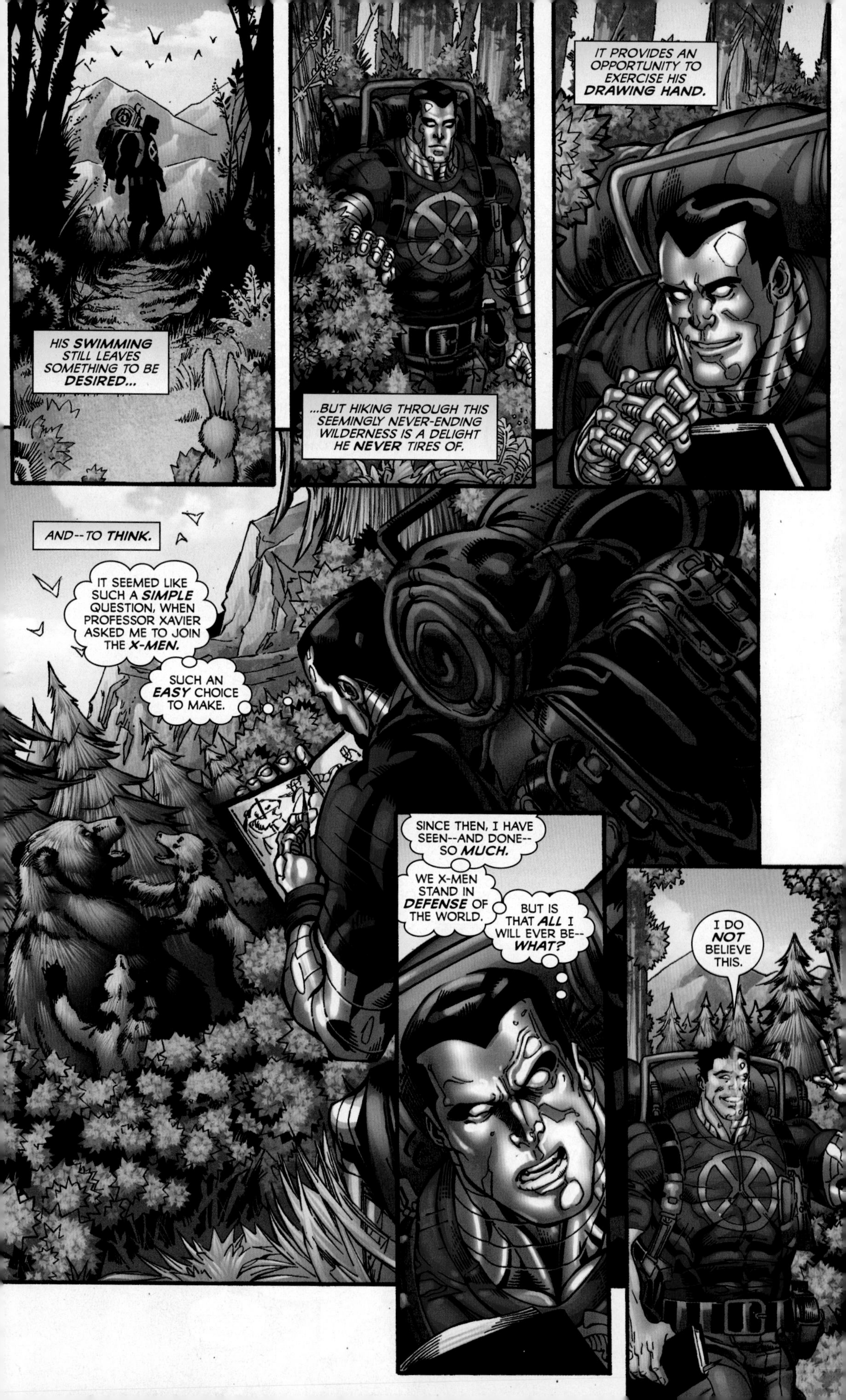
HIS SWIMMING STILL LEAVES SOMETHING TO BE DESIRED...
...BUT HIKING THROUGH THIS SEEMINGLY NEVER-ENDING WILDERNESS IS A DELIGHT HE NEVER TIRES OF.
IT PROVIDES AN OPPORTUNITY TO EXERCISE HIS DRAWING HAND.
AND--TO THINK.
IT SEEMED LIKE SUCH A SIMPLE QUESTION, WHEN PROFESSOR XAVIER ASKED ME TO JOIN THE X-MEN.
SUCH AN EASY CHOICE TO MAKE.
SINCE THEN, I HAVE SEEN--AND DONE--SO MUCH.
WE X-MEN STAND IN DEFENSE OF THE WORLD.
BUT IS THAT ALL I WILL EVER BE--WHAT?
I DO NOT BELIEVE THIS.

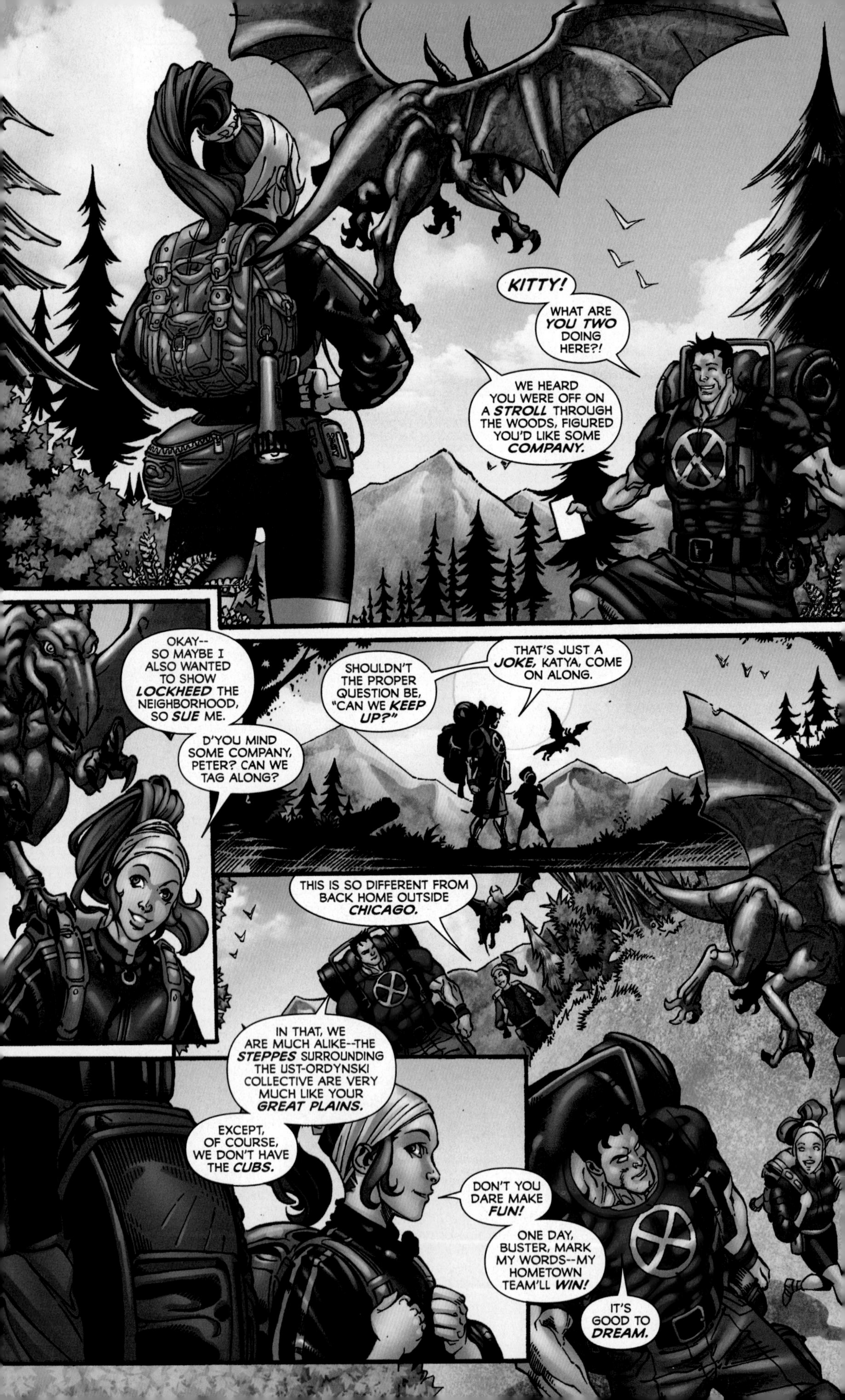
KITTY!
WHAT ARE YOU TWO DOING HERE?!
WE HEARD YOU WERE OFF ON A STROLL THROUGH THE WOODS, FIGURED YOU'D LIKE SOME COMPANY.
OKAY-- SO MAYBE I ALSO WANTED TO SHOW LOCKHEED THE NEIGHBORHOOD, SO SUE ME.
D'YOU MIND SOME COMPANY, PETER? CAN WE TAG ALONG?
SHOULDN'T THE PROPER QUESTION BE, "CAN WE KEEP UP?"
THAT'S JUST A JOKE, KATYA, COME ON ALONG.
THIS IS SO DIFFERENT FROM BACK HOME OUTSIDE CHICAGO.
IN THAT, WE ARE MUCH ALIKE--THE STEPPES SURROUNDING THE UST-ORDYNSKI COLLECTIVE ARE VERY MUCH LIKE YOUR GREAT PLAINS.
EXCEPT, OF COURSE, WE DON'T HAVE THE CUBS.
DON'T YOU DARE MAKE FUN!
ONE DAY, BUSTER, MARK MY WORDS--MY HOMETOWN TEAM'LL WIN!
IT'S GOOD TO DREAM.

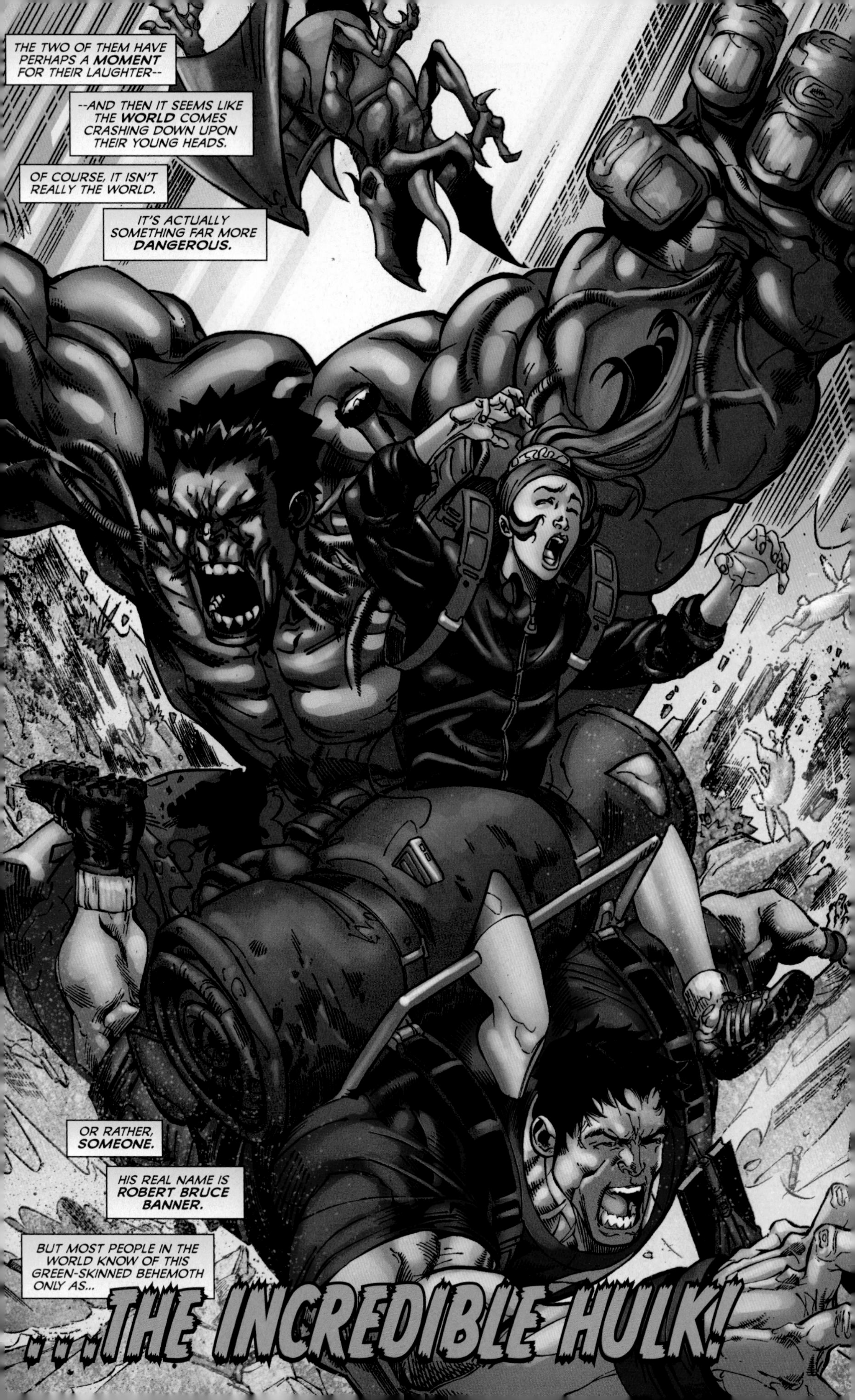

THE TWO OF THEM HAVE PERHAPS A MOMENT FOR THEIR LAUGHTER--
--AND THEN IT SEEMS LIKE THE WORLD COMES CRASHING DOWN UPON THEIR YOUNG HEADS.
OF COURSE, IT ISN'T REALLY THE WORLD.
IT'S ACTUALLY SOMETHING FAR MORE DANGEROUS.
OR RATHER, SOMEONE.
HIS REAL NAME IS ROBERT BRUCE BANNER.
BUT MOST PEOPLE IN THE WORLD KNOW OF THIS GREEN-SKINNED BEHEMOTH ONLY AS...
...THE INCREDIBLE HULK!

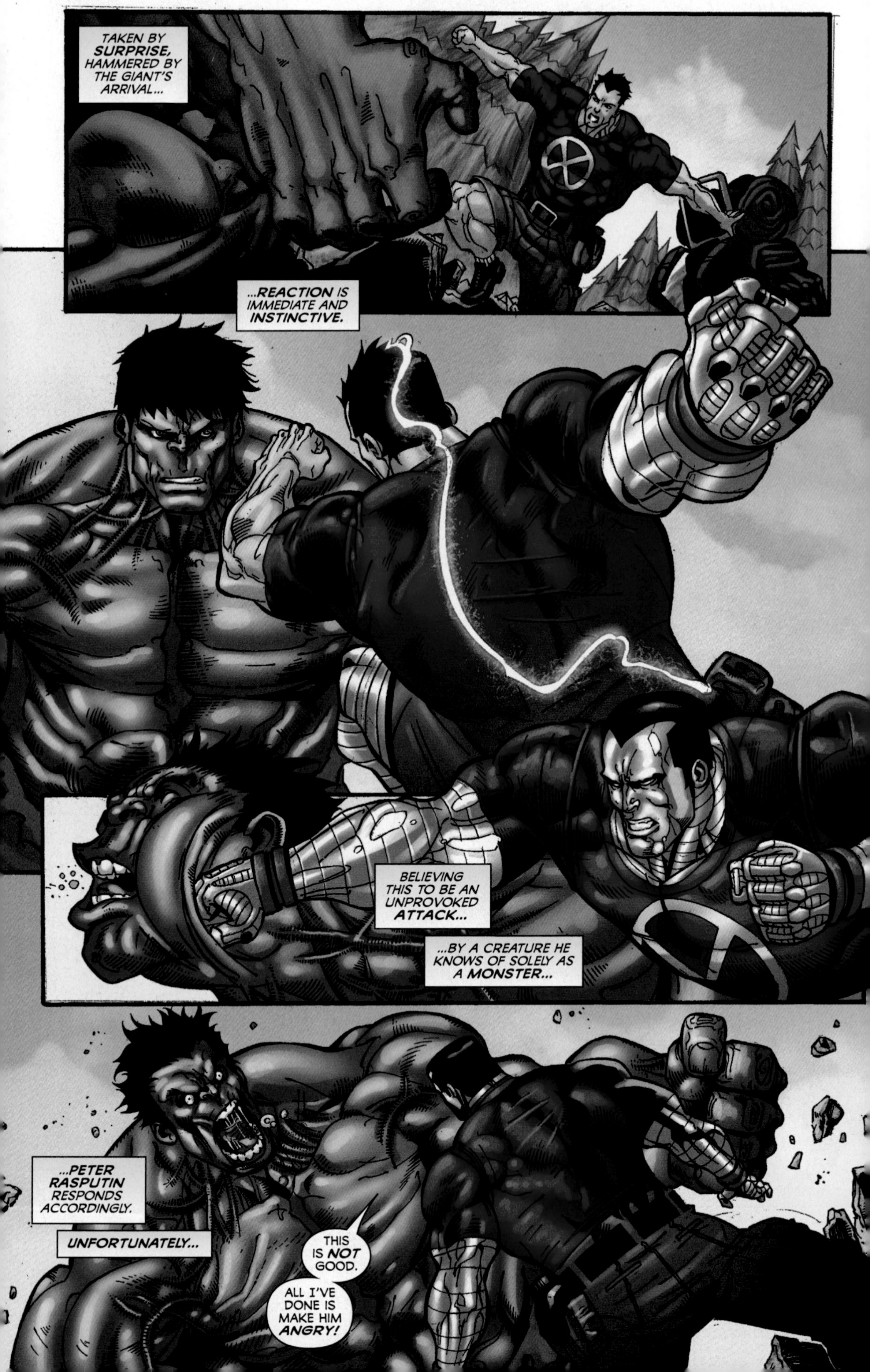

TAKEN BY SURPRISE, HAMMERED BY THE GIANT'S ARRIVAL...
...REACTION IS IMMEDIATE AND INSTINCTIVE.
BELIEVING THIS TO BE AN UNPROVOKED ATTACK...
...BY A CREATURE HE KNOWS OF SOLELY AS A MONSTER...
...PETER RASPUTIN RESPONDS ACCORDINGLY.
UNFORTUNATELY...
THIS IS NOT GOOD.
ALL I'VE DONE IS MAKE HIM ANGRY!

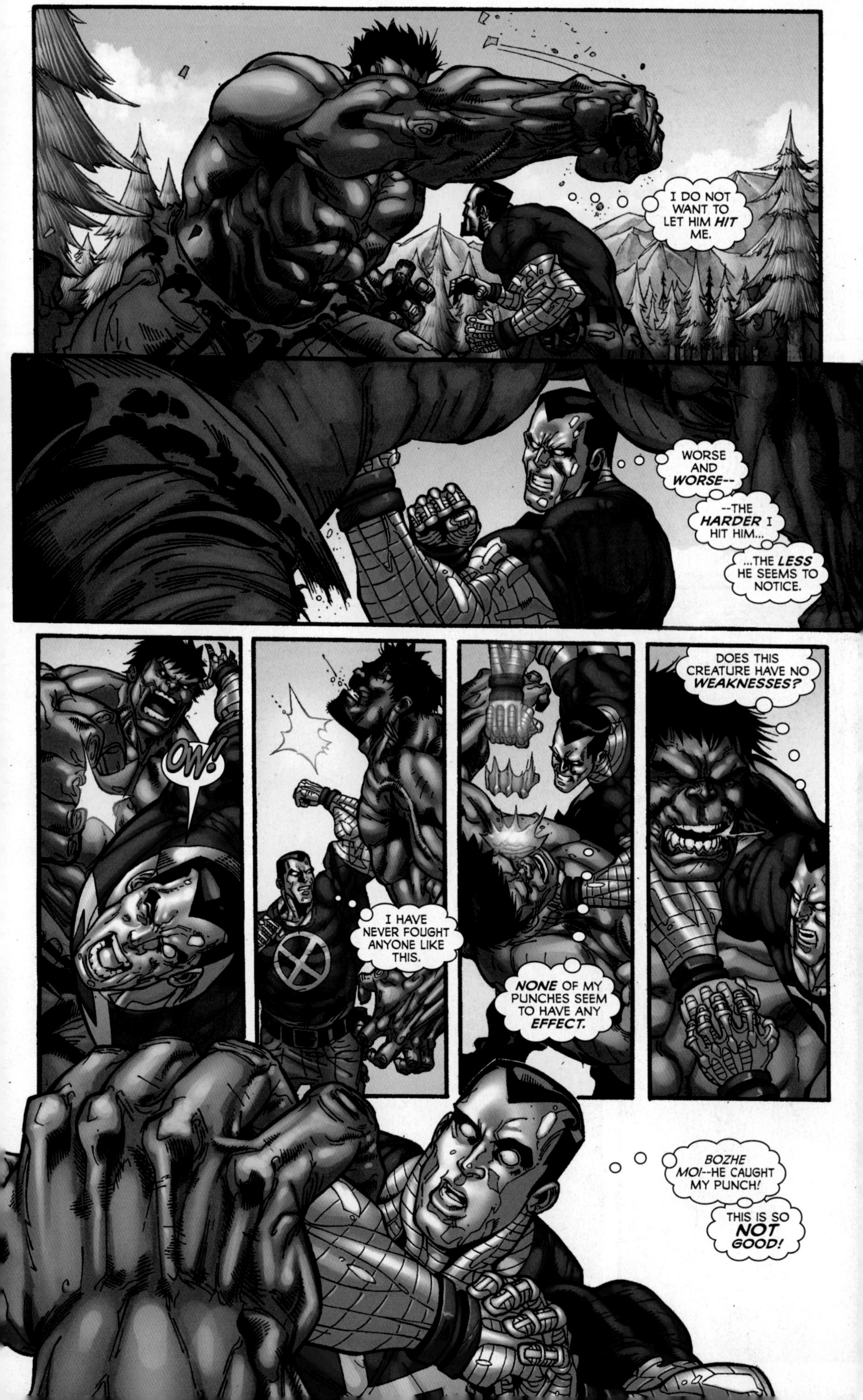
I DO NOT WANT TO LET HIM HIT ME.
WORSE AND WORSE--
--THE HARDER I HIT HIM...
...THE LESS HE SEEMS TO NOTICE.
OW!
I HAVE NEVER FOUGHT ANYONE LIKE THIS.
NONE OF MY PUNCHES SEEM TO HAVE ANY EFFECT.
DOES THIS CREATURE HAVE NO WEAKNESSES?
BOZHE MOI--HE CAUGHT MY PUNCH!
THIS IS SO NOT GOOD!

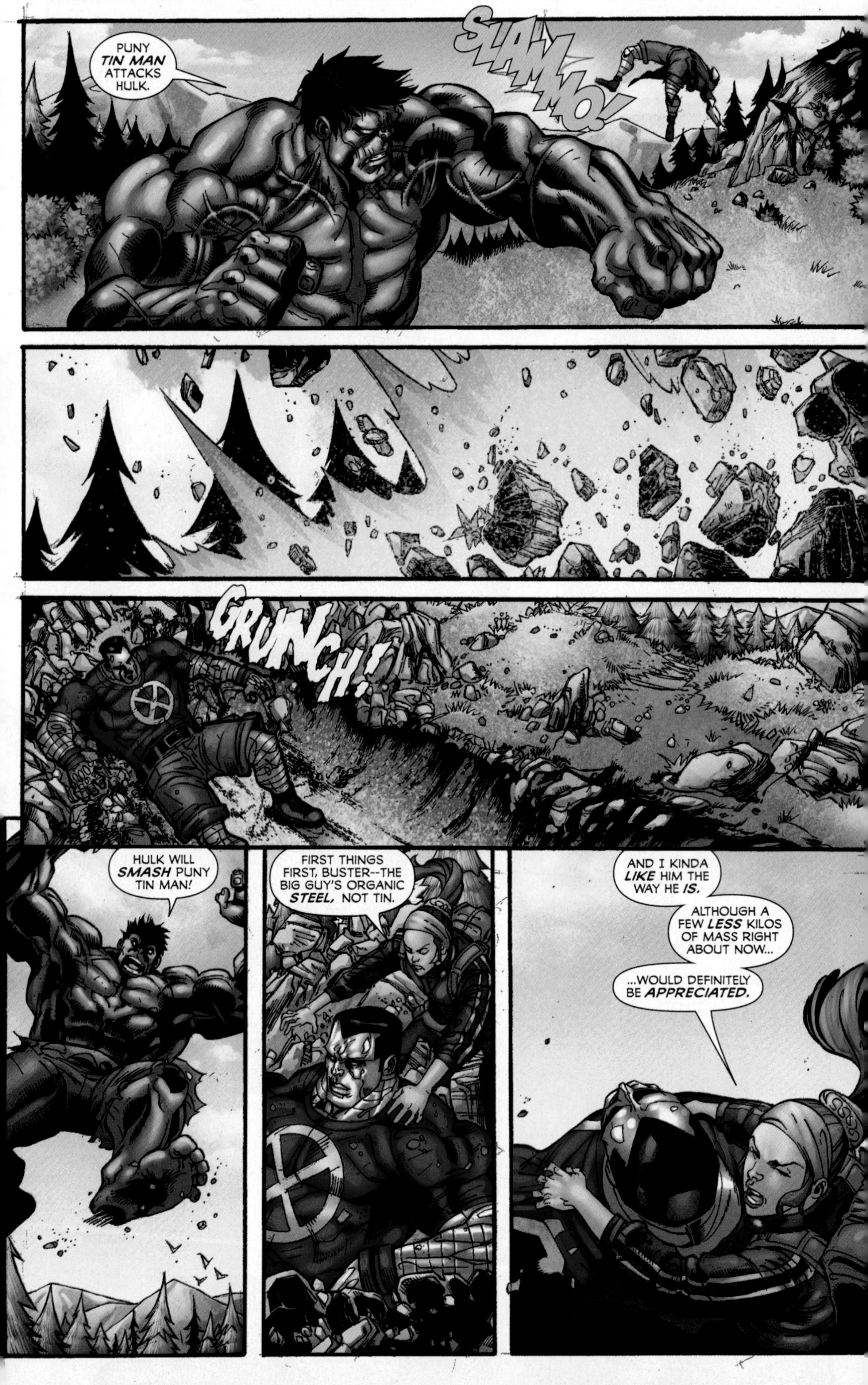
PUNY TIN MAN ATTACKS HULK.
SLAMMO!
GRUNCH!!
HULK WILL SMASH PUNY TIN MAN!
FIRST THINGS FIRST, BUSTER--THE BIG GUY'S ORGANIC STEEL, NOT TIN.
AND I KINDA LIKE HIM THE WAY HE IS.
ALTHOUGH A FEW LESS KILOS OF MASS RIGHT ABOUT NOW...
...WOULD DEFINITELY BE APPRECIATED.

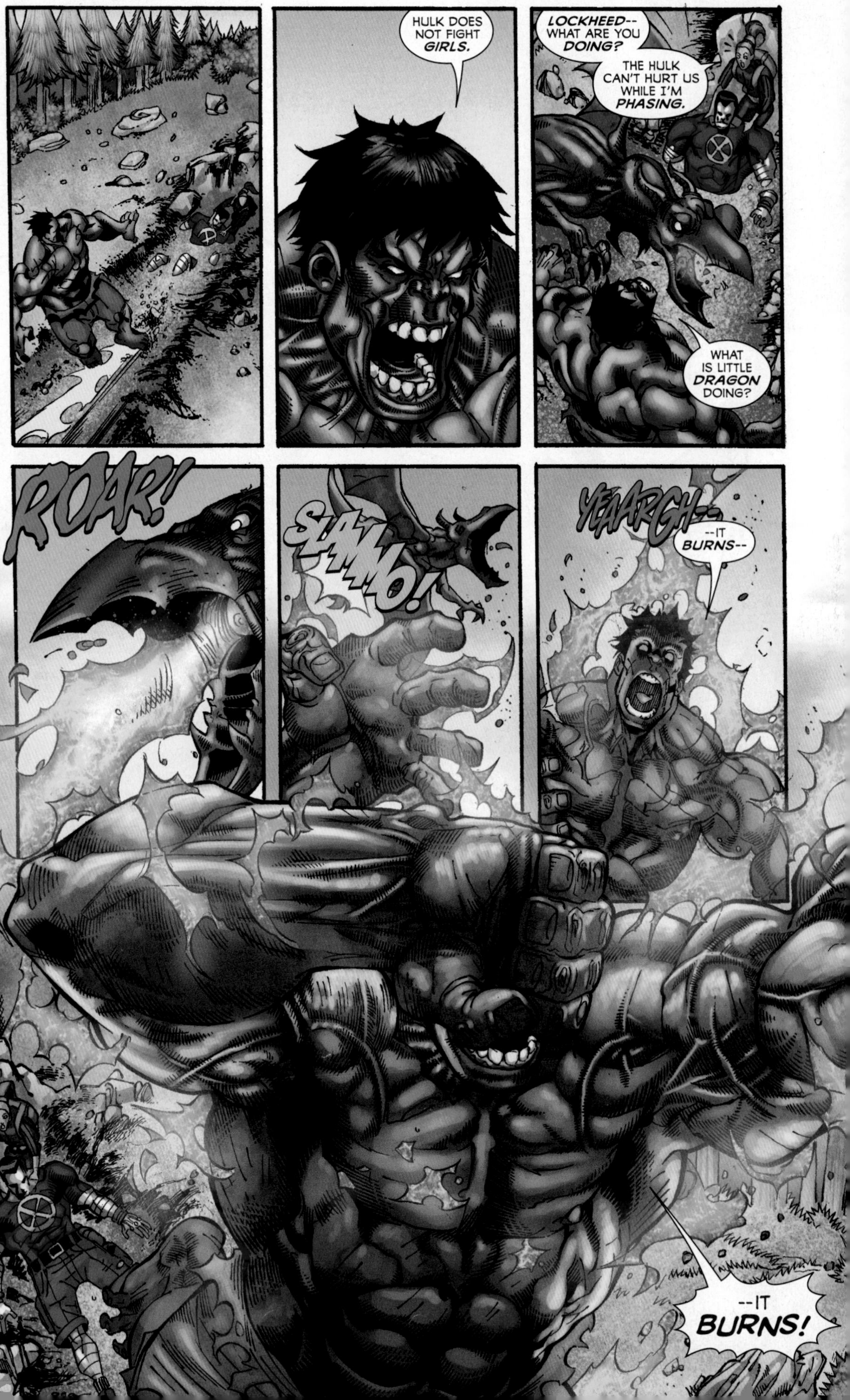
HULK DOES NOT FIGHT GIRLS.
LOCKHEED-- WHAT ARE YOU DOING?
THE HULK CAN'T HURT US WHILE I'M PHASING.
WHAT IS LITTLE DRAGON DOING?
ROAR!
SLAMMO!
YEAARGH--
--IT BURNS--
--IT BURNS!

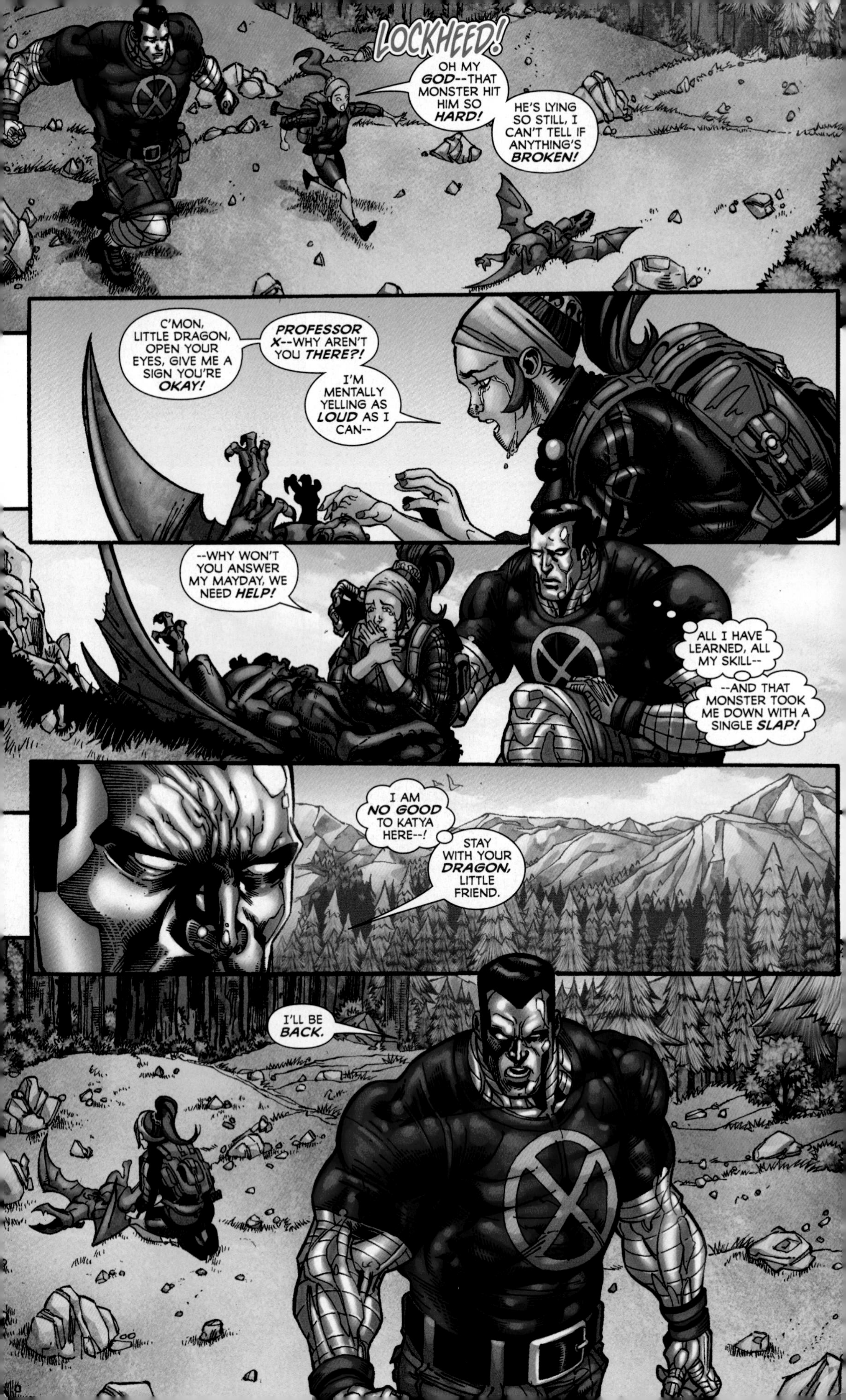

LOCKHEED!
OH MY GOD--THAT MONSTER HIT HIM SO HARD!
HE'S LYING SO STILL, I CAN'T TELL IF ANYTHING'S BROKEN!
C'MON, LITTLE DRAGON, OPEN YOUR EYES, GIVE ME A SIGN YOU'RE OKAY!
PROFESSOR X--WHY AREN'T YOU THERE?!
I'M MENTALLY YELLING AS LOUD AS I CAN--
--WHY WON'T YOU ANSWER MY MAYDAY, WE NEED HELP!
ALL I HAVE LEARNED, ALL MY SKILL--
--AND THAT MONSTER TOOK ME DOWN WITH A SINGLE SLAP!
I AM NO GOOD TO KATYA HERE--!
STAY WITH YOUR DRAGON, LITTLE FRIEND.
I'LL BE BACK.

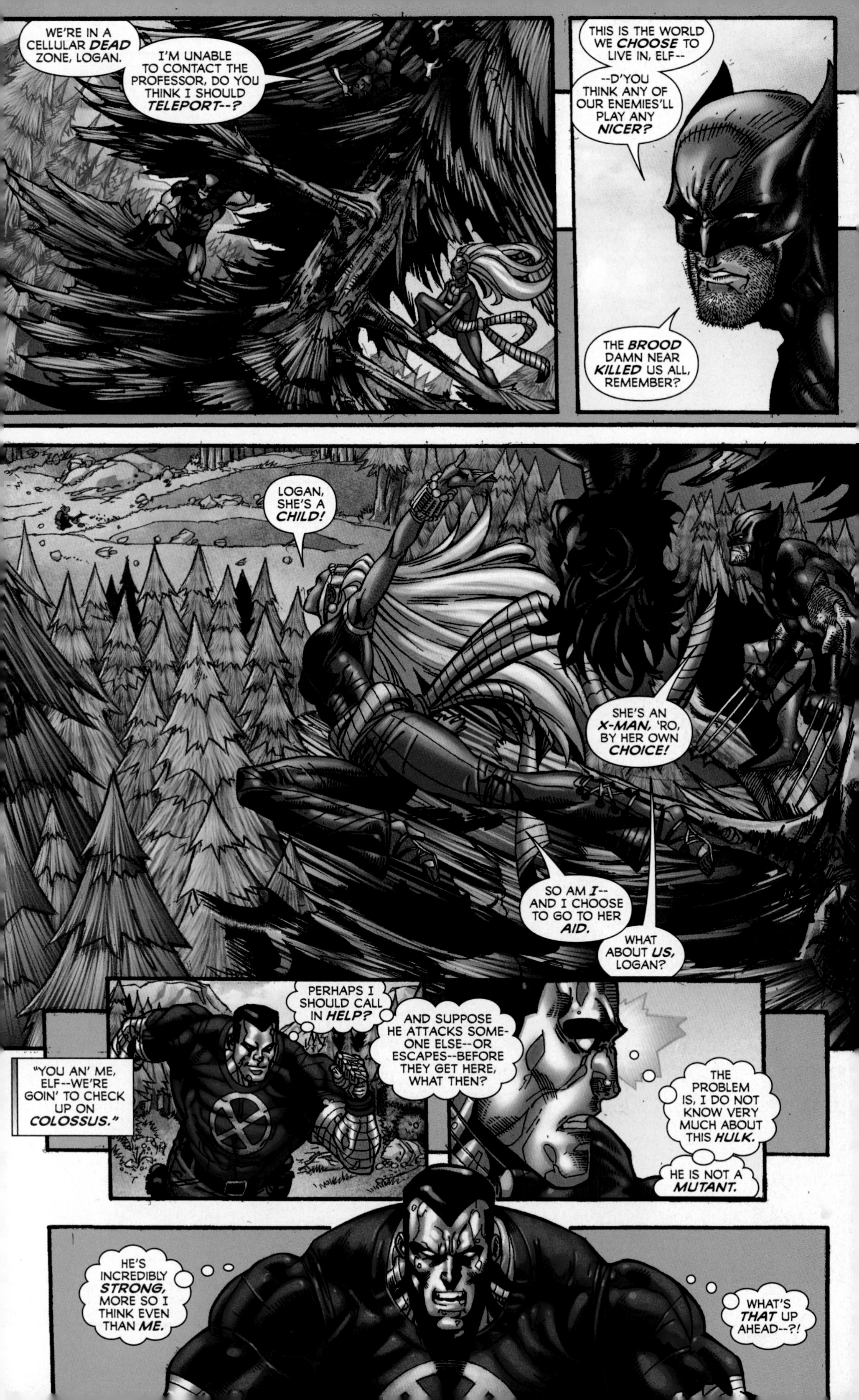
WE'RE IN A CELLULAR DEAD ZONE, LOGAN.
I'M UNABLE TO CONTACT THE PROFESSOR, DO YOU THINK I SHOULD TELEPORT--?
THIS IS THE WORLD WE CHOOSE TO LIVE IN, ELF--
--D'YOU THINK ANY OF OUR ENEMIES'LL PLAY ANY NICER?
THE BROOD DAMN NEAR KILLED US ALL, REMEMBER?
LOGAN, SHE'S A CHILD!
SHE'S AN X-MAN, 'RO, BY HER OWN CHOICE!
SO AM I-- AND I CHOOSE TO GO TO HER AID.
WHAT ABOUT US, LOGAN?
"YOU AN' ME, ELF--WE'RE GOIN' TO CHECK UP ON COLOSSUS."
PERHAPS I SHOULD CALL IN HELP?
AND SUPPOSE HE ATTACKS SOME-ONE ELSE--OR ESCAPES--BEFORE THEY GET HERE, WHAT THEN?
THE PROBLEM IS, I DO NOT KNOW VERY MUCH ABOUT THIS HULK.
HE IS NOT A MUTANT.
HE'S INCREDIBLY STRONG, MORE SO I THINK EVEN THAN ME.
WHAT'S THAT UP AHEAD--?!

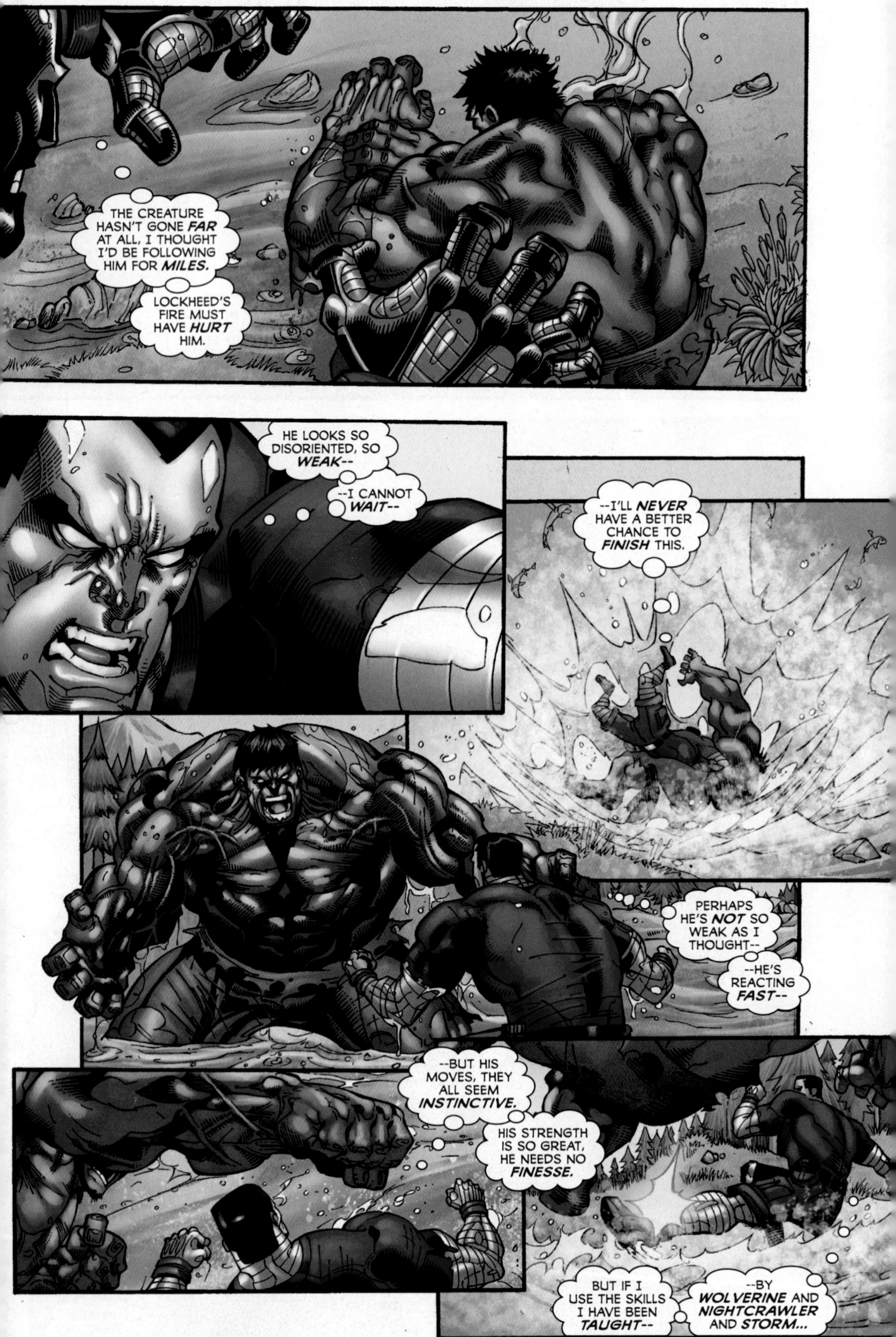

THE CREATURE HASN'T GONE FAR AT ALL, I THOUGHT I'D BE FOLLOWING HIM FOR MILES.
LOCKHEED'S FIRE MUST HAVE HURT HIM.
HE LOOKS SO DISORIENTED, SO WEAK--
--I CANNOT WAIT--
--I'LL NEVER HAVE A BETTER CHANCE TO FINISH THIS.
PERHAPS HE'S NOT SO WEAK AS I THOUGHT--
--HE'S REACTING FAST--
--BUT HIS MOVES, THEY ALL SEEM INSTINCTIVE.
HIS STRENGTH IS SO GREAT, HE NEEDS NO FINESSE.
BUT IF I USE THE SKILLS I HAVE BEEN TAUGHT--
--BY WOLVERINE AND NIGHTCRAWLER AND STORM...

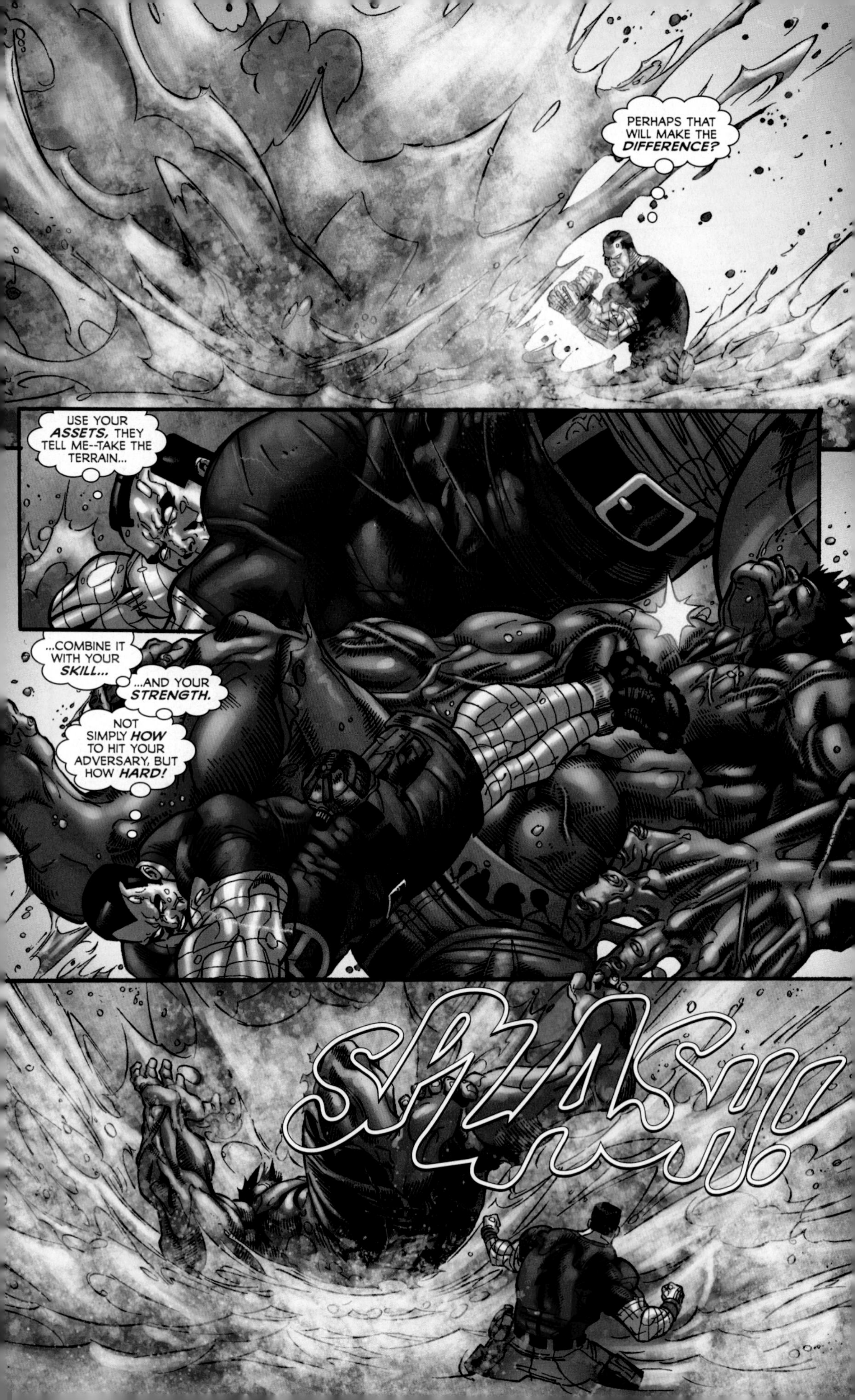
PERHAPS THAT WILL MAKE THE *DIFFERENCE?*
USE YOUR *ASSETS,* THEY TELL ME--TAKE THE TERRAIN...
...COMBINE IT WITH YOUR *SKILL...*
...AND YOUR *STRENGTH.*
NOT SIMPLY *HOW* TO HIT YOUR ADVERSARY, BUT HOW *HARD!*

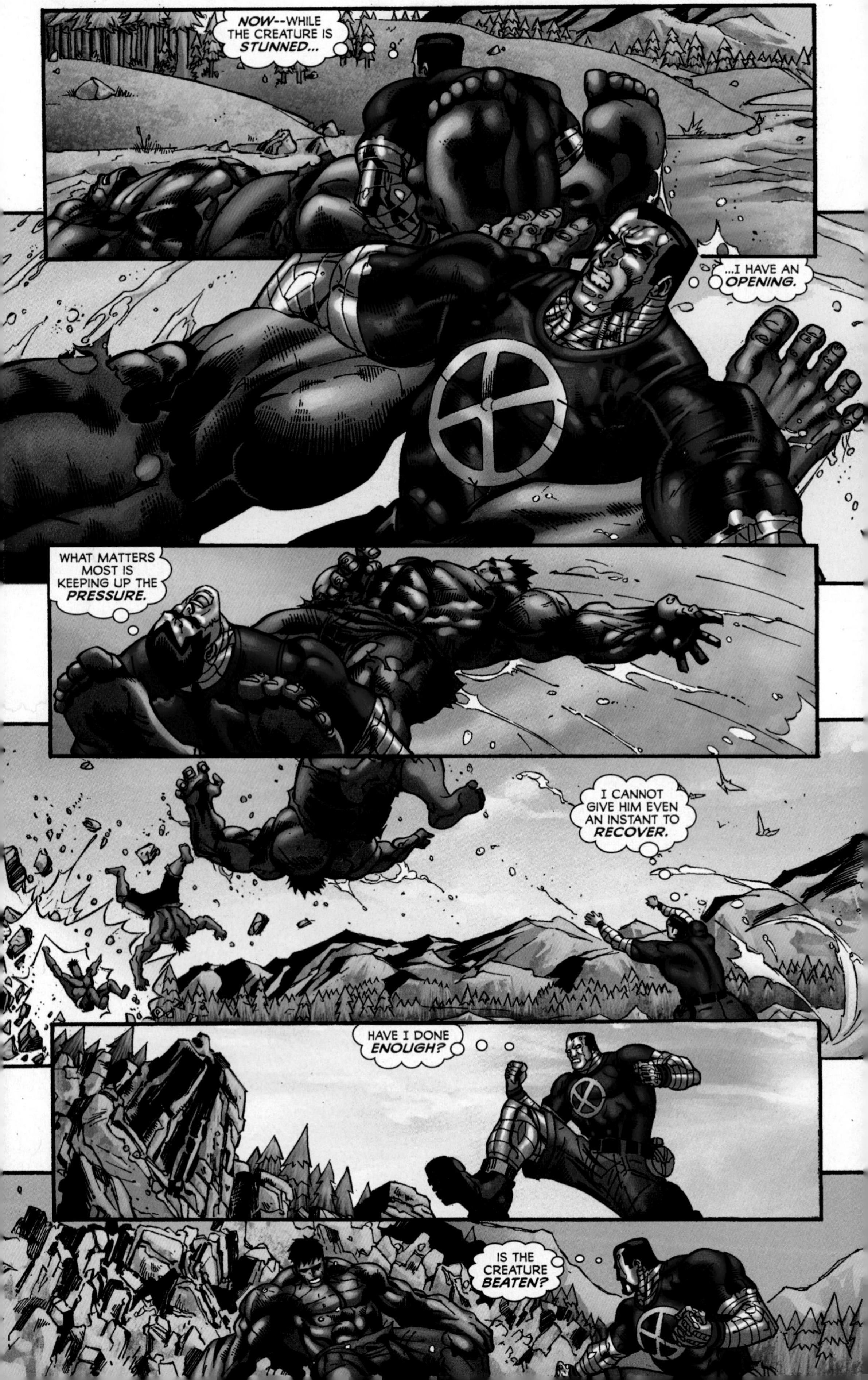
NOW--WHILE THE CREATURE IS STUNNED...
...I HAVE AN OPENING.
WHAT MATTERS MOST IS KEEPING UP THE PRESSURE.
I CANNOT GIVE HIM EVEN AN INSTANT TO RECOVER.
HAVE I DONE ENOUGH?
IS THE CREATURE BEATEN?

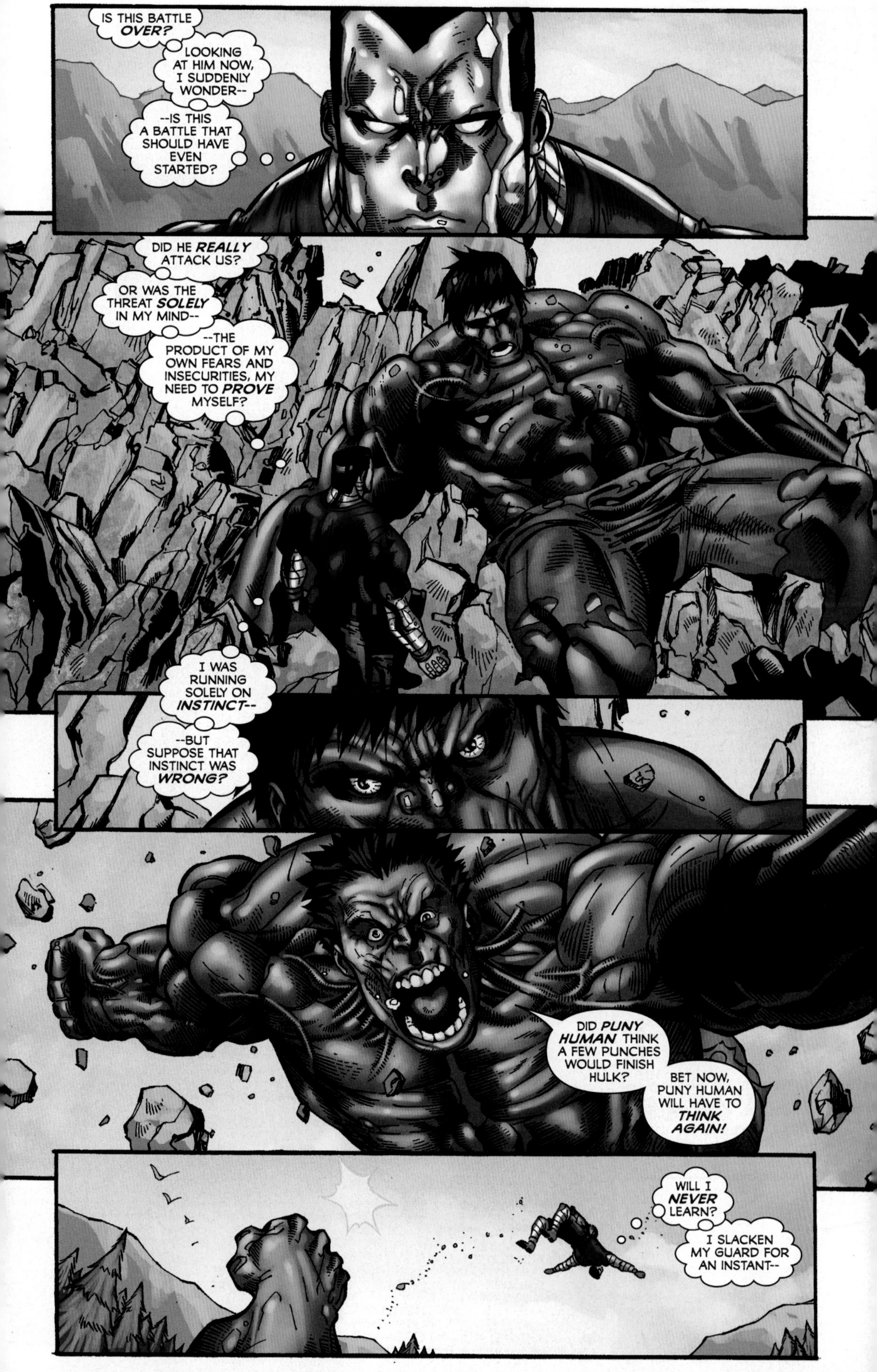
IS THIS BATTLE OVER?
LOOKING AT HIM NOW, I SUDDENLY WONDER--
--IS THIS A BATTLE THAT SHOULD HAVE EVEN STARTED?
DID HE REALLY ATTACK US?
OR WAS THE THREAT SOLELY IN MY MIND--
--THE PRODUCT OF MY OWN FEARS AND INSECURITIES, MY NEED TO PROVE MYSELF?
I WAS RUNNING SOLELY ON INSTINCT--
--BUT SUPPOSE THAT INSTINCT WAS WRONG?
DID PUNY HUMAN THINK A FEW PUNCHES WOULD FINISH HULK?
BET NOW, PUNY HUMAN WILL HAVE TO THINK AGAIN!
WILL I NEVER LEARN?
I SLACKEN MY GUARD FOR AN INSTANT--

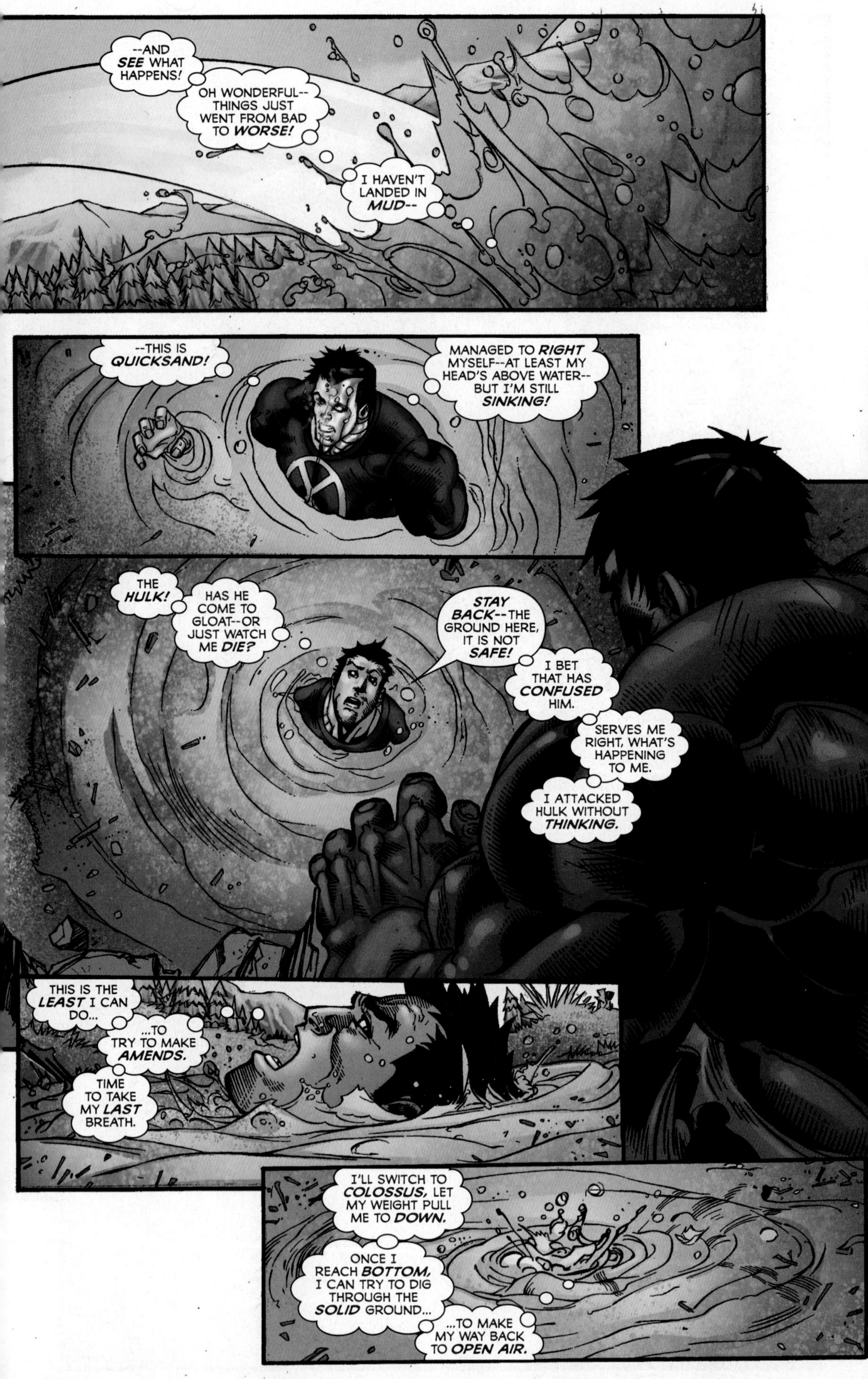

--AND SEE WHAT HAPPENS!
OH WONDERFUL-- THINGS JUST WENT FROM BAD TO WORSE!
I HAVEN'T LANDED IN MUD--
--THIS IS QUICKSAND!
MANAGED TO RIGHT MYSELF--AT LEAST MY HEAD'S ABOVE WATER-- BUT I'M STILL SINKING!
THE HULK!
HAS HE COME TO GLOAT--OR JUST WATCH ME DIE?
STAY BACK--THE GROUND HERE, IT IS NOT SAFE!
I BET THAT HAS CONFUSED HIM.
SERVES ME RIGHT, WHAT'S HAPPENING TO ME.
I ATTACKED HULK WITHOUT THINKING.
THIS IS THE LEAST I CAN DO...
...TO TRY TO MAKE AMENDS.
TIME TO TAKE MY LAST BREATH.
I'LL SWITCH TO COLOSSUS, LET MY WEIGHT PULL ME TO DOWN.
ONCE I REACH BOTTOM, I CAN TRY TO DIG THROUGH THE SOLID GROUND...
...TO MAKE MY WAY BACK TO OPEN AIR.

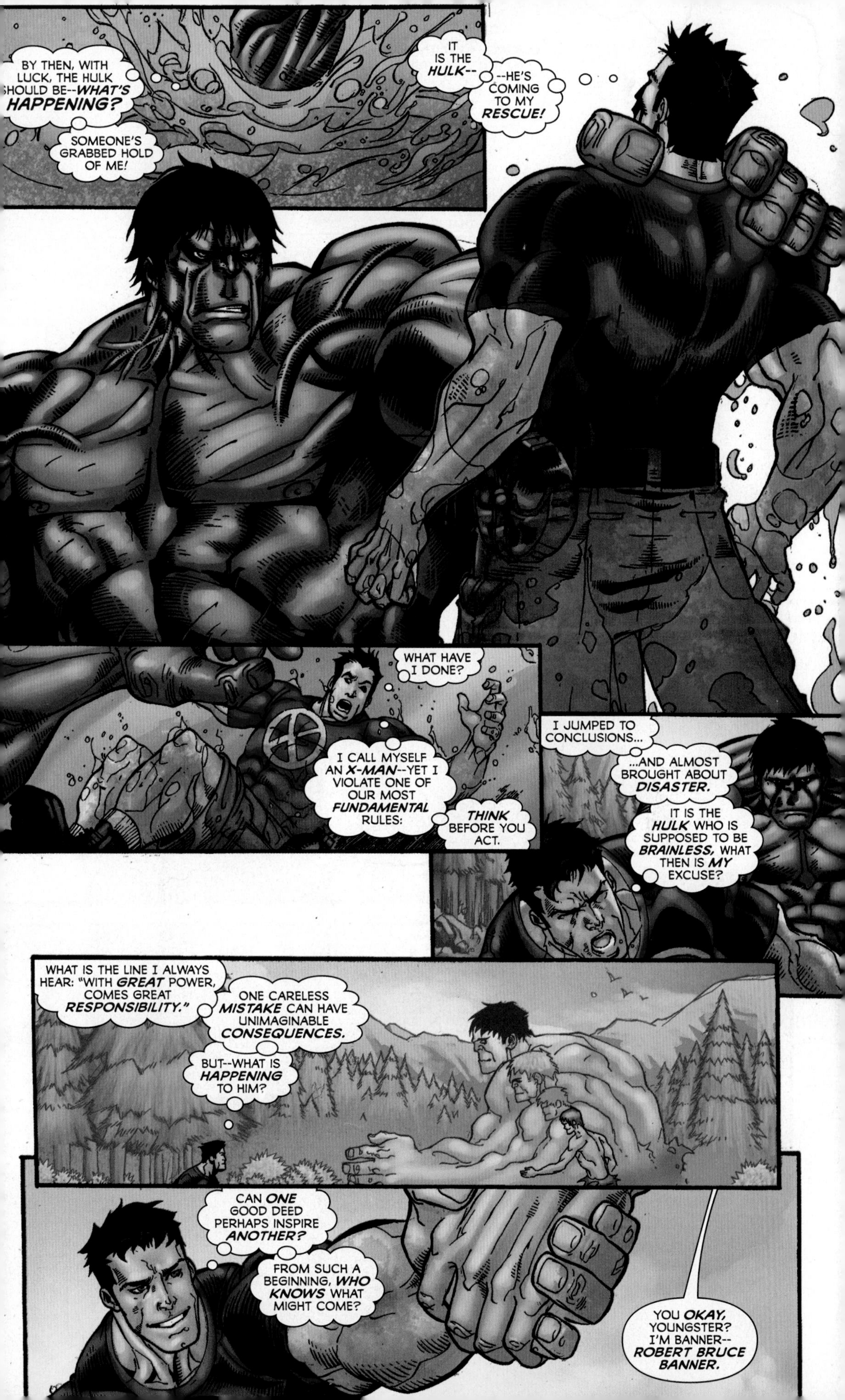
BY THEN, WITH LUCK, THE HULK SHOULD BE--WHAT'S HAPPENING?
SOMEONE'S GRABBED HOLD OF ME!
IT IS THE HULK--
--HE'S COMING TO MY RESCUE!
WHAT HAVE I DONE?
I CALL MYSELF AN X-MAN--YET I VIOLATE ONE OF OUR MOST FUNDAMENTAL RULES:
THINK BEFORE YOU ACT.
I JUMPED TO CONCLUSIONS...
...AND ALMOST BROUGHT ABOUT DISASTER.
IT IS THE HULK WHO IS SUPPOSED TO BE BRAINLESS, WHAT THEN IS MY EXCUSE?
WHAT IS THE LINE I ALWAYS HEAR: "WITH GREAT POWER, COMES GREAT RESPONSIBILITY."
ONE CARELESS MISTAKE CAN HAVE UNIMAGINABLE CONSEQUENCES.
BUT--WHAT IS HAPPENING TO HIM?
CAN ONE GOOD DEED PERHAPS INSPIRE ANOTHER?
FROM SUCH A BEGINNING, WHO KNOWS WHAT MIGHT COME?
YOU OKAY, YOUNGSTER? I'M BANNER-- ROBERT BRUCE BANNER.

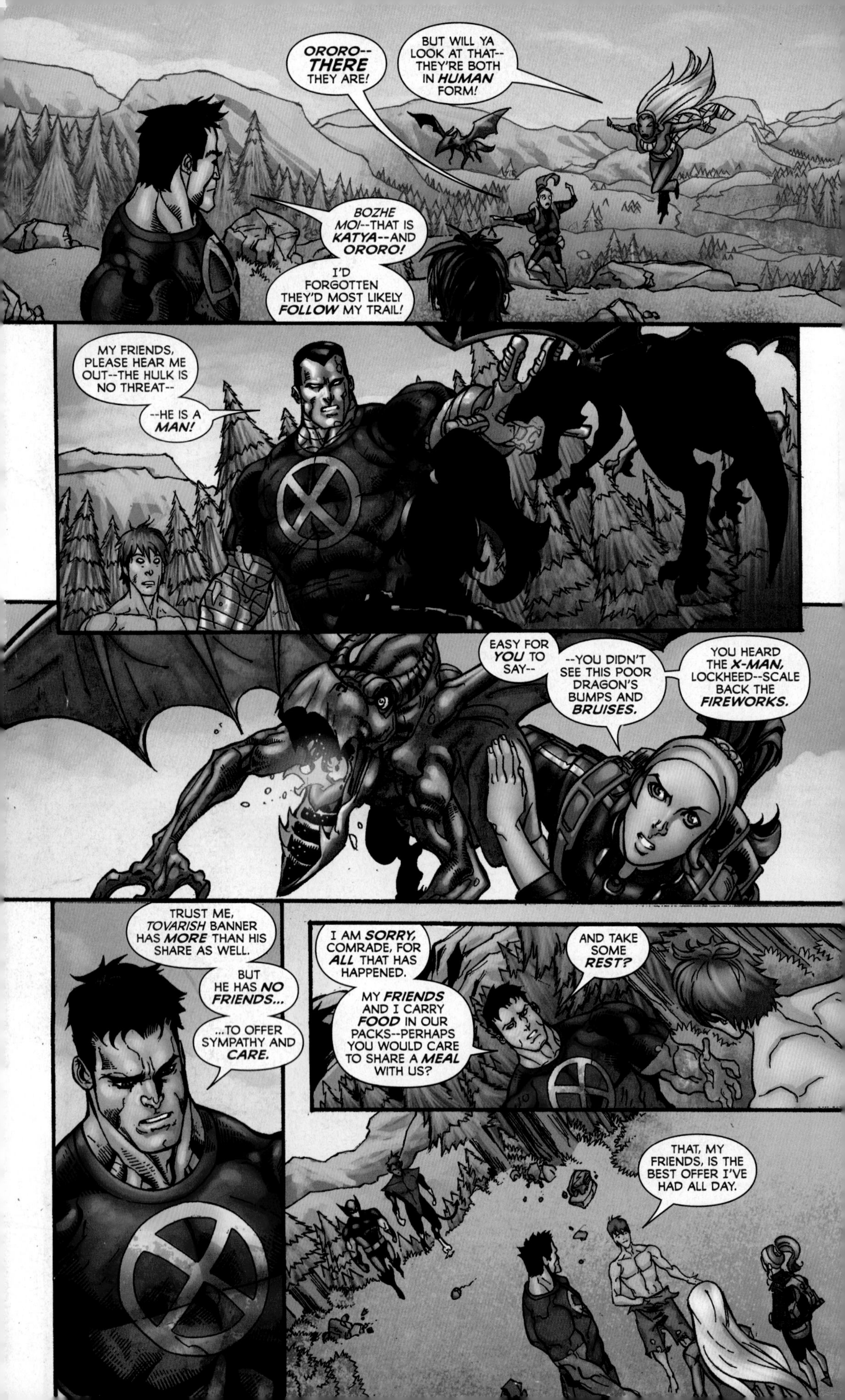
ORORO--THERE THEY ARE!
BUT WILL YA LOOK AT THAT--THEY'RE BOTH IN HUMAN FORM!
BOZHE MOI--THAT IS KATYA--AND ORORO!
I'D FORGOTTEN THEY'D MOST LIKELY FOLLOW MY TRAIL!
MY FRIENDS, PLEASE HEAR ME OUT--THE HULK IS NO THREAT--
--HE IS A MAN!
EASY FOR YOU TO SAY--
--YOU DIDN'T SEE THIS POOR DRAGON'S BUMPS AND BRUISES.
YOU HEARD THE X-MAN, LOCKHEED--SCALE BACK THE FIREWORKS.
TRUST ME, TOVARISH BANNER HAS MORE THAN HIS SHARE AS WELL.
BUT HE HAS NO FRIENDS...
...TO OFFER SYMPATHY AND CARE.
I AM SORRY, COMRADE, FOR ALL THAT HAS HAPPENED.
MY FRIENDS AND I CARRY FOOD IN OUR PACKS--PERHAPS YOU WOULD CARE TO SHARE A MEAL WITH US?
AND TAKE SOME REST?
THAT, MY FRIENDS, IS THE BEST OFFER I'VE HAD ALL DAY.

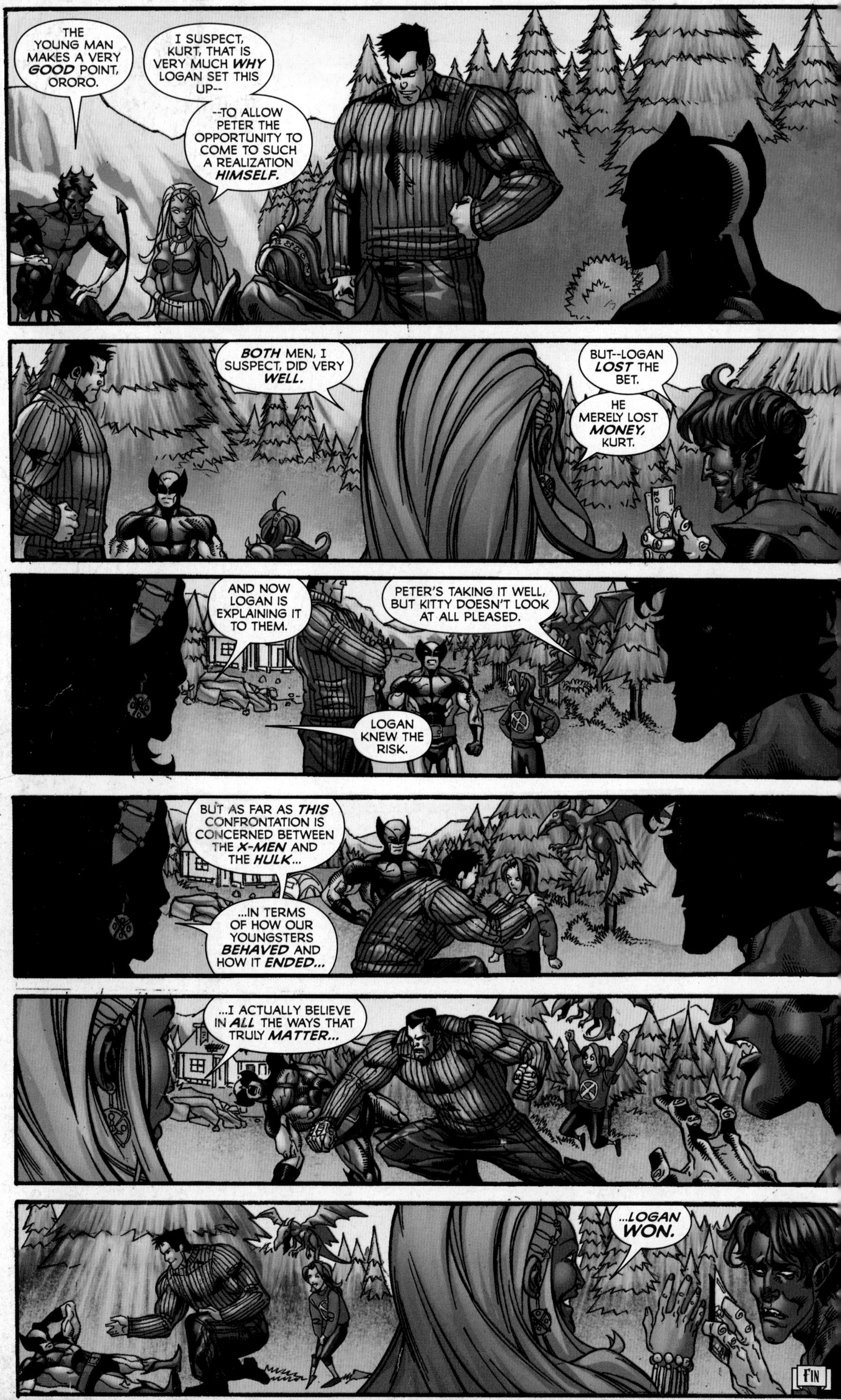
THE YOUNG MAN MAKES A VERY *GOOD* POINT, ORORO.
I SUSPECT, KURT, THAT IS VERY MUCH *WHY* LOGAN SET THIS UP--
--TO ALLOW PETER THE OPPORTUNITY TO COME TO SUCH A REALIZATION *HIMSELF.*
BOTH MEN, I SUSPECT, DID VERY *WELL.*
BUT--LOGAN *LOST* THE BET.
HE MERELY LOST *MONEY,* KURT.
AND NOW LOGAN IS EXPLAINING IT TO THEM.
PETER'S TAKING IT WELL, BUT KITTY DOESN'T LOOK AT ALL PLEASED.
LOGAN KNEW THE RISK.
BUT AS FAR AS *THIS* CONFRONTATION IS CONCERNED BETWEEN THE *X-MEN* AND THE *HULK*...
...IN TERMS OF HOW OUR YOUNGSTERS *BEHAVED* AND HOW IT *ENDED*...
...I ACTUALLY BELIEVE IN *ALL* THE WAYS THAT TRULY *MATTER*...
...*LOGAN* *WON.*
FIN

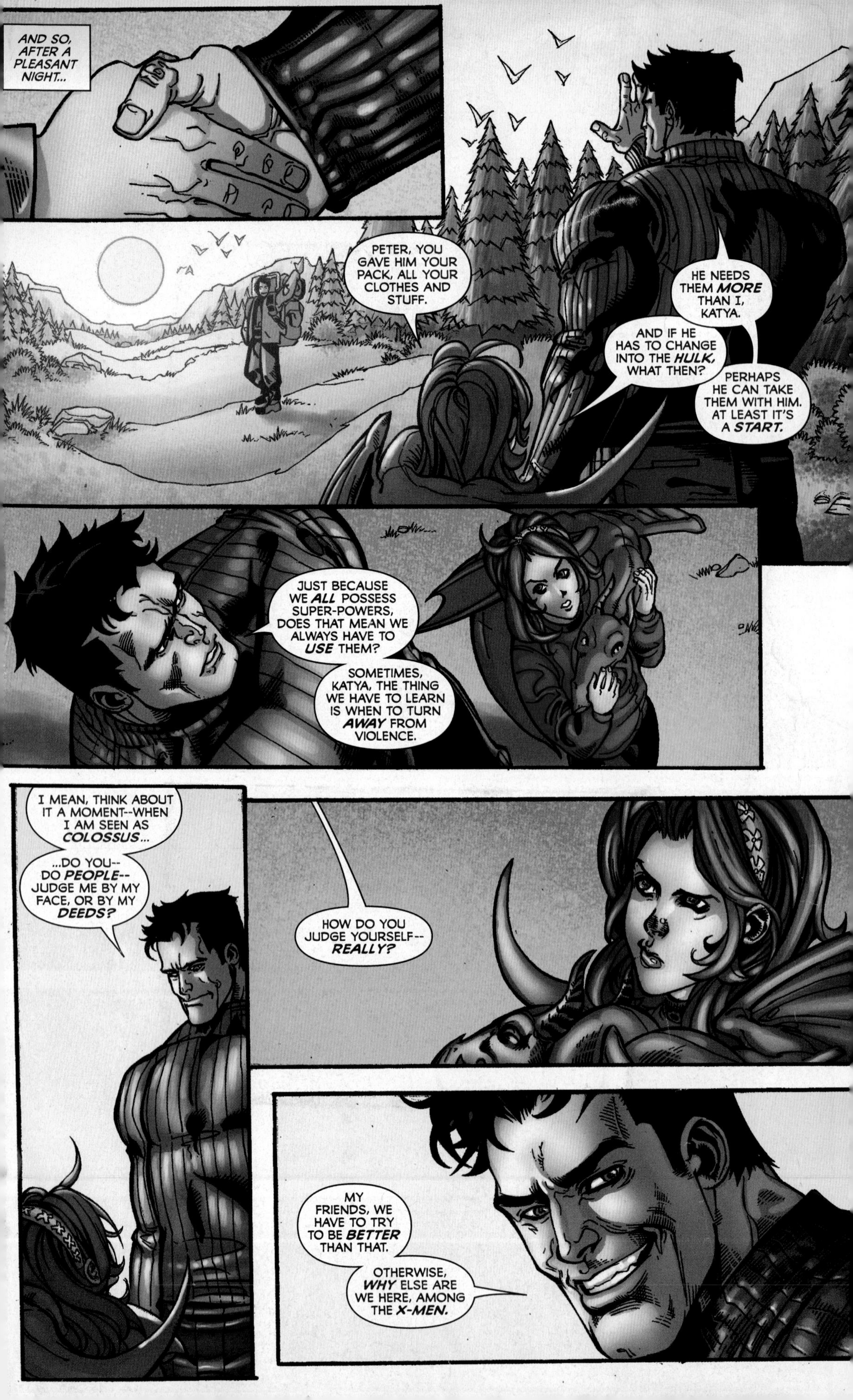
AND SO, AFTER A PLEASANT NIGHT...
PETER, YOU GAVE HIM YOUR PACK, ALL YOUR CLOTHES AND STUFF.
HE NEEDS THEM MORE THAN I, KATYA.
AND IF HE HAS TO CHANGE INTO THE HULK, WHAT THEN?
PERHAPS HE CAN TAKE THEM WITH HIM. AT LEAST IT'S A START.
JUST BECAUSE WE ALL POSSESS SUPER-POWERS, DOES THAT MEAN WE ALWAYS HAVE TO USE THEM?
SOMETIMES, KATYA, THE THING WE HAVE TO LEARN IS WHEN TO TURN AWAY FROM VIOLENCE.
I MEAN, THINK ABOUT IT A MOMENT--WHEN I AM SEEN AS COLOSSUS...
...DO YOU--DO PEOPLE--JUDGE ME BY MY FACE, OR BY MY DEEDS?
HOW DO YOU JUDGE YOURSELF--REALLY?
MY FRIENDS, WE HAVE TO TRY TO BE BETTER THAN THAT.
OTHERWISE, WHY ELSE ARE WE HERE, AMONG THE X-MEN.